C000173728

THE LONDON, CHATHAM & DOVER RAILWAY

THE LONDON, CHATHAM & DOVER RAILWAY

by

ADRIAN GRAY, M.A.

'One of the most remarkable works of our age.'

Herapath's Railway Magazine, 3rd August 1861

'One of the most gigantic frauds ever perpetrated.'

Railway Times, 10th December 1870

MERESBOROUGH BOOKS

1984

Published by Meresborough Books, 7 Station Road, Rainham, Kent ME8 7RS.

Meresborough Books is a specialist publisher of books about Kent. A list of sixty titles available December 1984 can be found at the back of this book.

© Copyright 1984 Adrian Gray

ISBN 0905270 886

Printed by Mackays of Chatham Ltd, Chatham, Kent.

CONTENTS

MAPS AND DIAGRAMS

Maps

Figures

Foreword

The history of the London, Chatham & Dover Railway is amongst the most bizarre of any of the multitude of railway companies that sprang up in mid-Victorian Britain. Because it was only a relatively small concern compared to giants like the Great Western or the London & North Western, the LCDR always visibly bore the marks of the men who struggled to control and direct it; throughout its life it was heavily influenced by the desires of landowners, contractors and financiers — it was never free to merely pursue the goal of efficiently serving the transport needs of south-east England.

Thus a history of the 'Chatham' must be more than a mere record of locomotives, carriages and cuttings — indeed the story of the line's engines has already been thoroughly attended to. In this book I have attempted to portray the life of this unusual Company by giving space to the men who actually made the decisions and have attempted to explain why the railway was built at all, relating it to the community it served. Unlike many books on railways, this is not full of nostalgia: the historian must be honest, and it can be said that few people in Kent mourned the old Chatham when it was absorbed into larger companies.

It is to be hoped that in treating the story of the LCDR in the way that I have done, I have shown that it is possible to cater for the interests of railway enthusiasts, local historians and historians with a wider interest in the social or economic affairs of the Victorian age.

Braintree, July 1984   A.G.

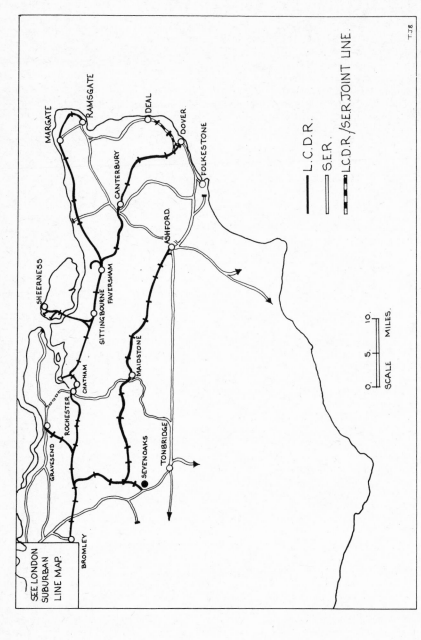

Map 1: General Map of the London, Chatham & Dover Railway, 1898 (details of lines and stations other than LCDR have been omitted.)

x

THE LONDON, CHATHAM & DOVER RAILWAY

CHAPTER ONE

The Foundation of the East Kent Railway

Most attempts to build railways in Kent were the result of efforts to secure two wholly different types of traffic: the purely local, and the continental. During the course of their independent existences the two main companies who developed the railway system in the County largely failed to reconcile the differing needs of these two types of traffic, although it was by no means impossible to have done so. Both companies, the South Eastern Railway and the London, Chatham & Dover Railway, imposed considerable capital burdens upon themselves in the attempt to exploit marginal advantages in the continental services and, later, in their services to certain of the major towns. The result was that the less glamorous sides of their businesses — the local and suburban services that were their bread and butter — were largely ignored and given a low priority in such matters as the allocation of stock.

That the two types of traffic were not irreconcilable is a fact which could not have been deduced from the route of the South Eastern Railway, which had been authorised by Parliament in 1836 and opened from London Bridge to Folkestone in 1843. There had been several years of argument over the course this line was to take, with Parliament and the landowners being largely responsible for the eventual unsatisfactory outcome. As it was opened, the South Eastern's contribution to the transport needs of Kent left much to be desired since from London it took a course due south to Reigate,[1] before turning sharply eastwards to pursue a route straight across the Weald to Ashford and so to Folkestone. Although Maidstone, Canterbury, Ramsgate and Margate were reached by branch lines by 1846, this left many of Kent's principal towns without a direct rail connection to London. The omissions of the SER were most obvious in North Kent, where a whole string of towns were neglected: Gravesend, Rochester, Chatham, Sittingbourne, Faversham and Sheerness all felt that they were suffering whilst Canterbury and Maidstone both had the impression that their honour had been slighted by being placed on branch lines. North Kent was also the traditional route for traffic from London to Dover, and indeed this route had been considered in the debate that led up to the South Eastern's Act of 1836. It was a varied area at the time, ranging from the resort town of Gravesend to the lime industry of Rochester and the brewing at Faversham; between New Brompton and Faversham lay an area rich in fruit and hops.

The dissatisfaction of North Kent was soon reflected in a proliferation of schemes designed to fill the gaps in the Kent railway network, and the interest in the schemes was such that they continued after the 'Railway Mania'. The

1

South Eastern Company was conscious of its own failings and also aware that the populous towns to the north of its line offered a profitable route to Dover for a rival. There were many plans to fill the gap, one of the earliest being the 'London & Chatham' scheme of 1841, of which the engineer was Charles Vignoles. This planned to branch off from the London & Greenwich Railway at Deptford and to travel via Dartford and Higham to the Frindsbury peninsula, a small neck of land on the west bank of the Medway opposite Chatham; it was proposed to cross the river by either a ferry or a floating bridge to a point very close to where the SER's Chatham Central station was eventually opened.[2] During the 'Mania' of 1845-1846 Vignoles expanded his plans to encompass a through line to Canterbury and Dover along the 'traditional' route, to which the SER replied by promoting its own line along the North Kent route from Deptford to Chilham on its Canterbury branch. This line secured the support of the Board of Trade and in 1846 was authorised as far as Gravesend, beyond which there were certain complexities surrounding the independent Gravesend & Rochester Company; however it was apparently necessary for the SER to bribe the promoters of Vignoles' line into not opposing their scheme before the House of Lords, Vignoles presumably being well satisfied with his share of the £30,000. The SER also pledged that it would complete a line to Dover by this route, thus holding on to the support of many local landowners.[3]

The situation became more complex in 1847 with the SER, the London, Brighton & South Coast Railway and an independent concern all in the contest. The SER had a whole variety of proposals, the most important of which was to extend eastwards from the Gravesend & Rochester's terminus at Strood[4] to Chilham on their own Canterbury line, with branches to Maidstone and Sheerness. At the same time it put forward proposals for a Mid-Kent line from Lewisham to Tonbridge which would cut off the 'elbow' of its main line via Reigate and which would also have had branches to Sevenoaks, Dartford and Maidstone; the latter included a 3¼ mile climb at 1 in 110 near Ightham and then continued on from Maidstone to rejoin the main line at Ashford.

The very magnitude of the South Eastern's plans for Kent in 1847 suggest that they were more defensive measures than serious proposals, for the cost of such a works programme would have been massive. The most serious threat to the SER's territory came from the LB&SCR which was planning a line from New Cross, 2¾ miles out from London Bridge, by way of Bromley, Sevenoaks and Maidstone to Canterbury, with a branch from Ightham to Tonbridge. The other competitor was a scheme for a London to Canterbury line via Riverhead, near Sevenoaks, and Maidstone. However all of these plans reflected the dissatisfaction of the principal towns and landowners with either being on a branch or isolated altogether; if it did nothing else, a railway increased property values. The SER must have been very conscious of attitudes in Kent since it had two Maidstone men on its Board of Directors.

Local landowners like Lord Sondes, who owned an estate at Lees Court near Faversham, decided to support the South Eastern project as it appeared to be the one most likely to succeed, but the Bill for the extension from Strood to Chilham ran into trouble on its second reading in the House of Lords in 1847.

Not only did the Kent railways have to consider local and continental traffic, but they also had to allow for defence needs — in this case the interconnection of Woolwich, Chatham and Dover. The Duke of Wellington doubted whether the SER's pledge to extend from Canterbury to Dover was sufficiently binding to protect the nation's interest should the Folkestone to Dover line be cut off at any time; the Duke can hardly have known how important his stand on this issue was to prove when, during the First World War, the South Eastern's line was cut by a landslide at Folkestone Warren. Rather than face the prospect of a clause compelling it to extend from Canterbury to Dover, the SER chose to abandon its Bill altogether — an action that was quite safe since the opposition had been defeated at earlier stages of the contest.

This precipitate action of the South Eastern's made it obvious to the North Kent landowners that if they wanted a railway they would have to promote it themselves, although it could subsequently be leased to the SER for operation. The result was the 1848 scheme, for which the engineer was Mr G. Taylor, to build a line from Strood to Faversham and Chilham, with possible extensions to Dover and Deal. A series of meetings to promote the line and assess the strength of local support began in December 1848 with a meeting at Faversham, chaired by Alderman C.J. Hilton who owned extensive cement works at Frindsbury, Lower Upnor, Rochester and Faversham, and who thus had commercial interests in the formation of a new line. It was decided that several influential land-owners, including Lord Sondes, were in support but the suggestion that eventual amalgamation with the South Eastern should be an aim did not find unanimous support.[5]

However it was not until the end of 1849 that the scheme really began to make progress. Taylor attended a meeting in Canterbury and outlined his plan for an extension from the SER at Strood to Dover, with branches to Sheerness and Maidstone, and from Faversham to Ashford. The Hon. Stephen Lushington, an important landowner, proposed the motion 'That the populous and important district ... is destitute of proper railway communication, and the inhabitants, as well as all parties having occasion to traverse it, are subject to serious loss, expense and inconvenience.' Many of the landowners had an interest in sending fruit and hops to London but had to face competition from other growers who could use a railway — particularly those in the Weald around Staplehurst.

Lushington was also active in meetings at Faversham and Sittingbourne in January 1850 at which the SER was criticised for saying that they would build a line when it suited them and not keeping to their word. Lushington said that he had supported the SER's proposals until 1845 because he believed that they had the good of the County at heart, but he no longer felt that this was the case; the depressed state of the capital market also made a positive SER contribution less likely.

Despite having been defeated on standing orders in 1849, Taylor's project now began to attract considerable interest. In January 1850 the *Railway Times* assessed the scheme's prospects: 'The agricultural wealth of the County of Kent, its beauties, its salubrity, and general importance, all concur in pointing to the commercial value of a railway traversing and penetrating into its interior.' The promoters also made much of the line's financial prospects, estimating annual receipts of £176,000 on a capital of £1,500,000.

On 22nd January 1850 the *Maidstone Journal* — representative of the landed interest — moved into support: '... the intermediate district between the terminus at Strood and that at Chilham, is left to the primitive resources of the tardy waggon, the rattling cart, the solitary coach, and that compromise of all dignity and comfort, the omnibus.' Clearly therefore, a railway was wanted, and the intimate connection between the railway project and the local land-owners was suggested by the proposal to 'pay' for the necessary land with a rent charge on traffic rather than a cash deposit.

The Duke of Wellington and Lord Grenfell of the War Office lent their support to the line and commented on the great importance of a Dover extension. It was reported that an enemy ship could cut the SER's line within half-an-hour.[6] However Taylor's proposal to obtain running powers, by which one Company's trains were afforded the right to run over another Company's lines, over the North Kent line of the SER west of Strood so enraged the established Company that they bitterly opposed the project and saw its rejection by Parliament in April 1850. The SER's opposition costs came to only £1,200.

The landowners were not daunted, however, and an announcement in the *Maidstone Journal* on 23rd April 1850 said that a new engineer had been obtained and the assistance of London capitalists was being sought for 'an entirely independent through line.' The concept of a purely local line, feeding into the SER, had been abandoned because of that Company's hostile attitude, the landowners feeling that they would rather control their own railway than rely upon such an uncertain partner. By September 1850 the 'Mid-Kent & Dover' plans were being publicised, having been prepared by George Bidder; Bidder had become famous as a child for his prodigious mathematical ability, rejoicing under the name of 'the calculating boy', but in his maturity was an engineer closely associated with the Stephensons. The new proposals were for a line from New Cross to Bromley, Otford, Snodland and Rochester to Chatham; from there it would follow the coast to Faversham and thus to Canterbury and Dover whilst there were also to be branches to Faversham Creek, from Faversham to Chilham, and from Burham — on the east bank of the River Medway — to Maidstone.

Much of the interest in this scheme centred on its proposed system of management and also the means by which it was proposed to borrow £2 million capital at 4% on the guarantee of tolls, and to cover the interest charges by a levy on the parish rates. It was estimated that the railway would add 16.6% to the annual rateable value of the parishes through which it would pass, so that they would not mind having to meet the interest charges.[7] The High Sheriff of Kent was given the responsibility of arranging a conference of landowners at Maidstone, at which twenty 'trustees' were chosen from various parts of the County to supervise the project. Under this system it was hoped that the different interests within the County would be represented and indeed, in its early days, the MK&D seems to have had an impressively co-operative air about it. Unfortunately this was not to last.

The Mid-Kent & Dover faced the opposition of a speculative scheme called the 'Strood & Dover District' which was promoted by London financiers although it was hoped to win over local support by allowing an option for each Kent town to elect a Director of its choice. The engineer, John Braithwaite, who had won a name for himself as co-designer of the Rainhill trials locomotive 'Novelty' and as engineer of the Eastern Counties Railway, emphasised that the scheme would cost only £980,000 for a line from Strood to Canterbury and Dover where it was to terminate close to Marine Parade. Predictably it was alleged that the Strood & Dover was a child of the SER and, although Braithwaite strongly denied this at a Rochester meeting in October 1850, the project performed badly in the 1850-51 Parliamentary session.

However the Mid-Kent & Dover was also running into problems and by January 1851 the community spirit that had at first catalysed it was beginning to look jaded. The system of management by trustees seems to have been easily adopted since it was already used by the administrations of Ramsgate Harbour and the Medway Bridge, but the proposal to add another rent charge to their properties to help pay for the line — with interest on borrowed capital being paid out of rates — did not please many landowners; 'this surely is gross oppression' one indignant man wrote to the *Maidstone Journal*. According to the *Railway Times*, the scheme had the support of six hundred important landowners,[8] but it faced growing opposition from the people of Maidstone.

Maidstone felt insulted by the proposal to include it only by way of a branch from Burham and its indecision over the scheme was heightened by rumours in April 1851 of a direct London to Maidstone line via Bromley. But the real crux of the matter was the proposal to meet interest repayments out of rates, for, because of the way rateable values were assessed, Maidstone would have had to meet these for 10% of the entire project even though it was only on a branch. Mereworth also objected to being taxed at 6d. in the £ when it already had an SER station nearby. The Maidstone area landowners switched their support to an extension of the SER from Strood, and the 1851 Bill for the Mid-Kent & Dover was lost.

Clearly therefore there were difficulties to be encountered when a railway was projected by landowners through the impossibility of planning a line that would satisfy everyone. All the Kent towns wanted to be on a main line from London to Canterbury or Dover, but it was very difficult to reconcile the interests of Chatham and Maidstone in this respect because of the configuration of the North Downs and the Medway valley. However the Maidstone interests on their own were insufficient to outweigh those from the North Kent towns between Rochester and Canterbury, so that the scheme projected in late 1851 and early 1852 made no serious attempt to accommodate the needs of Maidstone. Although the end of 1851 saw rumours of a Wimbledon-Croydon-Maidstone line and an independent Strood-Dover line, it was the project supported by influential landowners like Lord Harris that once again attracted public attention.

In the autumn of 1851 interest began to centre upon a project referred to as the 'East Kent & Maidstone'. At a series of meetings in Canterbury, Sittingbourne, Rochester, Chatham and Faversham it was emphasised by Lord

Harris that the scheme was to be financed for the most part with London money, but that it was necessary for 3,000 of the 32,000 £25 shares to be taken up by Kent people as an indication of local support. Harris chaired a meeting at Canterbury in October 1851, saying that initial plans were for a line from Rochester to Canterbury at an estimated £780,000, together with £78,000 for land. There was the possibility, he said, that once the line had been built it could be operated by the South Eastern. Reference was also made to the extent of support amongst Kent landowners; the report of the meeting in the *Railway Times* stating that 43 out of 45 principal landowners had agreed to the scheme, whereas the *Maidstone Journal* chose to report that only 1 in 8 of affected landowners had so far assented.[9] The most influential landowner seems to have been Lord Sondes, with estates near Faversham and at Elmham; in late October he appears to have been converted into a supporter of the line and started to appear at its meetings although Lord Harris remained the guiding light. By the middle of November, 154 out of 513 affected landowners had assented to the proposals. At about the same time it became commonly accepted that the project's ultimate goal was not Canterbury but Dover; one of the committee, Sir J. Tylden, was reported by the *Maidstone Journal* as having 'no doubt whatever that eventually it would be extended as far as Dover.'

During the various meetings the question of the relationship with the South Eastern arose repeatedly. Sondes was reported by the *Railway Times* as saying that '... under certain stipulations, the South Eastern might be justified in withholding its opposition....' indicating that there was always the possibilty of co-operation.

However local opinion was generally antagonistic towards the SER, who were at the time promoting a line from Chilham to Faversham Creek. It was feared that this would allow the SER to '... deluge the County with cheap coal and timber, but only till they had ruined every trader, and then up would fly their price to a monopoly height.'[10] Meanwhile the East Kent promoters assured the peoples of both Rochester and Faversham that their towns were to become the major port for central Kent.

The committee which was administering the project by late 1851 included several names that were to be closely associated with the London, Chatham & Dover Railway's subsequent history. They included Lords Harris and Sondes, the Rt. Hon. Stephen Lushington and C.M. Lushington, C.J. Hilton and J. Lake amongst others.

Some more details of the scheme had emerged by late 1851 and, in December, it was decided to start only from a station at Rochester Bridge on the east bank of the Medway until the new road bridge over the river had been completed. There was to be a station in Military Road, Chatham, and a branch from Rochester to Maidstone that would cross the Medway on a nine-arch viaduct at Allington Lock. The latter was insufficient to secure Maidstone support and only fifty people attended a meeting in that town; they were more interested in the SER's plan for a line along the Medway's west bank from Strood.

However in January 1852 the scheme was abandoned as not enough shares had been taken up in the County, a fact which is worthy of consideration in assessing whether the line that was eventually built was a landowners' line or a speculative venture financed from outside of the County.

There was then a very definite lull in the railway proposals until a new campaign commenced in July 1852 — one that was to bear fruit at last. A new project called the 'East Kent Railway' was launched at a meeting in Faversham

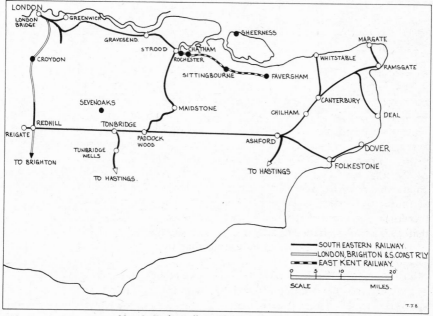

Map 2: Early Railways in Kent, to 1858

on 31st July for a line from Strood to Faversham, Boughton and Chilham with access to Canterbury, although it was understood that extension to Dover was inevitable — even though plans for this were abandoned in the hope of ensuring SER support. At first the engineers of the line were J.S. Valentine and W. Mills, but these gave way to Sir Charles Fox as London financial interests became involved. Fox was already well known in the district as he had been engaged in the construction of a new road bridge over the Medway at Rochester. Fox and his friends subscribed for 14,500 shares on the condition that a further 5,000 were taken up within the County, which meant that the landowners only had to contribute a sixth of the £700,000 estimated cost; it would also mean that Fox's firm could get the contract for building the line on their own terms. Others were not enthusiastic about the East Kent Railway's financial prospects and the General Manager of the SER, perhaps with an interest at stake, wrote to its promoters in November 1852:

> 'Your profits will be nil: it is a line that by no possibility can pay; the South Eastern Company would not take it at any price; and if you, the gentry, embark on it, you will all be ruined.'

The opposition of the SER must have been a bitter blow to the EKR promoters, though the more senior Company later paid dearly for their early hostility. A number of the EKR supporters were in favour of an eventual union with the SER, but such attitudes helped to ensure that they remained a minority. The EKR also faced competition from an independent scheme for a 'Chatham & Canterbury Local' which was to run from the Sun Pier in Chatham to Faversham and Chilham on a single track; this was a project emanating from London financial circles and it did not meet the local people's desire for a through route. Local support remained firmly behind the EKR which was chaired by Hon. Stephen Lushington of Norton Court near Faversham, and also supported by Lord Harris and C.J. Hilton, the cement manufacturer. However it was feared that without the SER's support, the EKR might sink into the clutches of the contractors (the evils of whom were aired regularly in the railway press), and with the arrival of Fox this became a very real danger. Late in 1852 the SER rejected the chance to lease the projected line in return for a guaranteed 3%; it was more interested in its own Maidstone plans and was content to let the EKR decline into bankruptcy — a result it confidently anticipated.

The Parliamentary conflict in 1853 over the East Kent's Bill centred on its plan to exert running powers over the SER from Strood to Dartford, with the longer term prospect of its own line from Dartford to Lewisham. The SER strongly opposed this proposal, but a compromise was reached allowing the EKR to use the Strood and Canterbury stations of the SER, to defend which the House of Commons inserted a 'facilitation clause' into the EKR Bill; this bound the SER 'to afford every necessary and reasonable facility to the East Kent Company for the transmission of their traffic.'[11] The facility to use Canterbury (SER) station was, however, unnecessary since the EKR decided on an independent entry to the city rather than following the SER from Chilham. The possibility of a later EKR extension to Dover was considered vital by the House of Lords, who extracted a promise from the SER not to oppose any such plan as a condition for the passing of their Strood to Maidstone line.[12]

The SER was the only opponent of the EKR Bill, which was supported by a petition from 9,000 landowners and occupiers. Although the conflict was eventually resolved peacefully it did have some lighter moments, such as when the SER claimed that the EKR Bill infringed standing orders 92 times. The EKR, whilst applying for its own Rochester to Maidstone line via Wouldham, claimed that it should have the pleasure of working the SER's Maidstone branch rather than the SER itself. The writer of a scurrilous pamphlet published in April 1853 concentrated on the EKR's swing-bridge over the River Medway, envisaging the SER hiring a fleet of tall-masted barges to sail constantly through and interrupt the trains. Perhaps, the writer mused, the SER might go even further than that:

'Who knows but that they may bribe the authorities some day to open the swing-bridge just as a train is expected, and deposit the unlucky East Kent passengers in the bed of the Medway? Who can say what such a dreadful company may not do?'[13]

8

Out of the 1853 Parliamentary contest emerged a state of affairs that seemed quite favourable to Kent, with the East Kent Railway authorised to build a line from the South Eastern's terminus at Strood to Canterbury and Chilham (16 & 17 Vic. cap.cxxxii; 4th August 1853) and an SER line from Strood to Maidstone (16 & 17 Vic. cap.cxxx). The EKR's task was the more difficult with an expensive bridge over the River Medway, three tunnels in the Chatham area and another near Selling. The cost of this line was estimated by Mills and Cubitt to be £674,000, with the works to be executed by Fox, Henderson & Co. The authorisation of a new company to operate in Kent was strongly in line with the findings of Cardwell's Parliamentary Select Committee on railway amalgamation of 1852-53, which had come out strongly in favour of competition — although at this stage the EKR was not officially claiming to be a competitor of the SER.

A company with a capital of £700,000 had been formed, but it was a company of many shadows. Much of the noise surrounding its promotion had been made by local people, but who really controlled the East Kent and was it a 'contractors' line?' The history of the early schemes in the region shows conclusively that the ideas for a railway generally originated in the locality. However the lack of local capital funds meant that it would often be outside financial interests that called the subsequent tune, and from the virtual start of the EKR's life Fox and his associates had agreed to take 14,500 of the Company's shares. Much evidence for the true state of affairs can be drawn from the *Railway Times* which in January 1853 had criticised the 'absence of real local support' for the EKR although it did point out that some of the promoters were of 'County' rank — a reference to the likes of Harris and Sondes. The arrangement negotiated with Fox was for local people to take up 5,000 shares at £25 each; according to the *Maidstone Journal* of 7th June 1853, 334 Kent people had subscribed to shares worth £135,375 — less than a quarter of the necessary capital. Lord Sondes later stated that 678 shares had been taken up in the Faversham area, always a centre of support.

Thus there was a degree of local interest but it was still necessary for meetings to be held to drum up enthusiasm for the shares. The *Railway Times* exposed the reality of the EKR's financial support with an article dated 15th January 1853, which examined the EKR's subscription lists and found that eighteen people provided £380,000 of the £700,000 capital. A subscriber for £50,000 was Mr J. Sadleir M.P., who later became Deputy Chairman before forfeiting many shares for arrears of payment. T.R. Crampton, the famous engineer, was down for £12,500 which allowed his firm to gain a more profitable interest later, whilst Fox himself was down for £31,875. Other people who stood to make a profit also subscribed — the stockbrokers for £87,500 and the contractor for rails for £18,750; the latter was possibly paid in shares 'in advance.' It was also revealed at a later stage that a man who subscribed for £40,000 was in actual fact a mere clerk in Fox's office — a time honoured way of disguising the true identity of a subscriber![14]

This uneven state of affairs amongst the subscribers was balanced by the first directorate, which was weighted towards the Kent men in terms of numbers though their holdings again reflected the strength of 'outside' interest. The Chairman was Lord Sondes of Lees Court near Faversham, who subscribed for £41,000 and thus accounted for a third of the Kent capital. C.J. Hilton (£5,050) and Hon. Stephen Lushington (£5,050) represented the Faversham area supporters, to whom must be added the latter's son C.M. Lushington (£7,550) who lived in London but may be regarded as a local man. There were four other Kent residents on the Board including D. Salomons of Tunbridge Wells (£7,550), E. Twopenny of Woodstock, Kent (£7,550), and Sir John Tylden of Milsted (£5,050). But the biggest shareholders with seats on the Board were all 'outsiders', including Crampton, a Birmingham banker called Scholefield (£25,000) and a Londoner named Wilson who also subscribed for £25,000. Of twenty-four other shareholders who subscribed for more than £2,000, four were from Sittingbourne and one each from Faversham, Hollingbourne, Tunstall, Torray Hill, Canterbury and Ashford; most of the rest were from London.

Local men were thus in a majority on the Board but it is doubtful whether they were fully in control of the Company. Fox was in a strong position and because of the financial support he provided was able to arrange a contract for the construction of the line virtually as he wished; hardly anything was put out to tender. Also of interest is the distribution of shareholders within the County, with a preponderance of subscribers from the Sittingbourne and Faversham area, but with no important subscriptions from the Medway towns of Rochester and Chatham, and only one from Canterbury. Agricultural interests in the Faversham area had particularly suffered from the advantage given to Weald farmers by the South Eastern, but those around Rochester and Canterbury had the use of branches. This demonstrates that local people were motivated by the chance to improve the financial prospects of their businesses, rather than the attractiveness of the Railway itself as an investment — subsequent events proved them right in their assessment! Outside 'capitalists' though had two reasons for their interest: either they hoped to make a clean financial profit out of the EKR, through healthy traffic or selling it off to the SER at an inflated price, or they stood to make money out of 'the works' as Fox did. However there were limits to even the latter group's enthusiasm, and by December 1853 interest in an EKR extension to Dover had 'expired' through lack of interest in its share subscriptions[15] though it was soon to resurface.

So most of the EKR's capital came from the traditional sources for Railway Companies of London, Birmingham and Lancashire. Some of these men provided funds in an orthodox way, others in manners that were becoming accepted more gradually: people like Fox, who were employed by the Company for the works, signed for shares in advance of the work starting, allowing loans also to be raised, and subsequently received their shares as part of the contract payment. In such circumstances work was rarely put out to tender and the East Kent began its plunge into an ever-tightening whirl of investment, loan and interest payment without a solid foundation of genuine capital.

Having secured its Act, the East Kent concentrated on the Strood to Faversham line which Joseph Cubitt estimated would cost £437,837; he recommended that

10

an immediate start should be made on the Medway bridge and the heavy works in the Chatham area which included three tunnels.

Even as the contract for the bridge was being worked out with Fox, Henderson & Co., the EKR was running into its first financial troubles. In January 1854 a call of £2-10-0d per share was met with complaints from the City shareholders and also from Scholefield, the Birmingham banker, who made comments about the state of the money market. There was an air of uncertainty in the City consequent upon the decline in Anglo-Russian relations, which was to lead to the outbreak of the Crimean War in March 1854. However the Kent shareholders paid up but then complained about the City shareholders in March 1854 when two-thirds of the shares were behind on payments. Despite becoming Deputy Chairman in 1855, Sadleir was one of the worst offenders and got £11,000 in arrears on his share calls, eventually forfeiting a large amount; so drastic was Sadleir's embarrassment that it was only eased by his death in early 1856.

Nevertheless work on the bridge began in June 1854 and on the Chatham tunnels in August but against a background of protest. Both the *Railway Times* and the Company's Minute Book record the complaints of shareholders who insisted that the line could be built more cheaply. Some argued that it would be better to build from Faversham to Chilham to avoid the cost of an independent line direct to Canterbury, others argued for a water's edge route in Chatham or the construction of only the Gillingham (New Brompton) to Faversham section. A deviation at Chatham and Rochester was seriously considered — especially as it would have increased the value of land held by some shareholders; the idea was put forward by a Director, Robert Lake (after whom the first effective locomotive on the line was named) of Milton, and work in the Chatham tunnels was suspended whilst a new route was surveyed. In November 1854 it was proposed to introduce a Bill for the deviation, but this had to be abandoned due to the opposition of the Board of Ordnance.

The year 1855 began very badly for the EKR; Fox was in financial difficulties and an argument between him and the Deputy Chairman, Salomons, resulted in the latter's resignation — he was replaced by Sadleir, one of Fox's associates. The shortfall on share calls was becoming serious and Fox was behind a scheme for using the £50,050 Parliamentary deposit to pay for the Medway bridge works; the authorisation of Parliament was eventually gained for this, despite SER opposition, because talk of a Dover extension was beginning to bear fruit and the completion of the East Kent was seen as vital for national defence. Lord Harding, of the War Office, wrote to Palmerston on 13th April 1855 that '... the completion of this line connecting Chatham and Dover is of great importance in a military point of view — the coast line between Dover and Folkestone being liable to sudden interruption....' Using the same argument, Fox was hoping to secure a loan of £400,000 from the Public Works Commissioners, but was unsuccessful.[16] However, for the EKR Harding's support proved conclusive and its 1855 Act allowed use of the deposit.

Fox's personal embarrassment during 1855 was such that another contractor offered to complete the line for two-thirds cash and one-third payment in shares,

11

but Fox managed to survive for a few more months. For the Strood to Canterbury works Fox was being paid 85% cash and 15% shares and during 1855 began to work out the details of the scheme. A swinging span was to be provided at the Strood end of the Medway bridge, whilst the Chatham station was to be built between the Fort Pitt and Chatham tunnels; early EKR plans show that the station buildings were to be to the north of the line, but they were eventually built on a bridge over the tracks — more appropriate given the cramped nature of the site. In August 1855 the EKR was asked to contribute to the maintenance of a chaplain for the instruction of the bridge workmen in Rochester. During the same month work commenced on the Chatham tunnels.

In June 1855 stockbrokers Carden & Whitehead suggested that the SER should take a controlling interest in the East Kent and work it instead of Fox, Henderson & Co., who intended to operate the line, take half the profits and pay the EKR 4% on capital for the privilege. It was to be a matter of considerable recrimination in later years that the SER passed up on this opportunity, though Parliament may not have been favourable in the light of the Cardwell Commission's views.

With Sadleir taking over from Salomons on the Board, Fox seemed to be getting stronger all the time — especially now that his Dover extension plans were making progress (see Chapter 2). The *Railway Times* was increasingly alarmed and, on the 30th June 1855, commented '... we do not see why Sir Charles Fox should not himself, publicly as well as practically, take the entire management into his own hands.' By November 1855 Fox had sunk into even deeper financial problems and the *Railway Times* seemed touchingly concerned for the rural innocents on the EKR Board:

'The East Kent is a contractors' line. The contractor has not been able to complete his bargain, and he is unwilling altogether to lose his hold.... These gentlemen, in our humble judgement, are exactly ten years behind the age. Have they been asleep since 1845?'

1845 had been the year of the 'Railway Mania', which had ended in scandal and charges of corruption. By autumn 1855 it seemed that the EKR was heading for a similar *dénouement* when it was revealed that the 2nd call on shares had gone unpaid on 20,937 of them.[17]

Early in 1856 Fox, Henderson & Co., had got into such difficulties that they were prepared to pay the East Kent £30,000 to be released from their contract. Although the EKR actually began negotiations with other contractors, Fox was able to rescue his company by forming an alliance with the firm of Morris, Burge & Crampton; the new contractors paid £100,000 for the privilege of being able to complete the whole line to Dover, now authorised, jointly with Fox, Henderson & Co. Crampton thus became a contractor as well as a Director, though he soon relinquished the latter post. The new partnership was authorised to start work on the Chatham to Faversham section on 19th March 1856, but although the works were to be for a double track only one line of rails was to be laid. One further embarrassment was removed in March 1856 with the death of Sadleir and the new contracting partnership seemed to offer hope of the line being completed by September 1857. In April 1856 work started on the Faversham to Canterbury section, commencing with the Ensden tunnel (as it was known at the time, later being Selling) and Boughton Hill cutting.

Meanwhile the basic arrangements for opening a railway were proceeding: a site for Faversham station was selected and it was decided to include a station at Newington after a petition from the local people. The Admiralty put in a request for a branch to Chatham Dockyard and in 1857 offered to guarantee 6% on this. In March 1856 the contractors again offered to lease the line, this time for 21 years with a guaranteed 5%, but the offer was firmly rejected by the EKR Board.

By early summer 1857, when the EKR was heavily involved in the arrangements for the Dover and St. Mary Cray (see Chapter 3), it was becoming clear that the Strood to Faversham section would not be open on 1st October 1857 as had been planned. At one stage it was suggested that the Ospringe to Gillingham section, both place names being specified in the Minutes on 20th June, could be opened as a temporary measure.

In July the Company received a request for a station at Boughton Blean (later served by Selling) and in August for a second station in Chatham. During December 1857 stations were under construction at Faversham, Teynham, Sittingbourne, Rainham and Chatham, it being resolved that 'the station at New Brompton be struck out of the timetables' which were then being prepared. The EKR contributed £300 towards the cost of a road being built from Milton to Sittingbourne station.

Rolling stock was hired from Crampton and arrived in December 1857, labelled 'L&C' for 'London & Chatham' in keeping with the Company's spiralling ambitions. The first five locomotives were named *Lake, Sondes, Faversham, Chatham* and *Sittingbourne*; the first two were named after influential Board members. Much of the stock had to be hired because the EKR could not pay £24,000 for the stock it had ordered; some of the Directors made last minute bridging loans to ease the Company's embarrassment. Given the financial difficulties, it is perhaps surprising that the EKR decided to run the traffic themselves rather than lease the operation to the contractors; but by 1857 the East Kent had pretensions to being a main-line Company, and so a Mr Finnigan from the South Eastern Railway was engaged as Traffic Manager.

The recruitment of staff commenced in November 1857, with porters being offered 16/- per week and gatemen 12/- together with a house. Kent was still a county that offered largely agricultural employment, with jobs in the fruit and hop trades being very unreliable and insecure, so that the railway was an attractive alternative. *General Order No. 6* from the EKR Board advised stationmasters on some of their responsibilites, which included '... daily inspection of the waiting rooms and water closets at their stations [to] see that they are kept in a cleanly state.'

Last minute financial worries struck in November 1857, with the EKR needing to find £114,000 to pay for the completion of the line to Faversham and also for the rolling stock, as mentioned above. Some of this came from

13

loans, but the situation was greatly eased by the contractors accepting £80,000 in debentures as part of the payment — at a healthy discount presumably, in the tradition of such arrangements.

Subsidence on the Strood side of the Medway approach embankment caused the EKR to apply initially to open only the Chatham to Faversham section. However the Board of Trade Inspector refused to sanction the opening at the beginning of January 1858 because of inadequate fencing and the lack of proper platforms at stations. The contractors were fined £200 for each day that elapsed until services between Chatham and Faversham commenced on 25th January, with horse-bus connections from Strood to Chatham and from Faversham to Canterbury.

To celebrate the opening a special train left Chatham for Faversham on 29th January, passing through triumphal arches at Rainham and Sittingbourne and conveying the traditional collection of Directors, shareholders and local dignitaries. An elegant repast was given at Faversham, about which the *Maidstone Journal* complained that '... for some unexplained reason, reporters were not admitted.' Nonetheless, its 6th February issue carried a report of the usual interminable speeches about trade, prosperity and progress. Reverend C. Hilton departed from the normal inanities of such speeches by enthusing about the way the railway would bring celestial light even to the pagans of Kent!

'The Rev. C. Hilton, in returning thanks, expressed an opinion that the extension of the railway to Faversham was a fact of great moral importance to the town. In one respect he had always been in favour of progress, and railways were progressive. They promoted commerce; commerce promoted civilisation; and civilisation was the forerunner of Christianity, because we must humanise people before we can Christianise them.'[18]

The theological basis of such remarks seems rather doubtful but the Kent audience, lost in the darkness before the dawn of commerce, did not argue.

An attempt was made to open the line between Strood and Chatham on 15th February, but in fact this was not achieved until 29th March 1858.

The initial timetable gave five through services from Strood to Canterbury, although this was operated by a four-horse coach beyond Faversham. By January 1860 there were six daily trains between Strood and Faversham, all with coach connections to Canterbury. The fastest 'up' train was the 8.10am from Faversham which, with a change at Strood, gave a London Bridge arrival at 10.20am.

During the latter part of 1858 locomotive shops were built at Faversham but these were never developed to the scale anticipated by local people as in 1860 the Company decided to have its principal shops at Longhedge in south London. The repair and maintenance sheds at Faversham appear to have been needed however, since the locomotive *Faversham* broke down nine times between 25th January and 13th March 1858. Mr C. Sacré was appointed Locomotive Superintendent in May 1858.

The railway showed an early ability to attract commercial development with the decision in January 1858 to build a new corn market close by Sittingbourne station. However progress was not so rapid at New Brompton (now Gillingham) and it is uncertain when the station actually opened for traffic; in March 1858 the EKR Executive Committee decided to start work on building a station there and in June 1858 the Board decided to open the station as early as possible 'before the Races.' It appears to have opened at some time during the late summer, land was sold for a station hotel in July, but by December 1858 the Board was considering closing it due to lack of receipts.

However the figures for the first receipts on the East Kent Railway seemed to suggest that the whole line was doing little better than New Brompton. After deduction of fees to the SER and for the Canterbury coach, total receipts for February 1858 were £725-6-11d and £1,807-4-11d for June. These were tiny amounts at a time when the EKR was trying to raise an extra £300,000 capital.

The East Kent had been initially promoted by local people to serve their own needs, with proposals that it should be leased to the SER — proposals that were rejected, probably because the South Eastern intended to wait until financial necessity forced the EKR to offer itself for sale at a discount. But during the later 1850s the EKR had begun to outgrow its origins, developing ambitions that arose in no small part from the minds of speculators and influential contractors. By the end of 1858 it had gained powers to extend to Dover in one direction and to Bickley, giving better access to London, in the other; it was thus in a position to challenge the SER for the cross-Channel traffic, and small ideas of serving the Kent community were mislaid in the headlong dash for glory. Visions of grandeur were dreamt up by stockbrokers and contractors and easily sold to the more naive Directors. Local men continued to be numerically strong on the Board — Sondes, Harris, Hilton and Lake were all regular in their attendance at Board meetings, but they appear to have been easily manipulated. Repeated attempts by the SER in 1858 to take over the EKR were firmly rejected; the SER was now alive to the dangers of a line competing on equal terms, but the EKR seemed to have already forgotten the financial problems of late 1857.

Psychological factors are perhaps as important as any in evaluating the policies of the EKR Board. Many of the Kent Directors were not experienced in industrial management and the railway was their first involvement in complex financial matters. Men like Fox and Peto seemed to exert a charismatic hold over successive, comparitively uninitiated directorates. Peto in particular was a man of great prominence in Victorian society, having achieved great fame through his connections with the Crystal Palace and the Crimean War when he had sponsored the famous 'navvy army' which went out to defeat the Tsar by building a railway. Also perhaps some of the local men treated the railway as an adventure and certainly the EKR's independence was a source of pride to many though the years increasingly revealed it to be a matter fit only for melancholy.

The mood was summarised in a speech by the Lord Mayor of London, himself an EKR shareholder, in a speech at Faversham on the opening day:

15

'... the Chairman and his brother directors would never be satisfied till they found themselves with a line finished to, and with an excellent terminus in, Dover. Hitherto they had endeavoured to make peace with the South Eastern, but now the South Eastern might without success endeavour to make peace with the East Kent.'

So by January 1858 the shape of the next forty years was already decided on. The East Kent Railway was not to be a local line, it was to become a plaything for the speculators and the contractors, the reason and excuse for promoting many miles of competitive line across the Kent landscape; miles that consumed capital voraciously and that were to lead the whole concern into Chancery in 1866.

An independent future of ruinous competition was the path the EKR chose in 1858, whilst the name of Sir Morton Peto was only a shadow on the horizon.

CHAPTER TWO

The Canterbury & Dover Line

The population of Dover proved to be amongst the most vocal supporters of the East Kent scheme and, later, of the independence of the London, Chatham & Dover Railway into which the EKR transformed itself in 1859. Dover people were closely involved with the promotion of the EKR plan in the early 1850s and consistently acted thereafter to ensure that it did not fall into the grasp of the South Eastern Railway. These actions had their origins in a profound distrust of the SER, a feeling which had built up from a very early stage in the railway history of Dover.

The 1836 Act of the South Eastern Railway had provided for a line from London to Dover via Ashford and Folkestone instead of by the traditional Rochester and Canterbury route. In itself this was no particular threat to the interests of Dover, but what they really objected to was the purchase of Folkestone Harbour by the SER in 1843 for £18,000. Folkestone was thus turned into a strong rival to Dover, for the Harbour there was served by an SER branch line and it was several miles nearer to London by rail than the senior port. It was also felt that the SER's ownership of Folkestone would prejudice that Company against Dover, though Folkestone Harbour was under the disadvantage of being severely limited by the effects of the tides. The *Railway Times* showed an early distaste for the complaints of the Dover residents, who had received their first trains to the Dover Town station in 1844; it commented that the SER had refused to 'knuckle to the sordid and grasping propensities of the "Men of Dover".... the little town of Folkestone is beginning to rival them and they are miserably jealous.'

Almost as soon as the SER was open there appeared a spate of schemes to provide Dover with a more direct link via Canterbury; many of these tried to secure Government support by arguing that the SER's cliff route between Folkestone and Dover was critically exposed to enemy attack. Dover itself supported most of these schemes, for example that of Vignoles in 1845-46. On 5th June 1846 the *Dover Chronicle* complained that '... the people of Dover are opposed to the roundabout course the South Eastern takes, and are favourable to a more direct line to London, which would also place them in communication with the populous towns on the road, and from which they are at present cut off.'

The SER failed to win over Dover's sympathies with schemes like its Canterbury & Dover Bill, which was dropped on the second reading in 1847; it was felt that this was just an attempt to block independent projects. However during the early 1850s it began to seem that Dover was not to be lucky; in1851

Canterbury East station, with the overall roof that was typical of LCDR practice on the more important Kent stations.   (A. Riley)

A recent view of Shepherdswell station, located at the bottom of a cutting. The sidings leading to the former East Kent Light Railway can be seen on the right beyond the station. (Author)

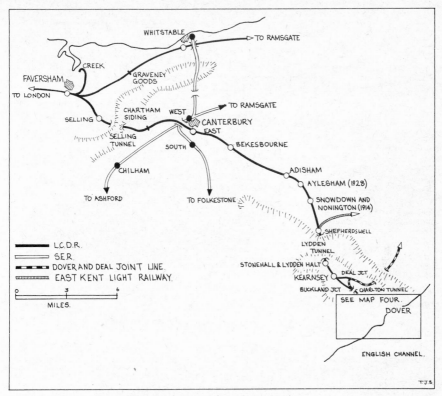

Map 3: The Canterbury & Dover Line

the 'Mid-Kent & Dover' decided only to go as far as Canterbury although late in 1853 the idea of a separate Canterbury & Dover Company was floated. This was to have had three Directors nominated by the EKR and was fostered by Fox, but in December 1853 the *Railway Times* reported that it had 'expired through lack of subscriptions.'[1] One of the overriding considerations in the promotion of a railway from Canterbury to Dover was the configuration of the land, for the scarp slope of the chalk downs faced Dover, so that even the Dour valley offered a difficult approach to the port.

However Canterbury was a far more promising possibility than Dover and, having been reached by the SER's line from Ashford in 1846, was included in the powers of the East Kent Railway's Act of 1853 to be the terminus of a line from Strood. Apart from the section through the Medway towns, the line from Faversham to Canterbury was the most problematic of the original EKR construction project. Leaving Faversham and heading south-east, the line had to cross a ridge of the North Downs in the neighbourhood of Boughton before it could descend into the Stour valley. Although Vignoles' plan of 1845/46 had envisaged a long tunnel through Boughton Hill, the EKR hoped to avoid this by the use of steep gradients (1 in 100) and sharp curves, though a short tunnel

19

at Ensden was still involved. During October 1854 the EKR Board considered abandoning this route and taking a more southerly line to join the SER's Canterbury branch near Chilham; this would have used a dry valley to obviate the necessity for a tunnel but would have been half a mile longer. Cubitt reported to the EKR on the subject and concluded that 'as a through line to Dover and the Continent to London the additional length has more weight;' so it was decided to press ahead with the tunnel rather than endure the inconvenience of a longer line, exposing the EKR's continental ambitions at an early date.[2] Robert Lake, the Director, was behind both this plan (which involved a single line) and another one to save money in the Medway area by building the line along the water's edge; it generally seems to have been the Kent people who pressed for the line to be built as cheaply as possible.

During early 1855 a new Bill for a Canterbury and Dover line was being actively promoted by Sir Charles Fox, who of course intended to profit from it through the contracting. However, his hopes for a loan of £400,000 from the Public Works Commissioners, based on the old argument of military importance, were disappointed. The line certainly did have some support from the War Office, however, and this was reflected in its Bill being allowed through Parliament without opposition in September 1855. The Dover extension Act provided for 20,000 shares of £25 each, but throughout the Parliamentary campaign the project had been bedevilled by lack of real local support and throughout the summer of 1855 a committee of Dover men had endeavoured to drum up local funds for the line to safeguard it from later sale to the SER. But again it was the outsiders who produced the greater proportion of the capital, with Fox subscribing for £40,000 in July 1855; the *Railway Times* noted soberly that the average local subscription was a mere £100-12-6d whereas ten outsiders put up £147,000 between them.[3] The *Railway Times* also reported a meeting held in Dover in July 1855 which resolved that the South Eastern 'sought to establish a most injurious monopoly, detrimental to all the other interests of this town.... this conduct has justified the local promoters of the East Kent in advocating a policy of entire independence.'

The Dover extension seems to have set the pace for the EKR and LCDR's later spectacular financial failures. Conceived under the tutelage of Fox, who ran into severe problems of his own late in 1855, the extension was to be watched over by the EKR but was financed entirely separately. Thus investors bought 'Dover shares' rather than EKR ones. When calls began to be made on subscriptions it soon became apparent that the subscription lists were a fantasy; by August 1856, the *Railway Times* was able to report, somewhat gloatingly, that calls on shares were already £20,500 in arrears. This was despite the panic in Dover due to the rapid increase in the popularity of Folkestone; in 1856 120,000 people used the Folkestone-Boulogne route across the Channel and only 70,000 the Dover-Calais route. Yet by 1858 the position of the Dover extension's finances was disastrous; in May the *Railway Times* claimed that 75% of the shares were unsold and a call for £22,000 in September produced only £9,000. Late in 1858 a new Dover Act had to be passed (21 & 22 Vic. c.li) to clear up the financial mess; this cancelled forfeited and unissued shares

20

and replaced them with preferred and deferred half-shares. In January 1859 the *Railway Times* claimed that only 6,686 shares had actually been paid up; 2,250 had been forfeited and 11,164 had been cancelled without having been issued. It is not surprising that when the EKR Board authorised the start of works on the Dover line in April 1857 it was to be at a rate of only £1,000 per month. Despite the 1858 Act, money for the Dover extension continued to be short so that in October 1859 Thomas Crampton, the contractor who replaced Fox, took a £60,000 deposit in debentures.

Whilst the problems of the Dover extension were being sorted out, work was proceeding very slowly on the Faversham to Canterbury section of the original line. On 19th March 1856, the EKR Board authorised Fox, Henderson & Co., to commence the works with assistance from Crampton, Morris and Burge, though only a single track was to be laid. Work started in April 1856 on the Boughton Hill cutting and at Ensden tunnel, which was later known as Selling.

Once construction work had begun the EKR began to receive the usual deputations about the siting of passenger stations. In May 1858 the people of Boughton requested a station at Crouch, a hamlet on the line near Selling. This idea obviously won the support of Hilton, who was arranging for a 'Selling' station in June of that year. As a defensive measure the South Eastern Railway opened a new station at Chartham in 1859, at a point where the EKR would be within half a mile of its Canterbury branch. In January 1860, by which time the EKR had changed its name to 'London, Chatham & Dover Railway', the Board decided to make an immediate start on building a 'Boughton & Selling' station though Cubitt, the engineer, had to redesign the station building with a separate lamp-room presumably as a precaution against fire.[4] The LCDR hoped to have its Canterbury line open in time for the Royal Agricultural Show, which was to be held there in summer 1860, even getting as far as planning to borrow extra stock for the traffic. But opening dates were set and then passed by without any public trains running: 15th June 1860 saw no public service and in fact the opening ceremony did not occur until 8th July 1860 with the full service commencing the following day. Selling was the only intermediate station on the ten-mile line but a siding was provided on the down side of the line at Chartham; there was a 405 yard tunnel which cost at least one life in its construction.

An immediate result of the opening of this line was that it brought competition into the railway life of Canterbury. The LCDR introduced very competitive rates from the outset, offering a 1st class Canterbury-London season ticket at £42-0-0d when the SER had been charging £52-10-0d.

Works on the Canterbury to Dover section had started in 1857 but the contractor, Crampton, was subjected to much criticism; in May 1859 the Board heard that only 250 men were employed on the entire section and in September Cubitt reported that he was dissatisfied with Crampton's progress. Nonetheless by November 1858 the debate over the siting of stations had commenced with a request for one at Adisham and in December the Directors decided that humble Bekesbourne did not merit a station. In February 1859 the Board

Adisham station during the Southern Railway days; the goods yard is noticeably prosperous.
(A. Riley collection)

received a deputation from Nonington and Sibertswold, asking for stations at Adisham and 'Butter Street' (Shepherdswell); the Company agreed to approve these providing that the land was given free together with £500 to cover the costs, conditions which also applied to the provision of a goods-only station at Bekesbourne; however by November 1859 the Executive Committee had opted to build a proper station at Bekesbourne instead.

During 1860 the Dover extension was finally approaching completion, though for Dover residents the good news was qualified by persistent rumours of an amalgamation of the LCDR with the SER. In January 1860 a Dover meeting resolved that a merger would be 'most prejudicial to the interests of the public and particularly to the Town and Harbour of Dover.'[5] During the 1860 enquiry into the LCDR's Bill for a Metropolitan Extension, much of the antipathy between Dover and the SER was revealed. Dover merchants complained that the coal dues charged at the port had been reduced to encourage the SER to develop the coal trade, which it had not done; dues had been waived to encourage the EKR as a result of this. In fact the SER had promised to develop a coal trade of 1½ million tons per year according to the merchants, but in 1860 the coal imports were running at only 4,000 tons. The SER had added insult to injury by manufacturing its coke supplies at Folkestone. Robinson, a Dover coal merchant who gave evidence to the committee of the House of Lords, was particularly vocal in his criticisms of the South Eastern: 'It is notorious that in consequence of Folkestone being fostered by the South Eastern Company, being their own port, they have done everything they could to injure the Town of Dover in every shape and form.' Robinson also commented,

22

Kearnsey station in about 1910. (A. Riley collection)

'You cannot call Folkestone a harbour, it is out of the question.' Dover people also claimed that the 1st class single fare of 22/- from London damaged Dover's chances of developing into a seaside resort, an area in which Folkestone, Margate and Ramsgate all had advantages; the SER's comparable fare to Canterbury was only 10/-.

Undoubtedly the SER made a bad mistake in its handling of Dover, especially after the possible amalgamation of 1858-60 fell through. In 1860 the the Dover coal merchant was able to describe the SER's treatment of the town as 'a course of deception from beginning to end;'[6] although this may appear to be an exaggeration, such feelings were typical amongst a large proportion of Dover's tradesmen and reflected a careless handling of public relations by the South Eastern. As far as possible the SER's image was fostered by the *Railway Times*, which had an intimate connection with Samuel Smiles, Secretary to the SER and author of *Self-Help* which was published in 1859. The *Railway Times* lost no opportunity to attack the EKR or its successor, the LCDR, whereas *Herapath's Railway Magazine* generally defended it. Clearly the people of Dover patronised *Herapath* rather than the rival publication.

However the South Eastern had been instrumental in a few developments at Dover. In 1851 it had constructed the impressive 'Lord Warden Hotel' and its presence certainly contributed to the decision to construct the Admiralty Pier, which was also opened in 1851. But the SER's situation in Dover was far from ideal because of its approach along a narrow space between the cliffs and the sea; indeed by 1860 local people were already claiming that a rough sea stopped the SER's trains from running past a point close to the Archcliffe

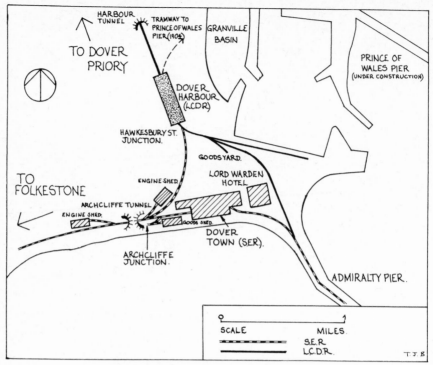

Map 4: Railways in the Dover Harbour Area, 1898

Tunnel. The SER opened its station at Dover Town, and in 1861 extended a short single-line branch from there to the Admiralty Pier.

In April 1860 the London, Chatham & Dover Railway was concerned about the advantage the SER would gain through its new direct link onto the Pier from the Town station, whilst its own passengers would be marooned several hundred yards away at Dover Harbour station; the provision of a 'tramway' of its own, from the Harbour station and crossing Hawkesbury Street onto Admiralty Pier, was therefore discussed but it was to be several years before the short extension was constructed. But at this time the Company's main concern was the tardiness of the works on the Canterbury-Dover line itself, even though the new line was inspected by the Directors on 4th August 1860 when they were hauled through Lydden Tunnel in contractors' wagons drawn by horses. In fact Sir Morton Peto was called in to advise on the situation in January 1861, when provision of a temporary station at Dover was also under consideration.

The Canterbury to Dover extension of the LCDR was eventually opened to traffic on 22nd July 1861, though only as far as 'Charlton' as the Board Minutes called it, known to the confused public as 'Dover Town'. The existence of two stations with the same name cannot have been well-received by the long-suffering local residents, and so the station became 'Dover Priory' from July

24

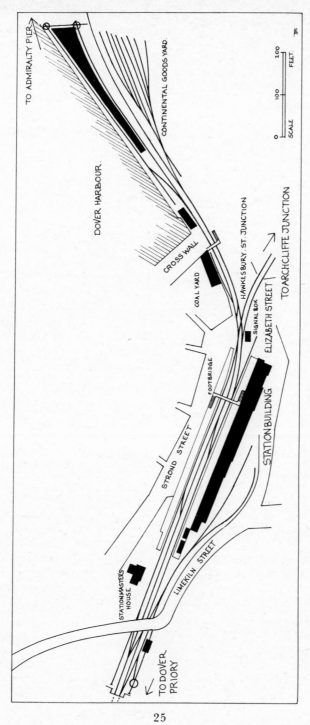

Map 5: Dover Harbour Station, 1898

TO ADMIRALTY PIER

DOVER HARBOUR.

CONTINENTAL GOODS YARD.

CROSS WALL

COAL YARD

HAWKESBURY. ST. JUNCTION

TO ARCHCLIFFE JUNCTION

SIGNAL BOX

ELIZABETH STREET

FOOTBRIDGE

STRAND STREET

STATION BUILDING

STATIONMASTER'S HOUSE

LIMEKILN STREET

TO DOVER PRIORY

0   100   200

SCALE   FEET.

Dover Priory in 1876, showing the Yard and sidings. Nearest to the camera is a 'Europa' class 2-4-0. (O.J. Morris/SECR Society)

26

1863; interestingly it was referred to as 'Priory' in the Minutes of August 1861, two years before the name was introduced. Beyond 'Dover Town (LCDR)' the line continued through Dover Harbour tunnel to emerge close to the seafront at what was to be the LCDR's 'Dover Harbour' station, but this section did not open until 1st November 1861 as the Inspecting Officer, Captain Tyler, reportedly found the tunnel 'too small'.[7] Only a temporary station was provided at Harbour to begin with and it certainly had no continental traffic until at least February 1862; a proper station was opened in June 1863 according to some historians, but the LCDR General Meetings Minutes of February 1865 recorded Dover Harbour station as still not completed.

This Canterbury to Dover extension line involved a considerable number of heavy engineering works in order to climb up the dip slope of the chalk downland and pass through the escarpment to Dover; these features of the landscape also accounted for the paucity of intermediate traffic. The principal feature was the 2,369 yard Lydden Tunnel, just south of Shepherdswell station. There were also considerable difficulties in the immediate vicinity of Dover itself, where the town had expanded to take up all the flat ground in the valley so that the railway was forced to tunnel through several outlying spurs of chalk in order to reach the harbour. Thus there were tunnels at Charlton (264 yards), Priory (158 yards) and Harbour (684 yards). Intermediate stations were at Bekesbourne, Adisham and Shepherdswell, though none of these places was sizable. Adisham had a population of 492 in 1861, though this was considerably swollen by the presence of railway workers as can be seen by comparing it with the 1851 and 1871 figures of 401 and 415 respectively. Sibertswold (Shepherdswell) had a population of 411 and Bekesbourne of 475 in 1861, though again both were swollen by the presence of navvies.

The growth of Dover was rapid after 1861. In that year the Dover Harbour Board was created, on which both the railway companies had a voice, and this pursued an energetic development policy. The Admiralty Pier, mentioned above, was a particularly important development since it reached out into deeper water and the LCDR opened a short, sharply curved link from Harbour station to the Pier on December 21st, 1864. This considerably improved the LCDR's facilities for continental passenger and mail traffic.

The most notable fruit of the formation of the Dover Harbour Board was the construction during the mid-1870s of a series of basins along the seafront, principally for freight traffic. These were served by an LCDR siding which curved sharply out of its Harbour station at the tunnel end, where space was so restricted that access to the branch could only be obtained by swinging aside part of the station's down platform. The branch was later extended to the Prince of Wales Pier as a street tramway because of the restricted space available.

A macabre event took place at Dover Harbour station on 1st March 1868, when stationmaster Edward Walsh was shot dead by eighteen-year-old porter, Thomas Wells. A request was made to the LCDR for an annuity to be granted to Walsh's widow, but this was refused. Great interest centred on the execution of Wells in August, 1868, since he was the first man to be executed within the

27

Dover Admiralty Pier in about 1900, shortly before the paddle-steamers were supplanted by screw-driven ferries. (Author's collection)

Prison walls at Maidstone rather than in public as had previously been the case; the execution was widely reported:

'The extreme punishment was carried into effect at half-past ten o'clock upon Thomas Wells, a culprit who only attained his 18th year in March last. There were very few, if any, strangers in the vicinity of the prison, and the town presented its ordinary appearance. A few of the tradesmen and other inhabitants might have been observed conversing together upon the sad spectacle that was going on within the walls of the prison, but the town generally presented a naked and extraordinary contrast to that which it has exhibited upon occasions when executions have taken place in public. No one was present at the execution but the under-sheriff, governor, serjeant, chaplain and representatives of the press. The culprit prayed fervently with the Rev. Mr Frazer, the chaplain, for a few seconds, and as the drop fell he was singing in a loud clear voice the 486th hymn. He appeared to die after two or three convulsive struggles.'[8]

Having found the people of Dover a useful ally in its initial struggles, the LCDR subsequently found them difficult to please when plans for amalgamation with the SER were being discussed. Dover had a very clear voice in the LCDR's policy decisions, since for the majority of the Company's history a Dover M.P. sat on the Board. Major Dickson was continuously involved from 1875 until his death in 1889, when he was replaced by George Wyndham who eventually rose to be Chief Secretary for Ireland with a seat in the Cabinet. A result of one such period of friendship between the two companies was the joint project for a Dover & Deal railway, authorised in 1874; this branched off from the LCDR's line near Kearnsey (where a station called Ewell had been opened on 1st August 1862) and is discussed in Chapter Nine. During the late 1870s the two companies got as far as depositing a Bill for their amalgamation but this was lost in August 1878, due partly to opposition from Dover Corporation. At the time plans existed for the creation of joint stations at Dover and Canterbury.

The joint nature of the Dover & Deal project necessitated some form of SER access to it other than the torturous process of reversing at Admiralty Pier. Because of this another short line was opened on the Dover seafront in 1881, probably on 15th June when the Deal line itself was opened. This was a new curve that ran from the SER at Archcliffe Junction to join the LCDR at Hawkesbury Street Junction, avoiding the SER's Dover Town station and wholly belonging to that Company. In March 1882 the Mayor of Dover, Sir Edward Watkin of the SER and James Staats Forbes of the LCDR met to discuss the possibility of a new and central Joint Station. Sadly nothing became of this proposal because relations between the two companies deteriorated shortly afterwards, though from 1914 onwards the Priory station virtually took on that rôle after the closure of the old Town station.

As the companies became more competitive again during the mid-1880s, the LCDR began to consider gaining access to Folkestone from off its Dover line. There had in fact been a long history of attempts to gain entry to Folkestone from the north, notably the Elham Valley Railway Act of 1866 which had authorised a line from the LCDR's Canterbury station to Folkestone. This project expired through lack of financial support, its authorisation coinciding with a period of deep gloom in the City. However in 1878 the LCDR proposed a line from Kearnsey to Folkestone via the Alkham Valley, a project which it revived in 1884. The SER's response was to reinvigorate the Elham Valley idea to fill the gap between Folkestone and Canterbury; this was authorised by Parliament on 28th July 1881 and opened on 4th July 1887. The line left the SER's Ashford to Ramsgate line at Harbledown Junction, near Canterbury, and ran through the Elham Valley to Cheriton Junction, near Folkestone. It is unlikely that the line did any damage to the LCDR's traffic, but it did block any attempt by the LCDR to reach Folkestone from its own main line. Later efforts by the LCDR to infest this SER stronghold came from the west.

One of the principal types of freight traffic on the northern part of the Faversham to Canterbury line was the hops which were moved from Kent to London for the brewing trade. The principal destination was Borough Market, the base of the hop factors, though these 'middlemen' declined in importance during the late 1800s. The growth of Kent hops increased very rapidly during the first three-quarters of the century, particularly during the 1870s; by 1877 the hop acreage had reached 45,984. Hops were grown at several locations along the main line between Rainham and Canterbury, though after about 1885 the acreage began to decline and the Kent hop trade became more

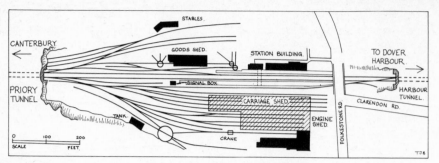

Map 6: Dover Priory Station, 1898

concentrated on Maidstone and Canterbury; acreage had fallen to 29,269 by 1906.[9]

The hop trade was very volatile with frequent and rapid shifts in prices: 'Marketing thus required special facilities in warehousing and transport, adequate market information and close contact between grower and factor.'[10] Thus the Wealden farmers gained an early advantage with the opening of the South Eastern line when other parts of Kent had no rail service at all, allowing them to undercut the prices of their rivals; in June 1851 the price of hops in the Southwark markets varied rom 70s. to 82s. for Weald hops, and 84s. to 140s. for hops from Mid-Kent or East Kent. The tendency of hop-growing to concentrate around certain 'nodal' points late in the nineteenth century was a result of the strong desire for good transport facilites in order to compete on price; thus in February 1867 land was sold at Canterbury station for a hop warehouse.

Another reason for the volatility of the hop traffic was that it was very sensitive to the weather. The *Railway Times* reported in 1879 that bad weather had reduced the LCDR's hop traffic by about £6,000 but in 1886, a good year, the fruit and hop traffic was reckoned to be 'up' on normal years by as much as £9,000. Bad weather in 1890 reduced the hop traffic from 56,000 pockets to only 20,000, a loss of traffic worth about £2,600.

The close dependence of the hop growers on the railway led to some charges that the railway was able to exploit a monopoly control. In November 1883 farmers from the Canterbury area complained of overcharging by both the SER and the LCDR, and a test case was brought before the Railway Commissioners concerning terminal charges applied to the carriage of hops from Selling to Blackfriars. In June 1884 the Commissioners found against the LCDR, so that in August the East Kent Chamber of Agriculture was encouraged to bring an action for the reduction of rates. Some farmers took to sending their hops by road, but this proved unsatisfactory due to the perishable nature of the some charges that the railway was able to exploit a monopoly control. In November 1883 farmers from the Canterbury area complained of overcharging by both the SER and the LCDR, and a test case was brought before the Railway Commissioners concerning terminal charges applied to the carriage of hops from Selling to Blackfriars. In June 1884 the Commissioners found against the

30

Dover Harbour station in 1921. On the left can be seen the unusual 'swinging' section of platform that could be adjusted to allow trains to gain access to the Prince of Wales Pier and Wellington Dock line. (Patterson Rutherford)

LCDR, so that in August the East Kent Chamber of Agriculture was encouraged to bring an action for the reduction of rates. Some farmers took to sending their hops by road, but this proved unsatisfactory due to the perishable nature of the product and in September 1884 the legal action was dropped. However in November both the SER and LCDR reduced their charges for hops and also for another perishable product, fish, when sent by passenger train.

During the later years of the nineteenth century there were several attempts to persuade the LCDR to build extra stations on the Faversham to Dover section. An 1886 request for a station at Chartham was turned down; though provided with a proper facility by the SER, Chartham was only ever afforded a goods station by the LCDR. In 1893 Dover Corporation supported a request for a station at Buckland, but this was turned down as was a proposal for a station to serve a new sports ground at Crabble, near Dover, in 1896.

The first years of the twentieth century resulted in a number of new developments along the line and also in the facilities at Dover, which are discussed in Chapter Sixteen.

CHAPTER THREE

'The East Kent is no more!'

— The Western Extension Line

i) Strood to Bickley

As it originated, the East Kent Railway had the appearance of a local line, but due to a number of pressures it transformed itself during the late 1850s and early 1860s into a major trunk route, the 'London, Chatham & Dover Railway.' In doing so it became involved in a financial tangle so labyrinthine that several years of bankruptcy — in Chancery — never really solved its problems. There were really three reasons for this transformation: firstly, a number of Kent interests — especially in Dover — wanted a viable alternative to the SER; secondly, the romantic appeal of railways continued to attract inexperienced investors despite the warnings of the railway press; thirdly, and of greatest importance, various stockbrokers, bankers and contractors stood to gain considerably from any railway project, whether or not it ever made a profit by running trains.

By early 1855 the fledgling East Kent Railway was beginning to show signs of ambition beyond its humble station. In particular it was concerned with making improvements in its means of access to London. The catalyst for this interest was a project named the 'Westminster Terminus Railway', which planned to establish a 'West End' terminus on the north bank of the Thames in Pimlico; at the time none of the Railway Companies operating in the southern counties had access across the River Thames. The Westminster Terminus Railway was authorised in 1854 and in November 1855 the EKR Directors voted to acquire an interest in the concern, despite the financial uncertainties caused by the Crimean War. However the EKR had no physical connection with the projected lines which led up to Pimlico (namely the 'West End of London & Crystal Palace', authorised 1853 and open by 1858), and so it drew up a Bill to authorise a connection between the SER's North Kent line, over which its services ran from Strood, and the Thames at Battersea.

The link-line between the North Kent and the Thames was a complicated project involving a line from Dartford to Lewisham, where it would have crossed the SER's Mid-Kent line to Beckenham (opened 1st January 1857), then passed via Nunhead and Camberwell to 'Victoria', as the West End terminus was being called by April 1856. Provision was to be made for branches to Greenwich, Deptford, Beckenham and Orpington; altogether a very ambitious project which would have provided 27 miles of new line for an estimated £600,000 construction costs. However the Bill was withdrawn during May 1856 and the Westminster Terminus Railway itself was replaced by a much healthier concern, the 'Victoria Station & Pimlico Railway' (Act passed 23rd July 1858) which was also backed by the London, Brighton & South Coast Railway.

grounds that it would damage the interests of the SER, but the real fight was to be in the Lords. The SER mounted a very effective attack including Lord Darnley of Cobham Hall, the principal landowner on the EKR route; Darnley disliked the railway and refused to have a station called Cobham.[3] Ashcroft, the SER's engineer, maintained that the line was unnecessary due to the SER's planned improvements; these included an extension into the West End from either Bricklayers Arms or New Cross, in south-east London. The SER had also planned a link from Dartford to the Crays line at Southborough Road (Bickley) in connection with the proposed leasing of the latter concern, though in fact only operation of the Crays line by the SER was allowed. Finally the SER criticised the complete lack of freight traffic on the EKR extension — citing only two mills in the Darenth valley and some fruit. The Bill was rejected.

As has been mentioned above, the subscription contract for the EKR's 1857 Western Extension Bill included four prominent contractors. To these were added a few Kent men and a number of London interests; the Kent men included Harris, Tylden, Hilton, E. Twopenny (Sittingbourne), W. Walter (Rainham), G. Cobb (Bredgar), J. Lake (Sittingbourne) and W. Dent (Bromley). The *Railway Times*, reporting on this in January 1857, noted that Hilton's interests now included banking.

In October 1857 the EKR produced a new Western Extension Bill for the 1857-58 session. In November the Crays Company rejected EKR approaches and granted the SER the right to work its line for ten years. However the Crays Company also intended to abandon its powers to build a line beyond Southborough Road (Bickley) and the EKR intended to take these over. The EKR was estimating its costs at £300,000 but this seemed rather academic when the Commons Committee rejected the EKR Bill in favour of the SER's link-line, on the condition that the SER improved its access to the West End. This was completely reversed by the Lords who passed the EKR Bill and rejected that of the SER, the Western Extension receiving its Royal Assent on 23rd July 1858. The Act allowed the EKR to build its own line from Strood to St. Mary Cray, to construct the line from there to Bickley in place of the Crays Company, and granted running powers over the Crays line and the WELCP to Battersea. The line between Bromley and Bickley had also to be doubled within a year to prevent undue obstruction by the SER. The decision, even whilst it was still only anticipated, aroused a storm of protests from South Eastern interests. An angry SER shareholder wrote to the *Railway Times* in May 1858:

'Had a direct line from London to Dover offered any advantages, save to the landowners and contractors, it would have been made long ago.'

The *Railway Times* itself, prompted by its close ties with the SER, unleashed a storm of abuse in a rampaging attack on the Parliamentary decision:

'The decision of Monday is an invitation to all the unscrupulous adventurers in the country to proceed in their nefarious attacks upon established property, until they are either recognised as competing powers or bought off

35

The terminal building at the Longfield refuse siding, opened in 1876 and variously used by the Vestry of St. Mary Newington and Lambeth and Southwark Borough Councils. After ten years of disuse, it still stands. (Author)

Sole Street station in 1984, virtually unchanged since its opening. Though it was built to serve Cobham, it has now fostered its own small community. (Author)

as brigands too strong to be driven out of their fastnesses.... It has pleased the Collective Wisdom of the Nation to plant a thorn in the side of the South Eastern....'[4]

Who were these 'unscrupulous adventurers'? None other than Peto, Betts and Crampton, who put in a request for the contract in July — as soon as the Act had passed. There seems to have been no tendering procedure and they were given the job in August. Crampton offered to advance the money needed to purchase the land in exchange for the contract, an offer which he applied to Strood-Bickley and Canterbury-Dover.[5]

During the 1858 Parliamentary contest the SER made repeated attempts to reach a negotiated settlement with the EKR, making offers to the EKR Board in May and June; on the latter occasion the EKR resolved that the SER proposals were 'utterly inadmissable.' Having so dismally failed in its attempts to grasp the implanted 'thorn', the SER seems to have descended to a policy of wilful sulkiness. Whilst the Western Extension was under construction, the EKR maintained the facility clauses which protected its use of the SER's North Kent line from Strood. However the SER fought back by withdrawing all facilities that it was not legally bound to provide, such as running its carriages onto the EKR tracks. EKR passengers were forced to change carriages at Strood, often incurring an extra charge of 1/- and if the EKR train was running late the SER refused to hold its own train that was supposed to provide a connection. Through tickets were also stopped. The result of this was that the tolls that the EKR paid to the SER for traffic worked onwards to London fell from £420 in July 1858 to £193 in August 1859.[6]

Two particular aspects of this dispute that galled the EKR were the SER's refusal, from 21st July 1858, to accept any through bookings from beyond Faversham and its insistence that all stock running through to London Bridge should be provided by the EKR. The Board of Trade was called in to investigate the case and found that the SER was not breaking its legal obligations in either case.

Work began on the Western Extension in November 1858, with the total cost estimated at £450,000. The new confidence and ambition that resulted from the success of these plans was made official in December 1858 when the East Kent decided to change its name to the 'London, Chatham & Dover Railway.' The change took effect from 1st August 1859 and was recorded by *Herapath*:

'The East Kent is no more! Start not, gentle shareholder. It is not of the demise of your railway that we write.... it is your name that is gone. Henceforth your Company is to be called "The London, Chatham & Dover Railway Company." You have outgrown the bonds which were properly described by the term "East Kent Railway Company." You are no longer a local line, but a great trunk railway from London, via Chatham, to Dover.'[7]

The reaction of the *Railway Times* was altogether more acidic:

37

Fawkham station looking east in about 1900. This is now the site of Longfield station.
(SECR Society)

Another view of Fawkham in about 1910, showing its isolated position amidst cornfields.
(E. Baldock collection)

'Under these circumstances it is considered expedient that the name of the original Company should be changed, blotted out of existence if not of public recollection and the thickest veil which can be procured is.... that described as the "London, Chatham & Dover Railway." But nature will break out. Wet blankets are of little use on the craters of volcanoes, except to hide the mysteries beneath from the spectator in a season of repose.'[8]

As construction of the Western Extension progressed, the usual discussions about the siting of stations began. The largest settlement between Strood and St. Mary Cray was Cobham, but Lord Darnley of Cobham Hall was implacably opposed to any station bearing the name of the village. The nearest site to Cobham proved to be Sole Street, which was considered by the Board as early as May 1858 though the final decision was not made until August 1859. Approved at the same time was a station at Meopham Road, so referred to as it was 1½ miles from the village of that name though it never carried the suffix in public service. These two stations were within a mile of each other and it was Sole Street that was rated as the most important since it was closer to Cobham. In fact the construction of permanent station buildings at Meopham was not decided on until March 1861, when it was seen as a good base for an omnibus link to Gravesend. Sole Street opened with the rest of the line on 1st February 1861 and from March 1861 its passengers were empowered to stop one express train each day by signal − presumably a concession to satisfy Lord Darnley. However Meopham did not open until 1st May due to the incomplete state of its buildings.

About a mile west of Meopham, on the up side, can still be seen the remains of Longfield Siding. This was opened in late 1876[9] to provide a waste disposal site for the Vestry of St. Mary, Newington (later Lambeth Borough Council). The project was sufficiently successful for the siding to require extension in 1892. It was in a rather isolated position providing difficulties for workmen, so in 1899 the Vestry erected six houses on the down side of the line which still stand.

Provision of a station at Longfield (pop. 188 in 1861) was discussed by the LCDR Board at length, starting with a letter from the local people in February 1859. In December the Traffic Committee resolved that 'for the present a station at Longfield is not necessary' although in October 1860 they decided that they would reconsider the matter once the line had been opened. In March 1865 a landowner, Robert Cobb, offered land and £200 for a Longfield station. A station was eventually provided at Longfield, under the name 'Fawkham', in June 1872. According to local sources[10] the station was close to a place often used for prize-fights and an earth mound beside the line had been used as an unofficial 'halt' for some time. However when the station was opened there was only one house visible from its platforms and the first nearby building to be completed was the 'Railway Tavern', which was for a while used as a home by the first stationmaster, Thomas Toms. After that growth came gradually − there were only 12 season ticket holders in the 1890s, but nearly 300 by the late 1920s and now the whole region has been built up. The only major incident

Fawkham, looking west in about 1910.   (A. Riley collection)

Looking east from Farningham Road, with the line descending to the viaduct; note the sign
advertising the station's convenience for the 'Homes for Little Boys'.   (A. Riley collection)

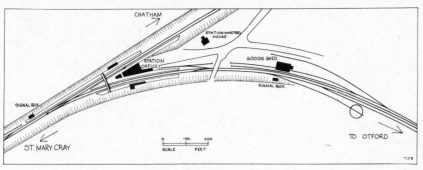

Map 8: Swanley Junction Station, 1890

in the life of this station occurred in 1900 when it was burnt down and for a
while a wooden shed by the signal-box acted as temporary facilities. Consideration
was given to moving the station to a new site, but this was rejected and it was
rebuilt in the same location. This station was known as Fawkham until 12th
June 1961, when it renamed 'Longfield for Fawkham & Hartley' following the
closure of Longfield Halt on the ex-LCDR Gravesend West branch. Since then
the name has standardised as 'Longfield' from 1968, though signs bearing the
extended name survived well into the 1970s.

Less protracted were the arrangements for a station at Sutton-at-Hone, where
there were two paper mills (1861 pop. 1,363). This location was also convenient
for Farningham and the station there was opened as 'Farningham & Sutton' on
3rd December 1860, making it — initially — the only station between St. Mary
Cray and Rochester Bridge. The station was built on the west side of the
Darenth valley, which the line crossed on a brick viaduct of ten arches.

This station changed its name to 'Farningham Road & Sutton-at-Hone' by
February 1862, and then to plain Farningham Road in January 1872.

There were two features of interest on the line west of Farningham Road.
These were a private station, with only a down platform, that was opened
on 11th October 1870 for the use of an orphanage, and Langlands Siding which
opened much later — in 1916 — and was out of use by the early 1970s.

The small village of Swanley became of significance since in 1859 an Act
was passed for a line from Sevenoaks which would link up with the LCDR
close by. For this reason 'Sevenoaks Junction' was opened there on 1st July
1862, being renamed Swanley Junction on 1st July 1872. Swanley's importance
as a junction was increased by the completion of the Maidstone & Ashford
line in 1884 which fed into the Sevenoaks branch, though a two-mile branch
to Park Gate, on the estate of Sir William Hart Dyke, which was requested in
1898, was not built. The railway did have a noticeable effect on the settlement
of Swanley, creating a daughter village around the station that has now sub-
stantially outgrown the original village that clustered around the church. In
1892 James Staats Forbes commented: 'A few years ago the Swanley Junction
neighbourhood was like a desert; it is now becoming a town.' This growth

41

The junction at Swanley, with the Sevenoaks line diverging to the right.   (E. Baldock)

An 'up' Dover express passing St. Mary Cray, showing the staggered arrangement of the platforms.
(A. Riley collection)

42

was further accelerated in the late 1930s by the Southern Railway's electrification projects, during which the site of the station was moved slightly to the west.

Between Swanley and St. Mary Cray there was a short siding on the up side called Bournewood Siding.

St. Mary Cray, with a population of 1,464 in 1861, was the most important intermediate station and was built with 'staggered' platforms. At the centre of a fruit-growing district, from an early date it received supplies of manure from London for which special sidings were provided. However the Crays area was most important for the growing of small or soft fruit which could not easily be transported by rail because of the transhipment that was necessary. The station here was demolished and rebuilt in 1958-59 when, as part of British Railways' Kent Coast electrification project, the line through St. Mary Cray was quadrupled.

Between St. Mary Cray and Bickley (Southborough Road), the LCDR's Western Extension skirted the southern edge of Chislehurst. A station in the vicinity was considered in October 1860 and in December two possible sites for it were investigated, though the fact that the area was already served from Bickley (where C.J. Hilton later lived) clearly affected the decision. In March 1861 the LCDR declared that a station could be opened if the landowner would construct a road and give the necessary land. This plan resurfaced in 1879, but again without success.

The opening of the Western Extension from Rochester Bridge to Bickley, where it joined the Crays line, was originally planned for 31st October 1860 but had to be delayed until 3rd December. On the first date a Directors' Special ran from Victoria to Chatham, hauled by *Sondes*; the Directors were treated to lunch near Cuxton, with a view across the Medway valley, and dinner at the Crystal Palace. On the official opening date the first train, hauled by *Aeolus*, broke down between Farningham and Meopham leaving the passengers stranded for 2½ hours. The breakdown was bad enough, but on the 'private opening' day Sir Morton Peto sat in the Chair at the dinner — thereby demonstrating his increasing hold on the Company.[11] The two main features of the line were the Darenth viaduct, 80ft. high, and a nine-arch, 45ft. high viaduct at St. Mary Cray; both these were to the designs of Cubitt. From the operating viewpoint the major problem on the line was the infamous Sole Street Bank, whereby 'up' trains climbed out of the Medway valley with nearly five miles of continuous 1 in 100 gradients.

The new line brought virtually no intermediate traffic to the LCDR, but it made it far more competitive over long distances; it was now able to offer a through time from London to Canterbury of 2 hours 10 minutes.

ii) Bickley to Beckenham Junction
The East Kent built its own main line from Strood to Bickley, but from there it was at first wholly dependent on the lines of other companies to gain access to London. In the space of four miles from Bickley to Beckenham, it used the tracks of two different Companies, thereby writing a complicated page in its

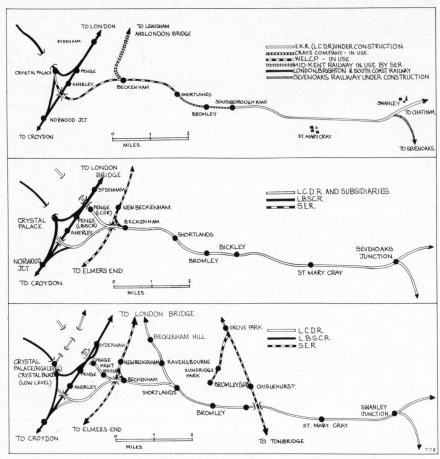

Map 9: Evolution of Lines in the Bromley Area — 1859, 1865, 1898

own history as shown in Map 9, 'The Evolution of Lines in the Bromley Area'. In the mid-1850s the area that now centres upon Bromley (pop. 4,127 in 1851) and is heavily built up was a mainly pastoral area but had nonetheless begun to attract a number of speculative railways. The West End of London & Crystal Palace Company was formed initially to operate a service between the two places of its title but in 1854 gained an Act of Parliament for its 'Farnborough Extension', under the powers of which it constructed a line to Norwood, Beckenham and Shortlands — this latter point being known as 'Bromley' from 3rd March 1858, when the line opened, until 1st July 1858.

Meanwhile, in 1855, the Mid-Kent Railway had also obtained powers for a branch off the South Eastern at Lewisham through Catford to join the WELCP at Beckenham. Another Act of 1856 allowed the Mid-Kent (Bromley & St. Mary Cray) Railway to extend from the WELCP at Shortlands to St. Mary Cray, as

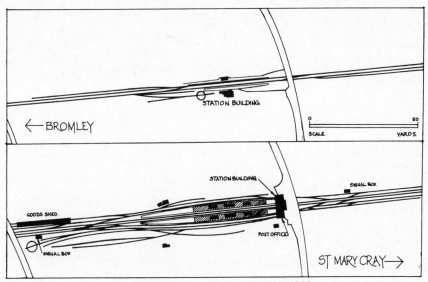

Map 10: Bickley Station — c.1860-65, 1898

described earlier in this Chapter; as we have seen, the powers of the Crays Company for the Bickley to Cray section were taken over by the East Kent. The section from Shortlands to Bickley (at first known as Southborough Road) opened on 5th July 1858 as a single line, operating on the 'one engine in steam' principle. This section included a new Bromley station, closer to the town of that name.

None of these three minor companies was wholly independent. The WELCP was closely associated with the LBSCR, who operated its trains, whilst both the Mid-Kent and the Crays lines were at first worked by the South Eastern.

When the East Kent Railway received powers for its Strood to St. Mary Cray line, and also powers to take over construction of the line from there to Bickley, it was faced with the problem of four miles of track controlled by the SER and belonging to the Crays Company before the comparatively friendly metals of the WELCP were reached at Shortlands. The South Eastern had, despite a number of arguments, managed to lease this section for ten years but fortunately Parliament was aware of the problem and in the Western Extension Act of July 1858 it ordered that the line between Bickley and Short-lands should be doubled within one year so that the East Kent's expresses would not be impeded. In fact an agreement to this effect had already been reached by the Crays Company and the EKR by 30th June in 1858 and the doubling work was started by contractors Smith & Knight in February 1859; it was finished in June. On 1st November 1859 the Crays Company wrote to the LCDR to declare that all their obligations had been fulfilled.[12]

Despite this provision the LCDR still regarded the situation as far from ideal and by January 1861 a row with the SER had broken out about control of this section. The LCDR wanted the line to be supervised by the Board of Trade, but in March 1861 began to promote its own parallel line; this received

45

One of the earliest known photos of the LCDR, showing Bromley station in about 1865. An indication that this photo was taken very soon after the station opened is the building work going on in the background — stations were rapidly surrounded with houses. Also notable is the light trackwork which gave the LCDR many problems in its early years.

(Bromley Library)

its Act on 6th August 1861 and would have rendered the Crays line almost totally devoid of traffic. Faced with defeat the SER gave up the struggle and the Mid-Kent Railway Leasing & Transfer Act of August 1862 provided for the lease of the Shortlands-Bickley section to pass to the LCDR from 1st September 1863.

Thus after the usual degree of animosity, the LCDR's problems began to be resolved. However the use of the WELCP's tracks was still not satisfactory, even though amicable arrangements had been arrived at. In April 1858 the EKR had promised to run at least five trains daily each way over the WELCP; in May 1858 the *Railway Times* said that the WELCP would gain 80% of the revenue from these, though EKR Board Minutes had earlier shown a desire to settle on a figure closer to 57½%. Clearly the WELCP held a strong position from which to negotiate, but by late 1858 it had become a virtual subsidiary of the LBSCR who used it as part of their main line between Norwood and Pimlico, whilst the section east of Norwood — to Beckenham — was of little use to them. In November 1858 the East Kent offered to buy the Norwood to Shortlands section for £105,000; in February 1859 they revised their offer to £106,200 and set a date of 1st January 1864. The transfer was authorised by an Act of 23rd July 1860, at an eventual cost of £120,000.

By this stage much of the LCDR's section of the WELCP was already in eclipse. In fact as early as August 1859 dissatisfaction was being expressed by both the LBSCR and the LCDR, who felt that the junction at Norwood was not suitable for the proposed services from off the LCDR into London Bridge via the LBSCR's tracks. Indeed in 1859 a direct link between Beckenham and the LBSCR's London Bridge line was promoted by the Beckenham & Sydenham Railway, in which Crampton, Peto and four LCDR Directors held interests; the Company's Bill was lost due to the opposition fo the LBSCR, who said they could not handle the traffic it would bring — the LBSCR's line was already in use by the SER. Both companies also accepted that the line through Crystal Palace station was not suitable for use by fast trains. In the light of subsequent events, discussed in Chapter Four, it would appear that the LCDR's decision to purchase the entire Shortlands to Norwood section was a misguided one.

Whilst the LCDR had been concerning itself with its approach routes to the West End of London, a number of developments had been taking place in the Pimlico area that need to be placed in perspective. A terminus on the south bank of the Thames, called 'Pimlico' though it was in fact adjacent to the present Battersea Park station, was opened on 29th March 1858. The 'Victoria Station & Pimlico Railway' constructed a line from there, across the Thames, to Victoria; the station here was divided into two sections, one for the use of the LBSCR (opened 1st October 1860) and one for the joint use of the Great Western Railway and the LCDR as explained in the next chapter.

The Bromley area rapidly proved attractive for 'villa development', with a dramatic impact on local population. Bromley itself increased from 5,505 in 1861 to 27,354 in 1901; Beckenham rose from 2,124 to 26,331 over the same period. A number of proposals and developments were put forward over

Bromley South station in about 1914.

(E. Course collection)

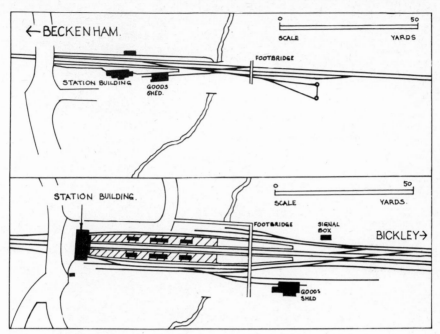

Map 11: Bromley Station circa 1860-65 (above) and in 1895 (below).

the ensuing years to cater for the growing traffic, and as early as September 1862 the LCDR was considering a 'third line' between Beckenham and Bickley.[13] In 1863 and 1864 a great deal of work went on to bring what had been built as a branch line up to main-line standards; money was spent on Bickley and Shortlands, whilst Fox was involved in resiting 'Bromley Common' station between August 1863 and March 1864. With the expansion of the LCDR's commuter services and the vast spread of the residential districts during the 1870s pressure on these lines became considerable. On 16th August 1879 the *Railway Times* referred to the possibility of doubling this section to four tracks on account of the suburban traffic. In March 1880 the LCDR bought land at Shortlands to allow for 'widening' and in January 1885 a Bill was presented for widening the 1m. section between Shortlands and Beckenham; in fact this short section has always remained double track because of the opening of the Shortlands & Nunhead line, which acts as a relief route. Quadrupling between Shortlands and Bickley was eventually authorised in 1892, with Lucas & Aird doing the contracting. Work carried out during 1893 included the re-building of Bromley and Bickley stations with their booking-offices on over-bridges across the tracks and Shortlands, on an embankment, also became a commodious establishment. The new tracks were put into use on 1st May 1894 and terminated at Bickley station, which was the outer limit for most of the LCDR's suburban services.[14]

49

A down express with both City and West End portions, approaching Bickley in 1911 with 4-4-0 No. 547. (Locomotive Club of Great Britain)

An early view of Beckenham station in about 1863-65, showing Michael Moore the station-master. (Beckenham Library)

West of Beckenham Junction station it is still possible to see the earthworks of an old spur that connected the original WELCP line to Crystal Palace into the LCDR's later 'Metropolitan Extension' line to Herne Hill. This west to north spur was originally authorised in 1864 but was not constructed until 1874. There is no evidence, so far as is known, that it was ever opened to traffic.

Bromley station, known as Bromley South since June 1899 to avoid confusion with the rival ex-SER establishment at Bromley North, appears to have been known as 'Bromley Common' for a short time after its opening on 22nd November 1858; this was probably a temporary measure to avoid confusion with Shortlands, which had been know as Bromley until 1st July 1858.

Beckenham was renamed Beckenham Junction on 1st April 1864. It would have become a major junction if the joint SER/LCDR plans of 1863-64 for a Beckenham, Lewes & Brighton Railway had reached fruition. The BLB had planned to join the LCDR main line on the level at Beckenham, but the LCDR itself expressed a preference for a flying junction. Beckenham was the second place on the LCDR system to be fitted with Saxby's patent signals.

A number of footpaths crossed the track between Bromley and Shortlands, and as the population in the area increased so too did the risk of accident. In the summer of 1887 at least three people were killed on this section, so that in October 1887 the Board decided to install footbridges instead of the crossings; at the time something like 170 trains per day travelled through this section.[15] A very serious accident occurred at Ivy Bridge, between Bromley and Bickley, on 23rd November 1882 when an overbridge collapsed onto a gangers' hut, killing six men inside.

51

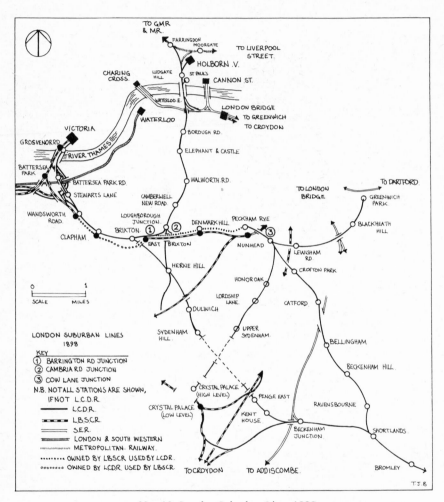

Map 12: London Suburban Lines 1898

CHAPTER FOUR

The Metropolitan Extensions

'I am in blood
Stepped in so far that, should I wade no more,
Returning were as tedious as go o'er.'
Macbeth, III.4[1]

i) The 'West End' Line to Victoria

As we have seen, a London terminus of its own was an early ambition of the East Kent's. In 1854 the Westminster Terminus Railway was formed to construct a station in the West End and in November 1855 the East Kent Board resolved to acquire an interest in this undertaking. Accordingly in 1855-56 they promoted various new lines from Lewisham to Camberwell and to 'Victoria', named after the new street that was being built through part of Westminster at this time. The WTR never succeeded but on 29th March 1858 the WELCP opened its line to a new Pimlico Terminus, which was in fact on the south side of the Thames at Battersea. On 23rd July 1858 the Victoria Station & Pimlico Railway was authorised to extend across the river from this point and to construct a new terminus just off Victoria Street near a canal basin. This was to be the East Kent's route into London, though from 1st July 1859 much of the WELCP passed into the ownership of the LBSCR.

So a route into London did exist, but by the end of 1859 the ambitious Directors of the LCDR were unhappy with it on two counts. Firstly, the tortuous line through Crystal Palace was unsatisfactory for express trains and, secondly, they still had no means of access to the City without relying on the South Eastern; the Beckenham & Sydenham project of 1859 might have provided a solution to the City problem but by planning to rely on the LBSCR's London Bridge line it secured the opposition of that Company. In November 1859 the LCDR therefore announced plans for its own line from Beckenham to Herne Hill, where it would divide to give separate routes to the City at Blackfriars and to the West End via Brixton and Battersea. The Bill specified three lines:

Railway No. 1: Beckenham to Herne Hill with two junctions at Penge.
Railway No. 2: Herne Hill to Blackfriars and Farringdon.
Railway No. 3: Herne Hill to Pimlico and connections with the London & South Western Railway at Battersea.

These lines were empowered by the Metropolitan Extensions Act of 6th August 1860, which passed only after a lengthy and bitter battle against the South Eastern, described in more detail in the next section of this chapter. The Beckenham to Herne Hill section was to form the 'trunk' of the new expansion; land costs alone on this section were to be £83,512 with three houses needing demolition,[2] but there was also the awkward problem of Sydenham Hill which necessitated the 2,200 yard Penge Tunnel. During construction a 16-acre brickfield was created on the Penge side and a 10-acre one at the Dulwich end to provide the 33 million bricks used to line the tunnel; after completion, the brickfield at Penge was quickly redeveloped for housing. During the debate over the Bill, the District Surveyor for Clapham had prophesied that the Sydenham area would be developed in this way. From Herne Hill, via Brixton to Battersea the land was to cost £84,098 and thirty-eight houses were scheduled for demolition. Despite the cost of the land, Sydenham Hill was the only substantial obstacle between Beckenham and the Thames, and in January 1861 the LCDR Board even considered applying for permission to divert their line round it instead of going through it.[3]

Having secured their route into London, which was being constructed by Peto's firm, the Directors turned their attention to the question of the Victoria station. The LBSCR opened its own section of the station on 1st October 1860 and from the same date an agreement between the VSPR, the LCDR and the Great Western Railway came into force. This stipulated that the LCDR's rent for the use of the eastern part of the station area was to be £13,250 for the first year, £18,000 for the second year and then rising to an annual maximum of £32,000; LCDR Minutes later recorded a payment of £11,250 for the first half of 1863. The eastern section of Victoria was to be shared by the LCDR and the Great Western Railway so mixed gauge track had to be provided from Longhedge Junction. The VSPR Act of 28th June 1861 sanctioned the lease of the eastern part of the station to the LCDR and the GWR.

The first LCDR trains from Pimlico began running on 3rd December 1860, offering a fastest time to Canterbury of 2 hours and 10 minutes. Once running had started the provision of locomotive facilities at the London end of the line became necessary and indeed the Board decided to concentrate their workshops in London rather than Faversham. Therefore in December 1860 they resolved to purchase 68 acres of Longhedge Farm for 'engine stables'. A running shed was opened there in February 1862 and a carriage works in December. Extensions to these premises were made in 1875-76 and 1880-81; a total of fifty locomotives were built there between 1869 and 1904.

However no progress had been made on the actual Victoria station until August 1861 when John Kelk was employed to do the construction work for £106,321;[4] he was instructed to decorate the premises with white brick facing and cement projections. This was one of the few major LCDR contracts in the early 1860s not to go to Peto's Company, but Kelk had been associated with them in the VSPR project. The eastern side of Victoria opened for LCDR services on 25th August 1862 and occupied a site of six acres, covered by a 740ft. iron roof. By 1869 it had nine platform faces, two of them offering

The LCDR's rather ramshackle facilities at Victoria in about 1895, a rather dismal contrast to the LBSCR's part of the Victoria facade which boasted the grand Grosvenor Hotel, seen here in the background.   (A. Riley collection)

mixed gauge facilities for the GWR whose services started on 1st April 1863. The station was not permitted to handle goods traffic.

Out of Victoria the lines climbed at 1 in 57 to reach the bridge over the Thames. This section of track was roofed over to minimise inconvenience to local residents. Construction of the bridge itself, which initially carried two tracks, started on 9th June 1859; the bridge was 930 feet long. Two mixed gauge tracks soon proved inadequate for the traffic and in 1864 powers were obtained to widen the bridge. This work was done by Sir Charles Fox who built a new bridge in parallel to the old one; this enabled three new mixed gauge tracks and one standard gauge to be added for the use of the LCDR and GWR, and one extra for the LBSCR, making a total of seven. Just on the north side of the bridge the LCDR opened its Grosvenor Road station on 1st November 1867; this closed on 1st October 1910.

Beyond the bridge the LCDR line dropped steeply to rejoin the level of the old line to Pimlico terminus. The tracks snaked past Stewart's Lane station, which was opened by the LCDR on 1st May 1863 and closed from 1st January 1867. At Stewart's Lane Junction the GWR trains diverged, providing a Victoria to Southall service from 1863 until 1915. This steeply graded and sharply curved section also proved unsuitable for the LCDR's traffic and the New Lines Act of 14th July 1864 provided for its improvement by the construction of a high-level line between Battersea Pier Junction and Factory Junction. Included in the project was the Longhedge Junction Railway, which provided direct access from the London & South-Western Railway's main line, towards

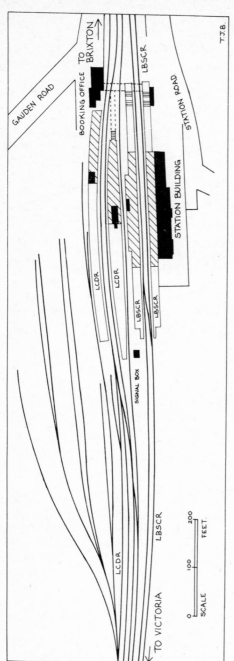

Map 13: Clapham Station, 1906

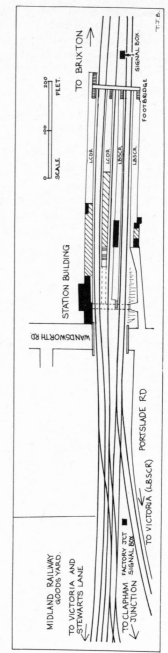

Map 14: Wandsworth Road Station, 1906

56

Brixton: thus it would have become possible for the LSWR to run through trains into Kent or over the LCDR to the City. This high-level line, entirely on viaduct, was opened on 1st January 1867 and included a station at Battersea Park Road which opened on 1st May as a replacement for the Stewart's Lane station. The high-level line was triple track.

From Factory Junction to Herne Hill the LCDR pursued a fairly level course through an area that was already developing some housing. The entire section was opened on 25th August 1862 and from 6th October 1862 carried a rather curious service between Victoria and Elephant & Castle; this ceased when the Brixton to Loughborough Junction line was opened on 1st May 1863 (see Chapter Ten), during which time it can hardly have built up much traffic since it was shut for three weeks in January 1863 due to slips in the engineering works near Clapham. The express service over this line did not start until 1st July 1863, when the Herne Hill to Beckenham section was finally completed; until then, main-line services continued to operate via Crystal Palace.

The early years of the Factory Junction (where the high and low level lines rejoined) to Herne Hill section saw a number of complicated events. There were three intermediate stations on this part of the route, with Clapham & North Stockwell and Brixton opening on 25th August 1862, whilst at first Wandsworth Road was only provided with a substantial goods depot which, however, opened on 15th January 1862 indicating that the line was partially open for freight some time before passenger services commenced.[5] Wandsworth Road opened for passengers on 1st March 1863, when a new service between Victoria and Elephant & Castle using the Brixton to Loughborough Junction link began.

As built the Factory Junction to Herne Hill line was double track, but again it became obvious that this would be insufficient since the LCDR intended to operate an intensive service between Victoria and the City and also because the LBSCR had obtained powers for a South London Railway which would provide a service between Victoria and London Bridge, running parallel with the LCDR from Factory Junction via Brixton, and across south London to Cow Lane Junction (see Chapter Ten). Accordingly the LCDR's proposed solution was to provide three tracks for its own use from Stewart's Lane to Barrington Road, and two tracks for the exclusive use of the LBSCR. These two tracks for the LBSCR were handed over on 1st May 1867; the LBSCR's route in fact used the old LCDR line between Clapham and Wandsworth Road but had an entirely separate station at East Brixton. The three tracks that the LCDR provided for itself between Stewart's Lane and Shepherds Lane opened some time earlier than this, probably on 1st May 1866 though station buildings at Clapham and Wandsworth Road were only temporary and were possibly not completed until July. The formation of a triple track east of Brixton, towards Loughborough Junction, was considered in 1866 but never completed. Thus Brixton station remained something of a bottleneck for the LCDR.

Herne Hill became an important junction, particularly as it was the practice of the LCDR to operate its expresses with 'City' and 'West End' portions which were joined and divided there. On 1st January 1869 a spur was opened to

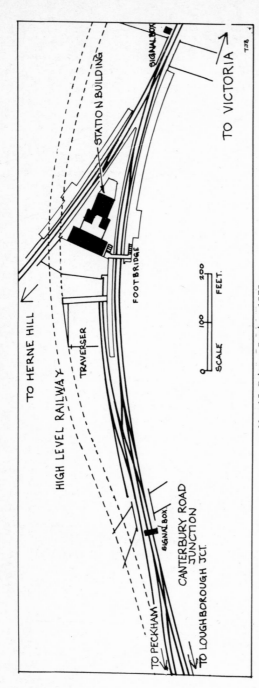

TO HERNE HILL

STATION BUILDING

SIGNAL BOX

TO VICTORIA

HIGH LEVEL RAILWAY

TRAVERSER

FOOT BRIDGE

SCALE
0   100   200
FEET.

TO PECKHAM

SIGNAL BOX

CANTERBURY ROAD JUNCTION

TO LOUGHBOROUGH JCT.

T.J.8.

Map 15: Brixton Station, 1878

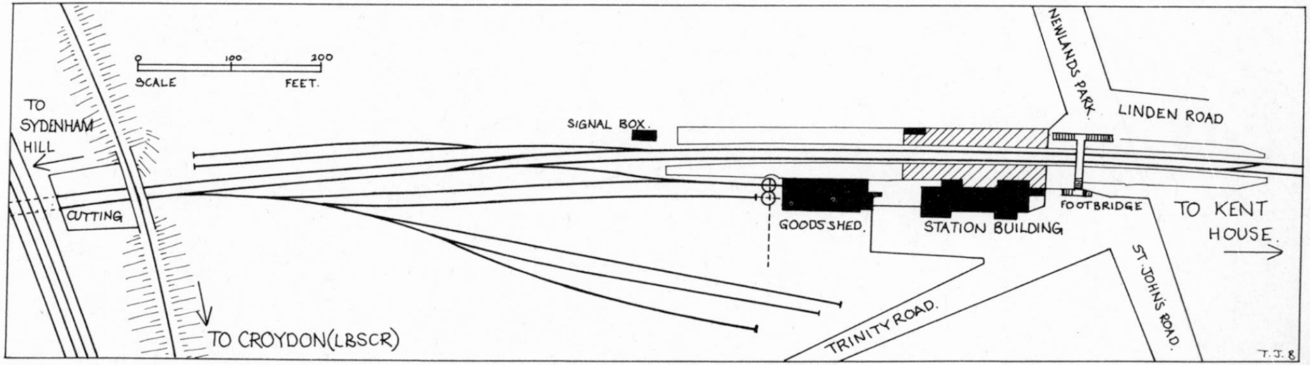

TO KENT HOUSE.

LINDEN ROAD

ST. JOHN'S ROAD.

NEWLANDS PARK.

FOOTBRIDGE

STATION BUILDING

TRINITY ROAD.

GOODS SHED.

SIGNAL BOX

SCALE
0   100   200
FEET.

TO SYDENHAM HILL

CUTTING

TO CROYDON (LBSCR)

T.J.8.

Map 16: Penge Station, 1906

connect the LCDR at Herne Hill with the LBSCR at Tulse Hill; this was partly a result of Peto's 1863 plan for a Herne Hill to Epsom line. Plans to provide a similar link between the companies at Penge never reached fruition.

The line from Herne Hill to Penge Junction, near Beckenham, opened on 1st July 1863 and completed the route to Victoria by-passing the old WELCP Crystal Palace line. This was the last part of the new approach to Victoria to be completed, the delay being caused by extensive tunnelling between Penge and Sydenham. Penge was the only intermediate station at first although as early as September 1861 the Board had discussed provision of a station at Sydenham to get some of the Crystal Palace traffic and in February 1862 they discussed a station for Dulwich. Work at 'Sydenham Hill station' had not started in May 1863 but it was mentioned in the General Report of the Directors in August 1864 as open, so it opened at some time in the first half of 1864, probably at the same time as Dulwich. Dulwich station was at first to be known as 'Knight's Hill', but in June 1863 the Board opted for 'Dulwich'. The nearby College insisted on ornamental bridges in the vicinity and extracted £40,000 compensation from the LCDR which contributed to the cost of its new buildings of 1867.

During the 1860s this line was interrupted on a number of occasions. Between Penge and Penge Junction the line crossed the Pool River and on 10th January 1866 one of the bridges was swept away; *Tacita*, hauling a goods train, plunged into the gap and the fireman was crushed to death, it taking some time to extricate his body. Being a fireman in the Penge district was clearly a risky business since another fireman was killed in September 1864 when *Snowdrop* on a Victoria to Dover express was derailed. The tunnel itself was in trouble in September 1868 when a shaft collapsed and held up services, and in February of the same year *Gorgon* was derailed actually inside the tunnel.

With the growth of suburban traffic the bottleneck of Penge Tunnel became a serious problem, as the line there could not be readily quadrupled. In August 1879 the Directors were so concerned about the situation that they said they were taking no steps to encourage traffic development since the line was over-burdened. However there were no immediate results from an 1879 plan to improve the capacity of the line between Herne Hill and Bickley by doubling to four tracks some sections of it, at a cost of £200,000.

Landowners had an obvious interest in suburban growth and correct railway facilities were a necessary precondition for this. In February 1883 Mr Cator, a prominent local landowner, gave some land for a station at Kent House which was opened on 1st October 1884. Given the impossibility of completely solving the Penge Tunnel problem, but also influenced by the promotion of a 'by-pass' line from Shortlands to Nunhead, the LCDR Board decided to increase the capacity of the line by providing up and down loops at Kent House; these opened on 10th May 1886, providing relief at a time when the LCDR's traffic was being further increased by the opening of the St. Paul's station.

ii) The 'City Lines' to Blackfriars and Farringdon
As we have seen, the original East Kent Railway became very concerned to find

The classic view of a minor railway station, in this case Penge, with station staff posing for the camera in about 1910. (A. Riley collection)

A view of Kent House station after the two loops had been added, probably taken shortly before the Great War. (A. Riley collection)

a direct way into London and because of the existence of schemes like the WELCP its initial attention became focussed on a West End terminus. However this soon proved insufficient for the Company's ambitions and by 1859 it was searching for a route into a terminus closer to the City as well. The obvious tactic was to secure access to the LBSCR's line into London Bridge, with a junction at or near Norwood the obvious method. As an alternative to this, in February 1859, Crampton and Peto proposed a link-line from the WELCP at Beckenham to the LBSCR near Sydenham; both plans failed because the LBSCR held that its own facilities were inadequate to meet the extra traffic.

Undoubtedly access to the City was important. The West End, where the Company was already secure, contained a large number of wealthy inhabitants who would make regular trips to the coastal resorts and the Channel ports — mostly on first class fares. But a good foothold in the City would provide a solid daily diet of commuter traffic such as that enjoyed by the Brighton Company from places like Croydon and by the SER along its North Kent line. This was particularly important to the LCDR as it had few settlements of any sort on its line between Bromley and Rochester, and only with good City access could it be sure of suburban development at places such as Shortlands, Bromley and Bickley. As will be seen in Chapter Ten, the East Kent was not alone in realising the vital nature of a steady income from commuter traffic.

By October 1859 the LCDR was completing its plans, prepared by Turner, for a major thrust into the middle of the City. When the Bill was deposited, in November, its ambition was plain: not only did it include the improved route to Victoria described earlier in this chapter, but it was based upon a line that transected the Camberwell district, crossed the Thames and then linked up with the Metropolitan Railway at Farringdon. There was also to be a junction with the LBSCR at Sydenham, and a ¾ mile loop from Brixton to Loughborough Park to connect the City and West End sections. Two features of this were distinctive: it would mean that the LCDR would be the first company to enter the City from the south and it would open up considerable possibilities for north-south travel between the LCDR and major northern companies such as the Great Northern Railway and the Midland Railway because of the connections afforded via the Metropolitan Railway — this through traffic would include not only passenger but coal traffic from the Midlands, and the LCDR was seriously short of reliable freight flows.

At the LCDR General Meeting in February 1860 the Metropolitan Extension Bill was discussed, and the provision of a branch to the new meat market at Smithfield was discussed. The Directors' Report commented on 'the immense relief this would give to the streets of London and especially the several bridges....'[6]

With such a major expansion the opposition was bound to be great and it proved so extensive that the Bill was in committee from April to July 1860. Particular interest centred upon the railway's effect on property since much of its route was through built-up areas, and details were provided by a land valuer:[7]

An LCDR Dover boat express passing Sydenham Hill behind M3 class No. 17.
(A. Riley collection)

The decrepit wooden buildings at Sydenham Hill during the days of the Southern Railway.
(R. Thomas)

Section	Land Value	Houses	Buildings to be demolished			
			Workshops	Shops	Inns	Chapels
Beckenham-Herne H.	£83,512	3				
Herne H.-Farringdon	£582,589	331	19	52	1	1
Smithfield Jct Line		19	8	13		
Snow H.-Metrop. Rly.	£78,238	8	5	21		
Herne H.-Battersea	£84,098	38	1	2		
Camberwell-Brixton	£21,239	14				
Battersea junctions	£6,170					
Station site in City	£254,749					

Various estimates for the scheme averaged the cost of land and compensation at approximately £1,450,000. This worked out at about £105,000 per mile, without any consideration for construction costs; with such a bill it is perhaps hardly surprising that plans for a branch to Crystal Palace were dropped after being rejected by the House of Commons committee.

One of the key witnesses against the Metropolitan Extension scheme was Samuel Smiles, Secretary of the SER and author of a scurrilous pamphlet about LCDR finances which had found favour with the *Railway Times*. Smiles based his criticism on the contention that the LCDR was financially incapable of proceeding with the scheme, claiming that it was disposing of its stock at 40% to contractors and already had annual interest charges of £122,536 to meet. Smiles' alleged interest figure becomes more significant when it is realised that the LCDR's profit on working for the year 1860 amounted to only £3,985 — a long way short of these alleged charges!

A great deal of attention focussed on the meat and vegetable traffic to the central markets like Farringdon and Newgate. The South Eastern's rival proposal, for a line to Charing Cross, was much criticised as being useless for meat traffic though it was, of course, convenient for Covent Garden. Most of the meat trade came from the North and East Anglia and animals were assembled at Copenhagen Fields before being taken through the streets to Smithfield and Newgate markets, the traffic to Newgate amounting to about 40,000 tons a year by this time. It was argued that the Great Northern Railway's link into the Metropolitan Railway would bring this street traffic to an end and also that the LCDR's extension would stop the practice of animals from the south being driven across London Bridge. A number of fruit and vegetable merchants gave evidence to the committee and discussed the usefulness of railways in conveying their traffic; details were even given by the City of London's solicitor about how the Great Western Railway sent 250,000 cauliflowers a year to the London markets from Cornwall, some sixty tons a day. But it was also claimed that the LCDR would not benefit greatly from the market gardening traffic as much of the produce was grown within fifteen miles of central London and brought in by cart; the returning carts carried loads of manure from the streets and stables of London for spreading on the fields, giving a fine example of rural-urban integration. This was a sizable traffic, approximately 1,500 carts reaching Borough market each day during the peak season. Traffic between the various markets was described by Mr F. Treadwell, a fruit merchant at Borough, who claimed that 10% of the produce went to Farrington market, 40% to Covent Garden, 30% to Borough and 20% to Spitalfields: this did not of course include the quite separate meat traffic. Farringdon market was generally reckoned to be a failure having been built by the City authorities for £240,000. Circumstances proved the pessimists to be correct for the fruit traffic was never ideal for rail carriage and the railways' hold on the soft fruit traffic was always tenuous.

The site of the main City station was to be at Ludgate Hill, just to the south of the main road. The line then crossed the street on a viaduct, the design of which caused some debate, and continued its route to the north by passing across part of the old Fleet Prison site. This site had been bought from the Government by the City Corporation for the knock-down price of £25,000 on condition that it was used for 'public improvement'[8] — not a phrase often used in connection with the LCDR's schemes! Much of the property south of the River Thames that would be affected by the line was fairly poor, but the SER felt that the houses on their rival route to Charing Cross were even worse; Hawkshaw, the SER's engineer, described them as having 'a very wretched character, indeed a considerable portion of it is built in wood — in fact I did not know such kind of property was in existence.' Demolishing the houses of the poor was generally considered an 'improvement', so the LCDR's opponents alleged that its line would affect the houses of the more comfortably off. The LCDR certainly believed that its line would improve property prices and stated its belief that the depressed values of houses in Camberwell were a result of the difficulties in commuting by bus — though the construction of the new Black-friars road-bridge was likely to improve this whatever happened to the railway proposals.

The LCDR also outlined its plans for stations — at Herne Hill, Newington, Camberwell, Elephant & Castle, Blackfriars Bridge and Ludgate on the City line. The Newington proposal seems to have been a rather indefinite one, though. Goods traffic, apart from market produce, was to be concentrated on the West End line and the LCDR suggested that because of the smell it would only convey 'deodorised' manure.

The balance of opinion seems to have been weighted towards the new lines despite barbed attacks from the usual enemies, notably with Samuel Smiles' pamphlet being circulated to a number of stockbrokers in an obvious attempt to undermine confidence in the LCDR. Of course some aspects of the project received more criticism than others, and in 1871 the *Railway Times* looked back with nostalgia and commented that 'the Ludgate station... excited the derision and contempt of every practically educated person when it first thrust itself upon Parliament....',[9] a statement which could perhaps be misunderstood.

But the opposition of the *Railway Times* was insufficient and the Metropolitan Extension Act was passed on 6th August 1860. The Act included a clause to ensure the LCDR would operate a cheap workmen's service because of the large numbers who would be displaced by construction work. This became the 5.05 am Victoria to Ludgate train. Not everyone was sad to see the end of

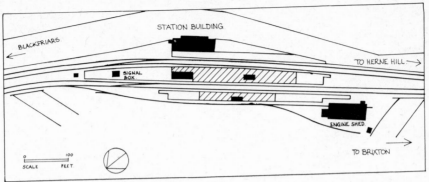

Map 17: Camberwell New Road Station, 1906

these workmen's houses however; in the Committee a Newington builder had complained that they were 'the resort of bad characters.' The Act allowed the raising of £1,650,000 new capital and the borrowing of £550,000 pushing the Company up to a new level in the financial world and sowing the seeds for its eventual downfall. The *Railway Times,* of course, felt that £2.1 million was far too low an estimate and suspected the joint stock banks of being behind the promotion.

It is clear that the *Railway Times* was not alone in its doubts because as early as August 1861 the LCDR itself was having cold feet about the whole prospect of bridging the Thames and building the 'Newgate Direct' link through the City. However, south of the River things were progressing and in February 1862 the Board approved plans for stations at Camberwell and Elephant & Castle. Work on the bridge was delayed for ten months with Peto, the contractor, blaming it on the City Corporation holding up their approval of the design; the Corporation also proved cantankerous over the Ludgate viaduct. This apparent explanation of the delay was insufficient to quell rumours about the abandonment of the Newgate Direct line, which were floating around by November 1862.

Some sections were virtually complete however. The line from Herne Hill to a station on the New Kent Road at Elephant & Castle was opened on 6th October 1862, enabling a Victoria-Elephant & Castle local service to commence. This service operated over a devious route via Herne Hill until the Brixton-Loughborough Junction line opened on 1st May 1863. At first there was only one intermediate station between either Herne Hill or Brixton and Elephant & Castle, but Camberwell Gate opened on 1st May 1863, being renamed Walworth Road in 1865; Camberwell New Road was opened on 6th October 1862. A station at 'Brixton Junction' was first considered in November 1863 and opened a few months later; this was the name given to the platforms on the west to north spur at Loughborough Junction where there was no station on the present site until 1872.

View of St. Paul's station and railway bridge from the street, c.1890.   (Author's collection)

Herne Hill from the south in about 1890.   (R. Thomas collection)

The LCDR's City Line near Loughborough Junction in early British Railways days. The line here was constructed on viaduct to reduce land costs. (R. Thomas)

Although part of the route was now open, problems and doubts continued into 1863. Not the least of the worries was the question of finance, with annual charges on loan repayments having reached £243,372 by that year.[10] Since the Farringdon, or Newgate, link was to provide through access, the LCDR was able to secure some investment from other companies — the London & South Western subscribing £310,000 and the Great Northern £320,000. By April 1863 the LCDR was still in doubt about extending its line right through the City, reports in the *Railway Times* suggesting that it favoured terminating the line at Little Earl Street, between the River and Ludgate Hill. It was suggested that the link to the Metropolitan Railway might be completed by an independent concern, the Ludgate Station & Junction Railway. Indeed it was Ludgate itself that was a problem, with Farringdon Ward insisting that the railway should tunnel beneath it — very difficult to achieve considering the limited space between Ludgate and the Thames bridge.

With the opening of the Beckenham to Herne Hill line on 1st July 1863, Elephant & Castle became the terminus of some more important services from outside the suburban area. This was followed by the opening of the Elephant & Castle to Blackfriars Bridge section on 1st June 1864, the new terminus being situated close to the new Blackfriars road-bridge on the south side of the River. This gave it a position amidst wharves and warehouses and there were early indications that the LCDR saw the site as a useful base for freight operations; it was certainly not a particularly attractive position from which to win commuter traffic. The one intermediate station on this section was Borough Road.

The Ludgate Hill viaduct in about 1918, clearly showing the City of London arms on the
bridge.   (Author's collection)

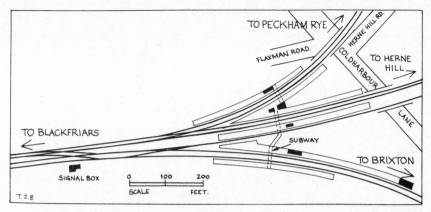

Map 18: Loughborough Junction Station, 1879

During 1864 the LCDR and the London and South Western Railway co-operated in promoting the Longhedge Junction Railway, for which an Act was obtained in July. This ran from the LSWR at Clapham Junction, via Longhedge Junction, to join the LCDR at Factory Junction and it was designed to allow the LSWR to operate services from the south-western suburbs, for example Kingston, via Loughborough Junction to Blackfriars, since the LSWR's terminus at Waterloo was inconvenient for City traffic. On 5th January 1865 the two companies reached agreement on LSWR access to the LCDR's Blackfriars and Ludgate line, by which the LSWR subscribed £316,000 in exchange for perpetual running powers; the LCDR agreed to quadruple its City line north of Herne Hill to cater for the extra traffic. An Act was passed on 5th July 1865 confirming this agreement and an LSWR Act of the same date provided that the part of the Factory Junction to Clapham Junction line that lay on the Clapham side of the bridge by which it passed under the main lines to Victoria and Waterloo should become LSWR property though with LCDR running powers;[11] this line had in fact opened a few days previously, on 1st July.

LSWR services from Kingston and Hounslow to Ludgate Hill did not commence until 3rd April 1866, the delay probably being due to the incomplete state of the quadrupling work on the LCDR's City line. The new tracks were opened progressively during 1866: Loughborough Junction to Elephant & Castle on 1st March, Elephant & Castle to Charlotte Street, near Blackfriars, on 8th August. Minutes also refer to the opening of additional tracks between Loughborough Junction and Herne Hill on 1st June 1866, though this may refer to the provision of a relief line and sorting sidings rather than an effective quadrupling.[12]

Whilst these negotiations with the LSWR had been progressing, the LCDR had been making final arrangements for the extension of its services across the Thames and into the City. On 21st December 1864 it finally opened its line to a temporary terminus at Little Earl Street, making it the first Railway Company

69

The battered remains of Ludgate Hill station as they appeared in 1957. Note the island platform and the remains of the walls that supported the station roof at one time. (R. Thomas)

Snow Hill curve, with Holborn Viaduct station to the right, in 1957. (R. Thomas)

to reach the City from the South. The bridge was constructed for four tracks and used some stones from the old Westminster bridge, which had been demolished in 1861. The main City station was to be at Ludgate Hill, on a site immediately south of what is now Pilgrim Street; however its construction was delayed when the roof collapsed on 26th March 1865 and when it was opened on 1st June it was in an incomplete state. The station was inconveniently sited on a viaduct in an area where property prices were high, so the booking office was built in the arches of the viaduct beneath the tracks. Above there were two island platforms serving four tracks. Despite its rather basic facilities, Ludgate Hill was in a far more useful position than Blackfriars and so the latter station never proved popular and eventually closed to passengers on 30th September 1885, after which it was entirely devoted to freight.

The final key piece in the LCDR's grand plan was the link through the City to join the Metropolitan Railway at Farringdon. This was opened from Ludgate Hill to Farringdon on 1st January 1866 and provided numerous possibilities for through workings, as discussed in Chapter Fourteen. Great Northern Railway goods services started to operate on 1st March 1866, and the through coal traffic immediately became very important; by November 1867 the LCDR was already making preparations to open coal depots at Clapham and Camberwell, then in March 1871 agreement was reached with the GNR for a coal depot at Elephant & Castle. The Midland Railway was also closely interested and opened its own depot at Walworth on 1st October 1871, later spreading further into Kent with a depot at, for example, Maidstone.

Steps were also being taken during the late 1860s to improve the passenger services; having invested a great deal, and being in a state of bankruptcy, it was in the LCDR's interests to bring as much traffic to the line as possible. The first of these improvements was the opening of the LCDR's Tulse Hill to Herne Hill spur on 1st January 1869, which was partly financed by the LSWR in connection with its Wimbledon to Ludgate service and which also allowed LBSCR trains to be worked through from Epsom and Sutton. Following that, the LCDR sought access to the Metropolitan Railway's station at Moorgate, east of Farringdon; this necessitated the construction of the 'Snow Hill spur' or 'Smithfield curve', opened by the Metropolitan Railway on 1st September 1871. In March 1870 the LCDR had reached agreement with the Metropolitan about this line, guaranteeing to operate a daily service of at least eighty trains over the Ludgate Hill to Moorgate section in return for which the Metropolitan arranged construction at an approximate cost of £40,000. An intermediate station on this curve, at Snow Hill, was opened on 1st August 1874.

By the early 1870s traffic had made sufficient progress for the LCDR to reconsider its station facilities on the City line. It was still recovering from a spell of financial anguish but also faced the problem that the SER's rival City terminus at Cannon Street, opened in 1866, was in a more attractive location and boasted rather better facilities — especially for main-line travellers. In December 1870 the LCDR Board decided that Ludgate Hill station was 'inadequate' and in January 1871 they resolved to build a new station at

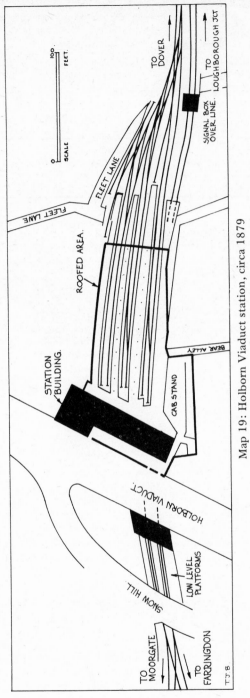

Map 19: Holborn Viaduct station, circa 1879

SCALE

FEET.

100

FLEET LANE

FLEET LANE

TO DOVER

SIGNAL BOX OVER LINE.

TO LOUGHBOROUGH JCT

ROOFED AREA.

STATION BUILDING.

CAB STAND

BEAR ALLEY

HOLBORN VIADUCT

LOW LEVEL PLATFORMS

SNOW HILL

TO MOORGATE

TO FARRINGDON

T.J.B.

The Newington Vestry refuse siding near Elephant & Castle in about 1910.
(A. Riley collection)

Holborn Viaduct since they believed this would be cheaper than extending the Ludgate station — the cost of land being the main consideration.

The Holborn Viaduct project was on a very small scale compared to the major extensions of the 1860s, but nonetheless a satellite company called the Holborn Viaduct Station Company was created, obtaining its Act on 13th July 1871. The station was reached by a short spur from Ludgate, at a cost of approximately £400,000 for all considerations. This six platforms were very short as it was envisaged that the station would handle only main-line trains which were customarily run in City and West End portions which were divided or united at Herne Hill. Suburban trains would continue to operate through to Farringdon or Moorgate to avoid complicated shunting on the congested City section where all empty stock and light engine movements needed to be kept to a minimum. Holborn Viaduct opened on 2nd March 1874; it was very close to the Smithfield curve, so a station was provided there on 1st August as mentioned above, changing its name from Snow Hill to Holborn Viaduct Low Level on 1st May 1912. A hotel was also provided at Holborn Viaduct and the LCDR leased this to caterers Spiers & Pond for a guaranteed 6% return; this opened its doors on 17th November 1877.

An extension that the LCDR did not view so favourably was the Blackfriars Junction Railway, proposed in 1872. At the time the City line was already proving its worth for freight traffic, so that the LCDR was prepared to spend

£50,000 on new warehouses alone at Blackfriars Bridge. The South Eastern Railway planned to share in some of this lucrative trade by connecting its own Charing Cross to London Bridge line into the LCDR just south of Blackfriars Bridge station, a plan in which it was encouraged by the northern companies, particularly the Midland Railway which saw the prospect of its coal traffic into south London and Kent being further expanded by direct access onto the SER. The spur opened on 1st June 1878, having been authorised by Parliament despite the LCDR's opposition. It was not only used by freight however, since the SER and GNR also operated a passenger service between Woolwich and Finsbury Park; this must have been a painful sight for the LCDR mandarins who had bankrupted their company in seeking to gain advantage over their bitter enemy the South Eastern, only to see that same enemy making use of their hard-won assets.

By the end of the decade traffic was again increasing to the point where LCDR station facilities were once more inadequate, notably for the suburban traffic which was only partially catered for at the new Holborn Viaduct station. Accordingly the Board obtained the LCDR (City & Suburban Traffic Station) Act of 1881, which authorised a new bridge across the Thames and a station close to the north bank. Some increased track capacity would also result from this plan since the new bridge, constructed on the east side of the original one, would carry five tracks: the LCDR was being subjected to a barrage of complaints about overcrowding on the Moorgate to Brixton and Snow Hill to Peckham services. The new station and bridge were only part of the plan, for the LCDR also introduced proposals to rebuild Herne Hill to cope with the extra traffic and also to widen the line at places like Kent House. However this major project caused financial problems and, according to the inevitable criticism from the *Railway Times*, the bridge and station were built on credit since the LCDR could not raise the capital. Construction of the bridge forced the closure of Blackfriars Bridge station to passengers from 1st October 1885, but there was then a growth of traffic at Borough Road where the service was improved. The opening of the new bridge and station, called St. Paul's, took place on 10th May 1886, with the Kent House loops opening the same day. St. Paul's was a combined through station and terminus, having three terminal roads; it also had the advantage of being closely connected to the Metropolitan District Railway's station, for which purpose stairways and passages were opened on 13th November 1886.[13] St. Paul's was, however, very close to Ludgate Hill and not in a position that was markedly better; because of this Ludgate Hill continued to see a large amount of traffic despite its notoriously dingy appearance.

Despite this major investment, the LCDR soon found itself with a new threat to face. By the mid-1880s tramways were eating into all short-distance passenger traffic, particularly within a six mile radius of Blackfriars Bridge. Another challenge was the advent of underground tube railways, such as the 'Clapham & City Subway' or 'City & Southwark Subway', against which the LCDR petitioned in March 1885. Particularly badly hit by the street tramways was the section of the LCDR between St. Paul's and Herne Hill, where inter-

St. Paul's station in about 1899.   (H. Patterson Rutherford collection)

mediate traffic fell away sharply; the *Railway Times* saying that this was because the LCDR had seriously misjudged its station facilities. Camberwell, it said, was a commodious station with little traffic whilst it described Walworth Road as a 'miserable little uncovered platform... a mine of wealth.'[14] Accordingly the LCDR decided, in 1891, to improve the facilities at Walworth Road but electric trams continued to provide strong opposition. It was largely because of this that some stations in inner London closed at an early date though most saw out the end of the LCDR's independence — Borough Road closed on 1st April 1907 whilst 3rd April 1916 was the last day on which passengers trod the platforms of Walworth Road and Camberwell New Road — their services succumbing to a combination of declining traffic and wartime economies.

By the end of the nineteenth century travelling patterns were starting to change and the LCDR's City line, with its trio of small stations, was hardly equipped to cope with the demands of the new century.

CHAPTER FIVE

Contractors, Corruption &

The 1866 Débacle

'The vilest scandal in railway ethics' — *Railway Times*[1]

The LCDR Directors' Report for the first half of 1866 contained a few words which reflected the fact that the Company's long decline into hopeless insolvency had at last reached its nadir: 'The Directors deeply regret the condition of the Company, which has rendered it impossible to pay the half-year interest due on the Debentures.' Speaking plainly, the LCDR was no longer able to pay the interest on its loans and, therefore, became bankrupt on 12th July 1866 — a state in which it remained for the next five years. It was in good company, for the same year saw the collapse of the reputable banking house of Overend, Gurney & Co., and also the disgrace of Sir Morton Peto who himself was declared bankrupt in 1868. The collapse of a number of banking and railway organisations in 1866 was sufficiently acute and scandalous to lead the Government to tighten up on standards of railway accounting with legislation passed in 1868.

There were a number of reasons for this disaster and the complexities of the collapse were sufficient to keep lawyers and financial experts involved in litigation for the next four years. In basic terms, however, the main cause was that the LCDR had continued to expand without sufficient capital behind it. The expansion had been financed mainly by loans, often in the form of Debentures,[2] raised on the security of share deposits which often existed only on paper. The whole situation can be blamed on the greed of the contractors and financial advisers of the Company who stood to profit from rapid expansion, but also on the naivety of a Board which seemed unaware of what was happening to them despite repeated warnings from the railway press.

To start with it is necessary to appreciate that the Board of the LCDR hardly ever operated as an independent concern. As early as 1855 they had become closely involved with Sir Charles Fox and had been warned by the *Railway Times* that they were a 'contractors' line'. From its very early days the Company was plagued by an inability to attract Ordinary shareholders, so that its chances of completing a line often depended on the favours of a contractor who was prepared to do the work in exchange for discounted shares or who arranged appropriate loans — at a high rate of interest of course. This led to the LCDR placing undue reliance on its contractors since not only were they building the line but they were also arranging the financing of it. The firm of Peto, Betts & Crampton was particularly dominant, though it was usually only Peto who was identified as the villain of the piece. Both Betts and Peto even had a certain amount of local interest in the Company since the former lived at Preston Hall near Maidstone and the latter had one of his residences at Chipstead, near Sevenoaks.

Following the severe problems that Fox had run into, Peto & Betts secured an interest in what was then the East Kent Railway through the Dover extension line, which had proved dismally incapable of enticing Ordinary shareholders to invest in it. In December 1859 the *Railway Times* reported that Peto & Betts had taken up a large portion of Dover extension shares and deposited them with a London bank as security for a loan at 10% interest to pay for the completion of the line. Such a financial manoeuvre was risky, since no cash had actually been paid for the shares and the 'security' therefore had no solid foundation. The shares would simply have been passed to the contractor in exchange for work, often highly discounted; the contractor would hope to make a profit on them by reselling the shares on the open market when the railway was in operation and — theoretically — producing attractive profits.

Having got involved in the LCDR via his links with Crampton and the Dover line, Peto really began to take his stranglehold with the promotion of the 'Western Extension' from Strood to St. Mary Cray. Again the public were not easily convinced that this was a wise investment and so the LCDR was forced to pay for the line through a multitude of loan schemes; the *Railway Times* of 16th February 1861 alleged that the LCDR were paying Peto the enormous rate of 14½% interest on a loan of £400,000. One result of this financial assistance was that a Company became inextricably bound to its contractor, and during the years of rapid expansion from 1861 to 1866 no major contract was ever put out to tender — all were simply taken up by Peto, Betts & Crampton. The LCDR Board was warned of this in March 1861:

'Are they not in the clutches of contractors, who compel them, under threat of immediate stoppage, to go on, year after year, with increase of liabilities, even while the capital of the original undertaking remains unsubscribed, and its works continue without prospect of ever being finished?'[3]

This warning was ignored since any withdrawal from the close relationship with Peto would have caused credit problems as many of the loans had been negotiated through Peto's friends in the City and, indeed, stood upon the security he offered. Thus, once involved, there was no escape. Peto went on to sign the infamous 'lump sum contract' in September 1862, though it did not become effective until 1863; this provided for the completion of all the lines in the London area at a cost of £5,979,160 — not even such a huge contract as this was put out to tender. In order to encourage the construction of these lines, from which they intended to make a handsome profit, Peto & Betts themselves stood as guarantors of the LCDR's loans. Sometimes Peto's involvement was indeed a great help to the LCDR, such as when he guaranteed 6% interest on the paid-up price of Metropolitan Extension 'A' stock in May 1865; this resulted in a four-fold increase in applications for them.

However contractors were not the only people to benefit from 'contractors'

77

lines'. Lawyers, bankers and stockbrokers all make substantial profits as well. Stockbrokers and 'jobbers' were often identified in the railway press as the evil power behind many competitive and duplicate lines, the object being to blackmail an established company into buying out the new rival at an inflated price. The EKR's Western Extension project was quickly identified as one such scheme and, following its authorisation in June 1858, the *Railway Times* bitterly attacked the Parliamentarians who had failed to identify its true purpose:

> 'Every nook of land may be invaded by the worst of all hostile interests, a beggarly knot of unscrupulous jobbers, whose only potency is to injure all they touch, to depreciate everything they approach.'[4]

A particularly notorious stockbroker associated with the LCDR was Cornelius Surgey.

Part of the guilt can also be laid at the door of the once-prestigious banking firm of Overend, Gurney & Co., who paid for their mistakes when they crashed on the infamous 'Black Friday', May 11th 1866. Overend, Gurney ceased payments with debts of at least £10 million and the same day the firm of Peto & Betts also ceased payments with debts of around £4 million; Peto himself managed to avoid being declared personally bankrupt until 1868. The collapse of these two empires triggered a whole run of failures, including the LCDR and some of its associated railway companies, but also a number of banking and finance companies with which the LCDR had dealings — for example, the Credit Foncier & Mobilier which had started to struggle as early as March 1866.

The *Railway Times* was highly critical of the behaviour of Overend, Gurney, who it was felt had precipitated the whole disaster by their reckless involvement with the use of 'Lloyd's bonds.' These were an acknowledgement of a Company's debt to a contractor and could be used to help raise further loans, but at a high rate of interest.[5] On 12th May 1866 the journal commented on the matter at some length:

> 'It is known that this once reputable house [Overend] departed from its legendary dignity by encouraging railway speculation in some of its crudest forms, and that it fostered speculative contractors and their marauding schemes in the idea that the great companies which were attacked would, in the end, be compelled to buy up the projects, which, like pestilent parasites, fastened upon them.'

Overend, Gurney were thus firmly involved with the promotion of 'contractors' lines' where the profit accrued to the stockbrokers, financiers (due to the schemes depending on large loans with handsome commissions) and the contractors. No one seemed interested in making money by actually running trains, except perhaps a few of the more rustic characters on the LCDR Board. The south of England became particularly riddled by such schemes, frequently with lines that were wholly inadequate in terms of traffic but which could be relied on to make paper profits for City interests. A classic example of the genre was the Beckenham, Lewes & Brighton (which was associated with the LCDR) for a duplicate line to the south coast but the chances of this being constructed were brought to an end by the events of 1866 and the temporary friendliness between the southern companies that resulted; another example was the present main line to Portsmouth which started life as a contractor's line and the work of Thomas Brassey, occasional associate of Peto, before being foisted onto the London & South Western Railway. The prevalence of competitive lines, and the need to build unremunerative defensive ones, accounted for the relative lack of profits among southern railway companies. It can be argued that a large proportion of the LCDR, including all lines west of Strood, were merely a contractor's speculation, the corrupting touch of Peto being present from Blackfriars to Ramsgate.

Many of these speculations were financed by stock market devices like Lloyd's bonds which ultimately represented a mortgage of what had already been acquired in order to gain some more! Much of the land that represented the ultimate security for Lloyd's bonds was itself only purchased by way of a loan through Debentures, so that one loan virtually formed the security for another. The *Railway Times* regarded Lloyd's bonds as very risky indeed and its attitude to Overend, Gurney's involvement with them seems to suggest that it felt justice had been done:

> 'It appears to have accepted Lloyd's bonds without limit — to have advanced cash to contractors in the most desperate circumstances, and to have gone so far as to encourage the rash rather than aid the careful or discriminating.'[6]

It was felt that the Limited Liability Company Act of 1862 had encouraged such unchecked speculation since individuals were no longer likely to have to make personal sacrifices if their business adventures misfired.

Undoubtedly Lloyd's bonds played a role in the failure of the LCDR to meets its debts, but what other factors were involved in the collapse of a major Victorian enterprise on 12th July 1866? Certainly of importance was the LCDR's continual inability to attract the Ordinary shareholder which, as we have seen, opened the door for contractor involvement. Ordinary shares should have provided the bulk of the LCDR's financial resources — by 1866 it had already invested £16 million — but in fact they proved a source of constant difficulty. Ordinary shares were issued originally at a nominal 100 for stock market quotation, but declined to 51 in January 1861 and to 38 in January 1863. In 1863 and again in 1865 these shares rallied due to rumours of amalgamation with the SER — rumours which it was said emanated from speculators trying to drum up the price of LCDR stock. The shares then collapsed again to 21 in July 1866 so that they never made an attractive investment. There were three principal reasons for the failure of the Ordinary shares: firstly there was little prospect of the LCDR paying a worthwhile dividend on them, secondly their value was undermined by offering them at a discount rate to contractors in exchange for work, and thirdly because the capital account was being drained by the practice of 'turning over' whereby interest on loans was paid directly out of capital.

The failure of Ordinary shares seemed a perpetual problem for the EKR and the LCDR. In 1859 the *Railway Times* was able to report that of 28,000 EKR shares 15,000 remained unissued or had been forfeited. The situation was even worse on the Dover extension, where only 6,686 shares out of 20,000 had been properly paid up; an Act of June 1858 allowed the cancellation of forfeited Dover shares. Despite the public's evident lack of faith in the LCDR finances, the Directors were planning to legitimise the payment of loan interest out of capital by the end of 1859; this was provided for in the Arrangements Act of August 1860.

During the years of rapid expansion in the early 1860s the Ordinary shares were quickly eclipsed by Preference shares[7] and Debentures. On 30th August 1862 the *Railway Times* reported that the Ordinary shares stood at £700,000 in theory, though only £663,275 had been paid up; in contrast there were £4,339,000 in Preference shares and £1,445,199 in Debentures. The situation improved somewhat during the next few years due to a combination of attractive discounts and handsome commissions to stockbrokers, so that by early 1866 Ordinary shares had reached a value of about £5½ million.

Lacking the ability to attract sufficient Ordinary share capital, the LCDR turned to raising money through Debentures, Preference shares and Lloyd's bonds. These were, in the case of Lloyd's bonds and Debentures, loans on which set rates of interest had to be paid using the security of the Company's land or revenues. Peto & Betts assisted in raising these loans by guaranteeing the interest on them during construction work — as they did with the Metropolitan Extension 'C' stock in 1862. Unfortunately the huge amount of capital raised this way saddled the LCDR with a vast interest payment, starting off in 1855 at about 5%, by the 1860s it was having to borrow at 10% and over, on top of which substantial commissions often had to be paid. The root cause of the 1866 failure for the LCDR was that its working profit never came near to meeting the interest charges it had incurred; the half-year from June to December 1862 brought in a working profit of £18,330 but, according to the *Railway Times*,[8] capital charges for the same period were £24,597. By February 1865 even the receipts on the Metropolitan Extension were unable to meet the Debenture charges. The Company survived until 1866 because it was supported by the City connections of Peto, but its own collapse became inevitable once Peto & Betts had failed on Black Friday.

The story of this descent into ruin makes sad reading. The Minutes of the LCDR are uninformative on the issue, but the *Railway Times* — which always opposed the role of Peto — chronicled it with great care. As early as 2nd June 1855 it reported that the EKR was paying interest at 5% out of capital at a time when there were already considerable arrears of payment on share calls; the arrears were so bad that it was possible to report their reduction to only £185,000 in August 1856, the *Railway Times* commenting that it was hardly a time for joyous celebration since 'we should not ourselves have been able to extract sunbeams from such cucumbers as these circumstances appear to be.'

By mid-1858, with the promotion of the Western Extension, the stranglehold of Peto, Betts & Crampton on the East Kent Railway's finances was beginning to form. By August of that year interest on Debentures had risen to 6%, producing a charge of £14,000 per annum. Between June and October 1859 Peto's firm took up £160,000 in Debenture stock alone; this meant that, in effect, Peto & Betts were loaning the LCDR the money with which to pay themselves.

Given such circumstances it became increasingly difficult to raise any further loans at all; in January 1861 the LCDR was advertising for loans at 5% interest, but to these it reportedly had to pay commissions of up to 25%. In August 1861 it borrowed £150,000 from Overend, Gurney, using £200,000 Preference shares as the security. By 1862 LCDR interest charges were £243,372 per annum, in a year when the working profit was only £25,500, and by 1864 this had increased to £423,562, with working profits improving at £110,913 for the year.

Despite the underlying financial gloom, the actual railway business was beginning to show signs of success by about 1863, though the working profits in the years up to 1866 never came remotely near to keeping pace with interest charges. The working profits for 1863-64 were four times higher than those for 1862-63 and in February 1865 the *Railway Times* commented that 'the average working expenses are being materially reduced while revenue is forcing its way into a condition of apparent if not actual respectability.' The working profit for 1865-66 reached £170,874, nearly a 70% increase over the previous year, but this was still far from meeting the interest charges even though they had been reduced to £255,340 p.a. by April 1866.[9]

Later investigations showed that the financial irregularities were particularly serious in the period 1863-64. In 1863 the LCDR had obtained its Act for the Peckham to Greenwich line and was seeking to increase its capital despite having a debt of £1,275,900 in Lloyd's bonds to pay off. Much of the Metropolitan Extension and associated works was being financed by Peto and his associates who, for example, took many Metropolitan 'A' shares at 50% discount. Further capital powers were authorised in 1864 and Peto took most of the £100 shares at £40. An inevitable result of this was that the Ordinary shares remained at a depressed price and when Peto tried to sell his 1864 stock on the open market in 1865 he found he had to repurchase much of it to ensure a reasonable price. 'It was necessary to repurchase a large amount in the market in order to keep up the price of the stock while the operation was going on,' Peto himself commented later.

One problem with the 1864 stock was that no Debenture loans could be raised until contracts had been signed for all the Ordinary stock and half had actually been paid up. Metropolitan Extension capital of £2,200,000 was therefore issued to Peto & Betts, in exchange for works, and the shares became 'paid up' even though no cash had actually changed hands. Despite this lack of real payment, the 1864 shares were then used as a security for total further Debenture loans of £500,000 with respect to City lines works; the share certificates, unsigned, were then lodged with Imperial Mercantile Credit — not surprisingly another of 1866's victims. In July 1864 Peto & Betts subscribed for half the Metropolitan 'C' shares so that Debentures could be raised to

81

purchase the land for the line which should really, of course, have been the security for such loans! These transactions at least enabled the Lloyd's bonds to be paid off. To compound the whole problem, the LCDR was guilty of issuing Debentures beyond its legal powers; an excess of £128,000 according to the admission of Lord Harris in 1866, of £133,200 according to the hindsight of the *Railway Times* in 1869.

In effect the entire line, land and works were being mortgaged several times over to pay for further expansion. The assets of both the LCDR and the contractors existed largely on paper only, though each guaranteed the loans of the other through Lloyd's bonds and Debentures. Dickens neatly encapsulated the problem in his novel *Little Dorrit*, published in 1857:

'A person who can't pay, gets another person who can't pay to guarantee that he can pay. Like a person with two wooden legs getting another person with two wooden legs to guarantee that he has got two natural legs.'[10]

Too much was being lent with too little capital as security, at a time when traffic receipts were insufficient to cover interest repayments. The City was already nervous given the deterioration of European affairs that led to the outbreak of the Austro-Prussian War in 1866 and signs of panic in March 1866 culminated in 'Black Friday', 11th May 1866, when Overend, Gurney ceased payment. The LCDR itself did not succumb until 12th July 1866, but its eventual collapse dragged down various allies like the Sevenoaks Railway and the Kent Coast Railway with it; such was the effect on the Sevenoaks Railway that construction work on its new Maidstone line was abandoned. Although Peto & Betts' contracting partnership was brought down too, Peto himself survived until 11th May 1868 when the LCDR's case against him was completed. Not everyone had expected him to prove a victim in this way:

'That the last few weeks must have been very painful to Sir Morton Peto we can well believe, but no one can doubt who really understands such matters that he will emerge from the cloud a very rich man still, and with a character for honour beyond the reach of any question.'[11]

But it was not to be. Peto, truly a pillar of the Victorian establishment and a man famed for his Baptist principles, was quickly singled out as a man worthy of discussion as soon as the recriminations commenced.

The *Railway Times* quickly identified Lloyd's bonds as a cause of trouble, particularly for Overend, Gurney and Credit Foncier & Mobilier. In fact it had been roundly critical of the whole practice for some time before Black Friday, condemning Lloyd's bonds in April 1866:

'By issue of these spurious acknowledgements for debts incurred, not merely have several railway companies been enabled to sink deeper and deeper into debt, but financial associations as well as other money lenders have been severely bitten by the transactions into which they had entered.'

With the collapse of several banking houses, many of these loans were called in and the fraud exposed. The house built on sand collapsed as soon as the weather started to become rough. After the LCDR resorted to Chancery, an investigating committee was set up in August 1866 under the leadership of Grosvenor Hodgkinson of Newark. It rapidly became obvious that LCDR interests were seeking to identify Peto as the *bête noire* of the case.

Another individual who received much criticism was Cornelius Surgey, a stockbroker who had been involved with the fund-raising in 1863-64. In October 1866 the railway press claimed that one of the factors behind the collapse was the ruinous commission being charged on Debenture loans by such people; it quoted one example of only £75 of a £100 Debenture reaching the LCDR. It was argued that large commissions encouraged jobbers to press their clients into taking unsafe stock. However Surgey argued that it was Peto who was to blame:

'A contractor is supposed to make a profit upon the contracts and works, and if he takes payment in shares and bonds and so on, he generally puts on something extra for the cost of those works. To my horror I find he not only had ample allowance for profit upon the contracts, but a tremendous allowance upon the bonds and shares besides. Now, the fact was, the candle was burned at both ends, and I think we have been tolerably well singed.'[12]

Surgey also felt that the practice of paying Peto in shares which were then used as a security for loans undermined the LCDR's credit rating.

Partly to counter such claims, Peto organised a public meeting in his Parliamentary constituency in Bristol on 22nd October. The proceedings started well, as he was received by wild cheers from the assembled crowd. 'The company rose *en masse* and gave vent to their feelings by waving their hats and hand-kerchiefs, and vociferously cheering for a considerable time', it was reported. Peto started by denying the LCDR's investigating committee's charge of 'selfish conduct'; he claimed that the LCDR Board had freely invited him to become its 'financial adviser' in December 1863 and that the blame for the issue of the illegal Debentures of 1864 rested with Messrs. Freshfield & Newman, a firm of solicitors who also worked for the Bank of England and who it was alleged had pursued the policy that an exchange of receipts rather than the actual cheques was quite sufficient as a formality before acquiring the magistrate's permission to issue the Debentures. Peto concentrated his speech on these 1864 Debentures, obviously keen to clear his name of dishonesty and immoral dealing. The allegation was that he had deposited the share certificates, knowing full well that only a paper transaction from the LCDR to himself had taken place instead of a cash purchase, so that he could falsely gain permission to raise the Debenture loan. Peto's defence was that they were not share certificates at all, but simply 'forms not filled up, not having the coupons attached and not placed on the register.' In Peto's opinion the forms were a mere acknowledgement of the LCDR's debt to himself.

Peto concluded his speech with a defence of his own character, paraphrased in the *Railway Times* report of the occasion: '... although the avalanche of May last had damaged temporarily the prosperity of his house, yet still he was perfectly conscious that there was one priceless jewel which he did not lose, and that was a conscious feeling of his own integrity.' But those who agreed with him seemed to be declining in number.

Peto had put up a spirited defence, but throughout the autumn of 1866 evidence against him continued to accumulate. In particular there was much concern over his acquisition of shares at massive discounts, with some claims that he was paying as little as 20% of the face value of the stock.

By mid-October agitation was building up within the LCDR. Lord Sondes had been replaced as Chairman by Lord Harris, who had distinguished himself as Governor of Madras during the Indian Mutiny, and five members of the investigating committee had gained seats on the Board; the Debenture holders were threatening legal action since they were being treated as partners and not as creditors. The report of the investigating committee suggested that a loss of £4,109,796 had been made on the share and loan capital, substantial portions of which had been absorbed by jobbers. The *Railway Times* of 13th October was not convinced that the blame could be handed out to the City interests like this, reckoning £275,305 nearer the mark. Nonetheless it foresaw a vicious fight amongst stock exchange interests: 'The Stock Exchange, so many members of which have made ample fortunes out of the Chatham and Dover, is now prepared to fall upon the wounded locust, and to devour it without remorse.'

During late 1866 a reconstruction plan began to emerge. Part of this was to treat Debentures as Preference stock and issue a new 5% Preference stock to rank over this with the aim of raising at least £1,500,000. Thus the Debenture holders were to lose their first claim on the LCDR's traffic receipts. By December 1866 a Bill was being drafted to implement this and also to stop all legal actions until 1st August 1868 and to allow for no Debenture payments until 1873. This plan created a furious outcry:

'The Bill is nothing less than the evidence of fatuitous madness or of sheer impertinence on the part of the Board; while its first and only result can be nothing else than an agitation which must shake the whole company to pieces, and bring down the entire fabric in hopeless and irretrievable ruin.'[13]

Particular concern was caused by the proposals for the Debenture holders, who still maintained that they were creditors of the Company and should be treated as such. Lord Redesdale, in a letter to the *Railway Times*, savagely criticised the plan:

'Their plan is to postpone their debenture debt to the sum they desire to raise to make their concern profitable, the bankrupts asking to be allowed to mortgage for their own benefit the income rightfully belonging to their present mortgagees, which I consider a monstrous proposition for a debtor to make.'[14]

In the event the Arrangements Act was passed on 17th August 1867, but only after a bitter fight. It suspended all legal proceedings for ten years and allowed £600,000 new stock to be raised. This was quickly condemned as inadequate to rescue a 'thoroughly and irretrievably insolvent concern.' Allowing for interest charges, the year to 30th June 1867 produced another loss — of £230,046, so debts were still accumulating.

But by June 1867 the LCDR was ready for an organised offensive against Peto. It had stated that Peto had been issued with £4,403,442 cash and £7,423,101 in stocks and Debentures; it credited him with works of £5,164,601 and so calculated that Peto owed the Railway Company £6,661,941, including approximately £2,500,000 on the Metropolitan Extensions contract alone. This ridiculous claim, based on nominal share values that had never had any currency, was laughingly refuted by the *Railway Times* who pointed out that stockbrokers' commissions and discounts had been ignored; for example many Metropolitan Extension 'A' shares had been issued to Peto at 50% discount.

The case was taken before the courts in 1868. The LCDR claimed that Peto had fraudulently negotiated an £150,000 loan from Overend, Gurney on the basis of non-paid up Metropolitan Extension 'C' shares. As the case dragged on attention continued to centre on the 1864 Debenture loan, it being alleged that Peto took £100 shares at only £40 in exchange for work done and used them to raise the Debenture loan without any cash changing hands. Whatever the claims, the LCDR's allegation that Peto owed them over £6 million was plainly ridiculous and in July 1868 the LCDR reduced its claim to only £484,000, apparently in recognition of Peto's lack of personal resources. It was all rather academic, since in March 1868 Peto's assets had been reported as a mere £4,000. A bankrupt himself, forced to resign from Parliament, Sir Morton Peto withdrew from public life, though he had surely proved to be one of the 'eminent Victorians'.

For 1869 the LCDR proposed another Bill to remove itself from Chancery and empower arbitrators to sort out its debts. This was again bitterly opposed by Debenture holders led by a Mr Hodgson, with interest now centring on the fact that the LCDR had exceeded its Debenture powers by £133,294 on a total of £4,297,693. Since the failure, Debenture holders had received no interest at all and the *Railway Times* reckoned the backlog of payments to be over £1,000,000. Led by the Metropolitan Extension Debenture holders, an injunction was obtained in May 1869 to stop the Arbitration Bill going to the House of Lords. The judge criticised the Board, who were meant to be trustees to ensure that the powers of the 1867 Arrangements Act were carried out properly:

'I have reason to doubt whether, from the complication of conflicting interests, these directors are not subjected to influences which make it desirable that they should govern the affairs of this Company.'[15]

However the judge's decision was reversed and the Arbitration Act became law. It was all too much for the *Railway Times* who, having compared the LCDR with Macbeth earlier in the year, now came close to expiring from apoplexy induced by rage — 'The vilest scandal in railway ethics, practice and presumption will not take shame or silence itself.'[16]

In November 1869 the arbitrators began work and their awards were known the next October. Mortgagees in the General Undertaking lost 32% of their stake, in the Metropolitan lines 45% and in the City lines 44%. As far as the usual critics were concerned, this broke all normal practice since the Debenture holders should have been repaid in full before other shareholders received anything. The *Railway Times* reached a conclusion about the 1869 Award that seemed to be an accurate summary of the LCDR's entire financial history:

'We look upon the award as a proclamation to the effect that the whole affair, from its first inception to the latest recognition of it acquired from the Legislature, was nothing less than one of the most gigantic frauds ever perpetrated upon the credulity of the investors in Great Britain.'

The LCDR was released from Chancery on 21st February 1871.

CHAPTER SIX

The 'Chatham &

South Eastern Comedy'

The feud between the South Eastern Railway and the London, Chatham & Dover was one of the longest running dramas in nineteenth century railway affairs. On several occasions the companies edged hesitantly towards friendship, but the very end of the century was reached before any truly significant progress was made. The whole issue became absorbingly melodramatic because of the two characters at its centre — James Staats Forbes of the LCDR and Sir Edward Watkin of the SER — two men who had built careers in railway management by dogged devotion to personal ambition and independence of action. Their rivalry was such that the *Railway Times* in January 1890 despaired of there ever being a rapprochement between the two Companies or men: 'It does not seem that the Chatham & Dover and the South Eastern Railway will ever be friends so long as Mr Forbes rules the one and Sir Edward Watkin is at the head of the other.' Both ruthless businessmen, each had amusing characteristics: Watkin seems to have been something of a dreamer, with his ambition of managing a through line from Manchester via London and a Channel Tunnel to Paris as well as his vision of recreating the Eiffel Tower in north-west London whilst Forbes was extremely fond of drawing-room performances of musical comedy. These two men dominated the struggle for ascendancy which took place between the SER and the LCDR for forty years; it was a struggle which, as they were repeatedly warned, wasted large amounts of money so that it is tempting for us to conclude that, even for these experienced industrialists, profit was not the only motivating force behind the railway business. Each, in his own way, became a type of king.

The struggle between the two concerns had commenced in the mid-1850s when the LCDR was still the fledgling East Kent. Talk of the EKR building an independent line into London caused panic in SER circles and a sharp drop in the value of South Eastern shares during the second half of 1855. Rumours were rife that the SER would be forced to take over the EKR; indeed stockbrokers Carden & Whitehead suggested that the SER should take £500,000 of the EKR's Western Extension stock and work the line. Speculation about a takeover in July 1855 helped to push EKR share prices upwards whilst reducing those of the SER — a pattern which was to continue each time such rumours circulated during the ensuing forty years.

It was generally felt that the SER would have to absorb the East Kent because of the geographical disadvantage it was placed under by its own main line which took all passengers between London and Kent almost halfway to Brighton, at Redhill, before striking eastwards. It is unclear why the SER

Directors failed to act positively at some time during the late 1850s, and they were later severely criticised by Watkin for failing to plan ahead. It may have been that the SER delayed its decision whilst watching the fortunes of its infant rival, acting in the belief that 'When the East Kent is reduced to beggary.... then the South Eastern may buy up the concern for about one-tenth of its actual cost.'[2] Some members of the EKR Board and later the LCDR Board, were aware that independence from the South Eastern would have to be bought and might not be worth the price; C.J. Hilton, the cement manufacturer, wrote to Lord Sondes on 1st October 1859 to say that 'Independence is very much to be desired but, it is becoming clear to me every day, that independence can only be bought at an almost murderous rate.'[3]

Even *The Times* itself was responsible for a takeover rumour that floated around in November 1859 but the only result was a rush to buy LCDR 6% 'B' stock. At the same time the SER was trying to undermine the reputation of the LCDR, notoriously with the anonymous pamphlet published in February 1860 that alleged the LCDR was being ruined by high interest payments. The printer of this pamphlet was actually called before the House of Lords committee on the LCDR Bill in 1860, and revealed that he had produced it at the request of Samuel Smiles, Secretary of the SER. Smiles then arranged for copies to be sent to over two hundred prominent stockbrokers.[4]

But when Forbes joined the LCDR from the Dutch Rhenish Company in 1861 the question became infinitely more complicated and the chance of an easy amalgamation disappeared; as Forbes developed the LCDR into a Company whose size rivalled that of the SER, mere undermining of financial confidence was no longer sufficient.

During the early 1860s the two companies engaged in a few preliminary skirmishes but also managed to reach agreement on a number of points. The air was soured by the LCDR's complaint to the Board of Trade in September 1860 that the SER was failing to comply with arrangements for through booking via Strood as included in section 42 of its 1853 Act. The issue of the diverse ownership of lines in the Bromley area also caused problems, with the LCDR seeking to run trains over the line between Bickley and Shortlands that was, for a time, in the control of the South Eastern; this problem was solved by the 'Bromley Traffic Agreement', which formed part of the 1862 Mid Kent Railway Leasing & Transfer Act. However it would seem that all agreements between the SER and the LCDR were made to be broken, so it was only twelve years until hostilities in the Bromley area were renewed.

During January 1863 there was another strong rumour of amalgamation, causing a 3% rise in the value of LCDR shares. The only concrete result of this was that the two rival Boards did manage to conclude an unofficial 'Continental Traffic Agreement' in February 1863. The exact details of this were not published immediately and there was a good deal of concern amidst SER shareholders that their Company would lose its advantage on the cross-Channel traffic; they were not made any happier by the *Railway Times*' claim in December 1864 that the agreement would lead to the South Eastern paying £150,000 per annum to the Chatham Company. Despite this a formal agreement was ratified on 7th September 1865, to be effective from 22nd September. The 'Continental Agreement' covered all traffic from London which crossed the Channel from any point between Margate and Hastings; all receipts from this traffic were to be placed in a 'common fund' which was then to be divided up with 68% going to the SER and 32% to the LCDR. However division of the fund was to be on a sliding scale thereafter, with the aim of a 50-50 division by 1872. This agreement represented a considerable improvement in the relationship between the two companies and in April 1866 the LCDR Board recorded a Minute favouring an extension of the idea to all competitive traffic.[5] The two railway companies were also jointly engaged in the promotion of a line from Beckenham to Brighton and by the end of June 1866 the rumours of amalgamation had been revived once more. But it was not to be; the collapse of the LCDR and the appointment of Watkin to the Chairmanship of the SER produced significant changes in the climate.

The financial problems of 1866 caused a temporary halt to the negotiations between the two companies, but as early as 1868 a major step forward was made. The major problem was that none of the southern companies were particularly profitable as independent units and therefore the South Eastern, the Chatham and the London, Brighton & South Coast Railways deposited a Bill to permit a joint working relationship. This would have meant that most of the railways in Kent and Sussex would have been controlled by one administration, thus ironing out wasteful competition, although the three companies would have kept their financial independence. There was to be a Joint Board of thirteen Directors to supervise the working arrangements, on which the LCDR would have had three representatives. However this plan encountered bitter opposition throughout Kent and Sussex, where it was believed that an end to competition would result in reduced services and higher fares; opposition was strongest where two companies competed directly, as at Canterbury or Dover for example. Although the Bill managed to pass the House of Commons it was lost in the Lords during May 1868 on the question of the fares to be charged. A residual result of this period of friendship was the decision in 1869 of the South Eastern and Chatham Companies to negotiate all cross-Channel mail contracts jointly.

In 1872 a Parliamentary Committee reported against allowing mergers between railway companies in future, arguing that amalgamations were prejudicial to the public interest as they would grant monopoly control over large areas of the country. This report was to prove a serious obstacle.

During the early 1870s the prospect of any further extension of friendship receded as several furious rows broke out during an era of expansion. Things had been quiet since 1866 as the money to finance competitive lines had been unavailable, but as the money market recovered confidence the flotation of a number of irritating schemes became possible. Firstly in September 1872 the SER angered the LCDR by starting independent negotiations for the French mail contract despite the 1869 agreement; the result of this was that the LCDR lost its share in the contract.[6] Also late in 1872 hostilities broke out over the question of lines to Maidstone; the Sevenoaks, Maidstone & Tonbridge Railway had received an Act to complete the Otford and Maidstone line (abandoned in 1866) in July 1872, thus threatening the SER's monopoly of one of Kent's most important towns. The SER only served Maidstone by devious routes via Strood or Paddock Wood, so that the prospect of LCDR trains running into the town over the shorter SMT route was very threatening. Accordingly in 1873 the SER emerged with its own plan for a new line from Sevenoaks to Wateringbury, on its Paddock Wood to Maidstone Branch, which in turn aroused the fury of the LCDR.

All seemed set for a savage and expensive 'war', but in the event a temporary truce was arranged. An LCDR Board Minute of 9th October 1873 recorded that the two Companies had agreed on 'the principle of absolute neutrality and forbearance from all encroachments, the one Company or the other, for a period of twelve months.' One important result of the 'truce' was the joint deposition in December 1873 of a Bill for a line from Dover to Deal. According to the *Railway Times* of 14th February 1874, the South Eastern was also in favour of an extension of the continental traffic agreement idea to cover all passengers between London and Ramsgate, Margate or Canterbury; truly the SER seemed to have fallen under the spell of St. Valentine's Day! However the LCDR was not so enamoured, asserting that the SER was only keen to come to an arrangement because the Chatham Company had gained an advantage in the struggle; it said that its new works at Holborn Viaduct and the Maidstone extension put it in a winning position.

The spirit of the 'truce' seemed to be wearing distinctly thin by May 1874 when a row erupted over the SER's support for the Bromley Direct Railway scheme, which the LCDR claimed to be a breach of the Bromley Traffic Agreement. The South Eastern countered this by claiming that the LCDR's association with the Crystal Palace and South London Junction Railway was also in conflict with the agreement. In this case Truth was probably on the side of the LCDR.

On 10th October 1874 the *Railway Times* reported rumours that negotiations were to start again between the SER, LCDR and LBSCR. The latter dropped by the wayside, but on 25th March 1875 the SER and LCDR signed the general terms for agreement. Fusion between the two was dependent on an Act of Parliament and interim arrangements being made, but the *Railway Times* felt that the official sanction of a railway monopoly of Kent was highly unlikely. LCDR stock prices rose, but during 1875 opposition began to develop from within the ranks of SER shareholders, led by Sir David Salomons; this was based upon the view that the SER could not benefit from an alliance with an insolvent Company. The railway press again blamed it all on City interests who, it was claimed, wanted to put some life into LCDR shares.

But in any case the talks broke down in June 1875, apparently because Watkin wanted to change the basis for profit distribution from gross to net and Forbes refused to go to arbitration on the issue.

Talks had resumed again by the winter of 1876, and on 16th December it was reported that agreement between the two Chairmen had been reached. Joint stations were to be provided at Canterbury, Margate and Dover whilst a friendly decision had also been reached concerning proposals for new lines east of Maidstone. Net profits were to be distributed out of a common fund at a rate of 33% to the

LCDR and 67% to the SER, but South Eastern shareholders again began to express doubts. Also unhappy about the fusion plans was the Sevenoaks, Maidstone & Tonbridge Railway.

A practical result of the 1876 talks was an evening out of the two Companies' fare structures in January 1877. Many of the fares were increased, producing a storm of opposition to the amalgamation idea. In March 1877 the *Railway Times* reported that 'Indignation meetings were held in all parts of the County, to whose locomotive wants the two lines minister. Town councils met and denounced the supposed projected monopoly, and petitioned against it.' It must be remembered that Kent had supported the inception of the East Kent Railway in order to break the supposed monopoly of the SER, and it was not proposed to let the advantages of competition fade away! Another Amalgamation Bill reached Parliament in February 1878 but was withdrawn after fierce local opposition, for example from Dover. The last fading hope of amalgamation at this time came in January 1880 when William Abbott, an influential South Eastern shareholder, prepared a plan for the fusion of the three southern companies.

The 1880s represented the nadir in the SER's and LCDR's relationship, during which huge sums of money were squandered on competitive lines and lengthy legal disputes. 1880 itself started with a fierce dispute over the Maidstone & Ashford line, which was being supported by the LCDR; to the South Eastern, this seemed a blatant attempt to secure LCDR access to Folkestone. The South Eastern was also unhappy about the LCDR's steamer service from Queenborough, on the Isle of Sheppey, to Flushing; this service had been running since 1876, but the SER waited four years before alleging that it broke the 'Continental Agreement' of 1863 and 1865, claiming that receipts from the service should be paid into the 'common fund'. The South Eastern's reply was comprehensive: they planned a new line from near Gravesend to the Isle of Grain where a port was to be set up on the banks of the River Medway opposite Queenborough — a scheme later described by Forbes as 'most idiotic'. This new branch was to be supported by a proposed loop line from Northfleet to Snodland, in the Medway valley, and planned branches to Loose and Charing to fill the gap east of Maidstone. Of these, only the Isle of Grain branch reached fruition, opening to its terminus at Port Victoria in 1882.

The dispute over the 'Continental Agreement' proved to be a lengthy one. However the South Eastern looked at Queenborough, there was clearly no legal argument that would convince a judge that it was between Margate and Hastings, the territorial limitations of the Continental Agreement. Unable to take legal measures, the SER decided to improvise. In 1863 it had opened a station at Shorncliffe, a few miles inland from Folkestone, and now it proceeded to use this as a means of avoiding the payment of continental receipts for Folkestone into the common fund, arguing that the agreement applied only to traffic from London to the ferry ports and that as Shorncliffe was neither London nor a port it was not affected by the agreement. Legal wrangles followed rapidly, going against the SER in 1881 when Justice Kekewich ruled that the Shorncliffe traffic should be paid into the pool of receipts. Getting continental passengers to use Shorncliffe instead of Folkestone stations was clearly an attempt to deceive. But the South Eastern decided to appeal against the judgement and continued to make only very irregular payments into the fund. In August 1884 the LCDR complained that traffic at Shorncliffe had risen from £6,020 in 1865 to £28,000 in 1883, much of the increase being continental in nature. Yet between August 1883 and October 1885 the South Eastern paid over nothing at all, eventually sending £6,545 when the LCDR reckoned it was owed £62,648. The LCDR's legal action against the SER for non-payment of the appropriate money extended from December 1884 until August 1887, when the House of Lords ruled that the South Eastern was to pay £45,000 into the fund as Shorncliffe was part of Folkestone. The SER appealed to the Lords against this decision, but again lost the case in May 1890.

Such protracted legal disputes as this absorbed huge amounts of money, and further large sums were being wasted on promoting competitive lines like the LCDR's 1884 plan for a line via the Alkham Valley into Folkestone. The result was that both companies obtained reputations for being distinctly poor in the facilities they offered to their passengers. The South Eastern was as frequently vilified as the Chatham: *Herapath's Railway Magazine* printed a particularly virulent attack on the SER on 15th March 1884, giving an impressive example of the Victorian style of vitriol:

'The South Eastern Railway *is* a railway! It is necessary to say so, because some people believe it is a canal, some others a tramway, and the great majority a steam plough in a field. The reason it is a railway is because it is so called by Act of Parliament. The reason it continues to be a railway is on account of the national respect for the majesty of the law.

The SER starts indifferently from Cannon Street or Charing Cross, and goes back there again. Sometimes, by mistake, it goes elsewhere. Occasionally it gets to Folkestone, and tries to throw itself into the sea. This is good for Folkestone, because multitudes of philanthropists reside there in order to assist the deed.

The SER is generous to excess. It will always buy old cabs, broken-down omnibuses, or mouldy perambulators from anybody who doesn't care to keep them till next cold weather. A number of these vehicles tied together in a string is called a South Eastern Railway train.

At the end of each train there is a stationary engine. It is because no more of these engines can be procured that there are no railways in China.

The SER is profoundly philosophical. Its time-table is the only instance of the human mind fully defining eternity.

The SER is going under a tunnel to France, and the Government is going to spend 20 millions on fortifications to prevent it ever coming back.[7]

If you want to travel by the SER, you take a ticket and walk.'

In the middle of the costly battles of the 1880s, the LCDR briefly indulged in another romance with the LBSCR. During August 1885 the *Railway Times* reported that the two companies were having talks with various limited arrangements in mind, with the LCDR apparently keen on eventual full union. Several factors influenced the situation, of which the economic 'depression' and consequent drop in traffic was one. The LBSCR was also keen to gain more satisfactory access for main-line services to a City terminus, such as the LCDR's Holborn Viaduct. A Bill was presented to Parliament in January 1886 but, like its predecessors, was lost.

With a final solution having been found to the Shorncliffe dispute, relations between the SER and the LCDR improved in 1890. Rumours of an amalgamation were again current in January 1890 but were dismissed by the *Railway Times* which felt that nothing was likely to happen whilst Forbes and Watkin retained power. Early in March 1890 Forbes was reported as saying that competition between the two Companies wasted £130,000 per year.[8] Unknown to the railway press an actual correspondence had begun between the two Boards, though it had not got off to a good start. W. Stevens, the SER Secretary, referred to the failure of talks in 1885 and 1888 in a letter to the LCDR Board: 'The position of the South Eastern Company has been much altered and strengthened since those fruitless efforts were undertaken, and there is less need, so far as the sounder section of the Railways concerned, for any alliance with a property so managed that it has Eleven Millions of capital condemned to perpetual exclusion from dividend.'[9] This letter stung the pride of the LCDR Board, who instructed their own Secretary to reply on March 7th: 'My Board deeply regret the tone of your letter and the unnecessary and unjustifiable innuendo contained in it, and for which there is no foundation whatever.' However talks over the revision of the Continental Agreement were expanded to cover other areas of competition, but they collapsed in November 1890 when the LCDR insisted on a 37% share in the receipts.

The overall mood of the two Companies seemed to have improved considerably when fusion talks resumed again in 1892 amidst rumours that the LCDR was now also flirting with the Midland Railway. In August 1892 *The Times* itself was in favour, though by November it had changed its mind. A powerful group of SER shareholders, led by Nathaniel Spens, was now pushing for amalgamation though the Mayor of Folkestone wanted an assurance that the two Companies would not transfer all their shipping services to Dover. By this time the amalgamation talks had become a music-hall joke, so that they were referred to as 'the Chatham and South-Eastern Comedy.' In December 1892 the Spens plan was rejected, but a Fusion Bill was deposited in Parliament; each Company was to have eight directors on a new Joint Board, though capital accounts were to be kept separate. Opposition from the Kent towns was strong, with Dover, Folkestone and Tonbridge among the protestors. The Bill was withdrawn in February 1893, Watkin blaming the 'temper' of Parliament. This was only one of a number of occasions when Parliament, acting through a dislike of 'monopoly', had rejected railway amalgamations that would benefit the general public. Watkin himself retired in 1894, helping to remove at least one more potential obstacle.

The LCDR's Act of July 1894 included provision, in clause 11, for the two Companies to work together from 1st January 1895. This was not an

The Amalgamation Public House, which is situated in Strood close to where the LCDR main line bridges the SER's Maidstone branch. The pub sign shows the heraldic devices of the two erstwhile rivals. (Author)

agreement as such, merely the creation of the opportunity for agreement. An immediate result was a 'levelling' of fares, which the *Railway Times* saw as a 'substantial gain to the public.' Shorter distance fares were increased: the 1st class single from Victoria to Beckenham rising from 1/- to 1/4d. Longer distance travel became cheaper with the 1st class single from London to Ramsgate falling from 10/6d to 8/3d. Rumours of complete amalgamation were rife by early 1895, with the SER finding it necessary to issue a denial that all steamship services would be transferred to Dover.

There was then a temporary lull until talk of fusion discussions and Forbes' possible retirement strengthened LCDR shares in June 1898. For once the talks made good progress, both Boards meeting at Charing Cross on 20th and 21st July 1898 to work out the details. It was agreed that profits should be divided on a formula of 59% to the SER and 41% to the LCDR and that all workings should be done jointly from 1st January 1899. These talks were held under the powers of the SER's Act of 1893 and the LCDR's of 1894, but it was decided to seek a proper Amalgamation Act to sort out questions over the financing of steamships. The amalgamation necessitated the retirement of Forbes.

The two started working together as the 'South Eastern & Chatham Railways Managing Committee' on 1st January 1899. The Amalgamation Bill, to formalise the new relationship, had a comparatively easy ride through Parliament with no opposition being put by Maidstone, Canterbury, Rochester or Chatham. It passed the 2nd reading in the Commons by the comfortable margin of 206 votes, but had to cope with opposition from the London County Council and the *Daily Mail*. The Act received its Royal Assent on 5th August 1899.

Under the new arrangement the two Companies maintained their financial separation, so the two Boards continued to exist merely to supervise various issues concerning land and money; the day to day running of the railway became the responsibility of the new 'Managing Committee' so that the identity of the LCDR was effectively lost for ever although its name continued to exist until absorbed into the Southern Railway by Act of 1921.

As will be seen from Chapter Sixteen, one of the first acts of the new combination was to develop physical links between the two systems and subsequently a number of purely competitive lines were closed. But eighty-five years of history have failed to totally erase the signs of a bitter struggle that lasted forty years and so relics of it can still be found throughout Kent, particularly in Thanet and the Medway towns where a pub, bearing the name 'The Amalgamation' and the arms of the two rival concerns on its sign, stands in the shadow of the viaduct by which the old LCDR main line crosses the Strood to Maidstone branch of the former SER. Even today there are still at least two different ways of getting from London to any of Maidstone, Canterbury, Ashford, Sevenoaks, Chatham and Ramsgate. That is the legacy of the era of Forbes and Watkin and the next few chapters describe in rather more detail how this campaign was fought out through a complex system of railway lines.

CHAPTER SEVEN

The Medway Towns

The 'Medway towns' has become a convenient way of referring to the group of towns near the mouth of the River Medway. Outlying ridges of the North Downs come right down to the river, so that settlement developed in the narrow strip of land between the Medway marshes and high ground; furthest west is Strood, then Rochester, Chatham and New Brompton, later swallowed up in the growth of Gillingham. This physical configuration had an important influence on the railways through the area because, although it was possible to serve four towns from one line, this could only be done at the cost of heavy engineering works. Indeed the difficulty of traversing the Medway towns may well have discouraged the South Eastern in the first place, for the East Kent eventually needed to construct a viaduct over the Medway and a high bridge across the Luton valley, as well as three tunnels — Fort Pitt, Chatham and Gillingham, of 428 yards, 297 yards, and 897 yards respectively.

Despite these physical difficulties, the Medway towns proved an enduring attraction for railway companies. The traffic potential, both passenger and freight, was probably greater than in any other area of Kent. Not only did the concentrated population (over 30,000 in 1851, over 100,000 by 1901) offer the possibility of lucrative passenger receipts, but the area also had great potential for freight. The proximity of chalk downland to the river had led to the early development of a cement and lime industry at Frindsbury, close to the river, whilst the Medway itself was busy with both commercial and naval traffic — including to the Royal Dockyard at Chatham.

The first railway to reach the towns had been the Gravesend & Rochester, which had been opened in 1845 following the simple operation of installing a line of rails beside the Thames & Medway Canal from Gravesend to Strood via the Higham tunnel. It was this line that had first introduced elements of drama and farce into the railway affairs of the region caused, as always, by a lack of money. Just before the line was scheduled to open a dispute had arisen between the contractor and the company over the cost of some additional works. Whilst the dispute was being sorted out, the contractor's men remained in control of the Gravesend terminus until, on 24th January 1845, the G&R forcibly took possession. The contractor replied the following day by sending a group of navvies who broke down the defences and threw out the G&R's men. According to the *Maidstone Journal*,[1] 'Another party of about forty navigators with spades, pickaxes, crow bars etc. were despatched down the line from Higham to Rochester [Strood] to destroy the terminus.' The contractor's foreman at Strood removed part of a locomotive to prevent a service being

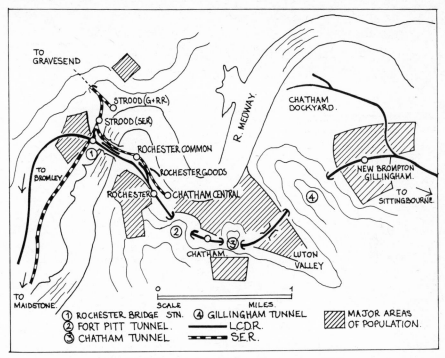

Map 20: Railways of the Medway Towns, circa 1890

operated. Full scale violence seemed likely, but magistrates intervened and the dispute was referred to arbitration, with the result that the stolen locomotive part was returned on 29th January.

Free trips to Gravesend and back began almost immediately and there were steamer connections across the Medway from Strood to the Sun Pier in Chatham. Passenger trains were running at least as early as 31st January 1845 and there were further experimental trips on 8th February. The official opening came on 10th February and the following Good Friday over 2,000 people travelled on the line of whom 1,500 used the ferry connection to Chatham. The fare from Chatham to London using this route and the Thames steamers upriver of Gravesend was only 1/3d. The line was soon absorbed into the SER and in 1849 became part of a through route to London Bridge, though its terminus remained at the original site close to the Strood canal basin until 1856. However the SER did not win many friends in the area, causing particular annoyance by doubling the fares over the line in 1850. The *Maidstone Journal*[2] took this as an opportunity to expound its theories of railway economics: 'Take two such places as Chatham and Gravesend; the one is a working town filled with mechanics and artisans, the other a pleasure town aiming to be the Margate of West Kent. Cheapen the communication between the two towns and you have a certain and constant stream of passengers.'

97

The three bridges across the Medway at Rochester in about 1900: nearest to the camera is the road bridge built by Fox, then Fox's LCDR bridge and furthest away Cubitt's SER bridge of 1891 which carries the main line today. Also visible is Rochester Bridge station.

(Author's collection)

When the East Kent line opened the only additional station that it originally provided for the Medway area was at Chatham, opened on 25th January 1858. This station was sandwiched between Fort Pitt and Chatham tunnels, with the booking hall provided on a bridge across the tracks, though it had been the original intention to site it on the north side of the line. Whether any additional station should be provided in the area had been discussed from the inception of the scheme, though little had been done about it before the line opened. By June 1858, however, the East Kent Board had finally decided that a station should be built at New Brompton which was close to the village of Gillingham and reasonably convenient for Chatham Dockyard. Board Minutes indicate that this station was to be constructed hurriedly and opened 'before the Races'[3] though in fact it did not open until some time in autumn 1858. The life of New Brompton station was nearly cut short at a very early stage, since in December 1858 the Board considered whether it should be closed!

Railways through the Medway towns showed an early ability to attract disaster. In July 1858 Sacré, the Locomotive Superintendent, was sacked following an accident at Chatham. Another result of this mishap was that a signalman was placed at the Strood end of Fort Pitt Tunnel, which curved so sharply that it was impossible for Chatham station staff to be aware of a train approaching from that direction. Even this provision did not solve all problems, for in July 1859 the Board decided to grant financial assistance to the widow of a man killed at Chatham. The Executive Committee resolved that '£5 be given to the widow of George Jarman who was accidentally killed whilst asleep in the Chatham tunnel.'[4] In June 1862 *Herapath's Railway Magazine* reported another accident in Chatham Tunnel. Two excursions going to Crystal Palace

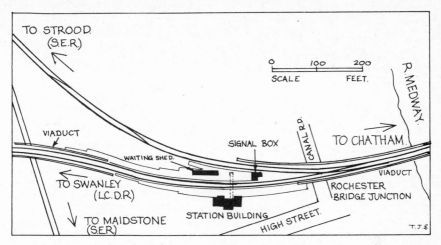

Map 21: Rochester Bridge Station, 1879

collided at 10mph and twenty people were injured: 'The shrieks and cries were of the wildest description, while the utmost confusion prevailed in the tunnel, added to which it was known that the ordinary continental express was then due.'

Railway developments in the area after the opening of the East Kent Railway in 1858 and the extension to St. Mary Cray and Bickley in 1860 largely followed three themes: the improvement of the LCDR's passenger facilities, the provision of a link into Chatham Dockyard, and the SER's search for a better way of competing for the Medway towns traffic.

As soon as the Western Extension to Bickley had begun to take shape a war of words developed between the EKR (LCDR from 1859) and the South Eastern. In July 1858 the SER began to cause difficulties at Strood, where the lines of the two Companies met. It was clear that, once the Western Extension line had been opened, this interchange would become virtually redundant, but in the meantime the SER began a policy of obstruction. This particularly affected the EKR's fast train passengers from Canterbury to London Bridge, who were forced to make a change of carriage and pay an extra 1/- for the privilege. The immediate result of this was a decline in the through traffic from the EKR or LCDR onto the SER; in July 1858 the EKR had paid £420 in tolls for the use of the SER beyond Strood, this dropped sharply to £259 in August 1858 and had declined to only £193 in August 1859.[5]

By 1859 the LCDR had to decide how it was to serve Strood and Rochester; this was not easy, since the line through Rochester avoided the city itself and ran along the waterside whilst it crossed Strood on viaduct and embankment. The LCDR Board showed a certain amount of indecision in solving this problem, having decided to buy land for a station in Strood in September 1859 it then deferred the decision in November. In August 1860 the Board discussed the

99

Chatham station viewed from the entrance to Fort Pitt tunnel in SE&CR days.
(A. Riley collection)

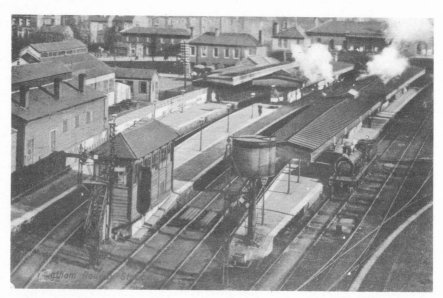

Chatham station in about 1905 showing the cramped layout necessary to fit in four main platform faces; also visible are the tracklevel buildings which may have been intended as the original facilities, though streetlevel ones were soon adopted.   (E. Baldock collection)

The imposing station building at Rochester Bridge, located on the Strood side of the River Medway. (Rochester Library)

'immediate need' for a station in Free School Lane, Rochester, but then in October decided not to provide a passenger station in Rochester at all, but only goods facilities. However it was decided to have a station in Strood instead; accordingly a station labelled 'Rochester' appeared in the timetables for November-December 1860, but without any trains stopping there. It was eventually opened as 'Rochester Bridge', probably in late December 1860, and was situated in Strood just to the west of Rochester Bridge Junction.

None of this altered the importance of Chatham, which remained the leading traffic centre in the area, with its stationmaster earning the comparatively princely sum of £150 per annum. In 1867 a lease was taken on 'No. 1 Ordnance Place' as the stationmaster's house.

With the opening of the direct Chatham to Bromley line services over the link between the LCDR and the SER into Strood station effectively ceased and Strood declined in importance. Although Strood and Rochester Bridge stations were only a few hundred yards apart, connections were not encouraged so that a journey from — for example — Gravesend to New Brompton was a difficult affair. The South Eastern in fact had the right to insist on through workings into Chatham and meetings were held to discuss arrangements for this in 1873. However the LCDR insisted that the SER should pay for the alterations that would be needed to allow through workings via Strood and terminating at Chatham, where operating facilities were very cramped. By October 1874 the SER was threatening to apply to the Railway Commissioners for a writ of summons against the LCDR, demanding that its legal right to effect through

101

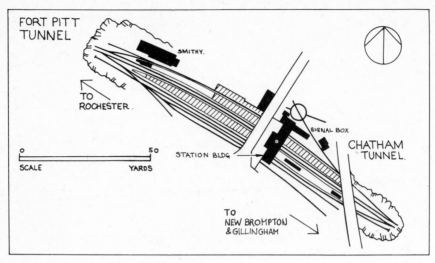

Map 22: Chatham Station, 1898

workings to Chatham should be recognised by 11th October. The situation was not resolved until the Mayor of Rochester, Mr Toomer, took the matter to the Railway Commission himself. Both Companies were subsequently threatened with heavy penalties if the through service was not restored and so the link, known as the 'Toomer Loop' for some years afterwards, returned to public service in April 1877.

Its confinement to the Strood side of the River Medway was a source of irritation for the SER, who in 1873 proposed their own extension line across the Medway and into Rochester. The main result of this was to encourage the LCDR to improve its own connections with Chatham Dockyard. The SER did not proceed any further with this project at the time, only going so far as to buy some land in Rochester in 1874, and during the later 1870s competitive schemes were largely forgotten whilst the railways enjoyed a more harmonious working atmosphere.

However in 1878 hopes of a union between the LCDR and the SER collapsed, with the *Chatham Observer* feeling that 'Sir Edward Watkin gets the credit for being the cause of contention.'

With the revival of competition Watkin cast greedy eyes on Chatham itself. In 1881 he complained that the LCDR was taking 70% of the traffic from Thanet, Canterbury and the Medway towns, so that the SER needed a more aggressive policy. Accordingly he revived the 1873 plan for an independent line to Chatham, which secured an Act of Parliament in August 1881. Part of the reason for this unlikely success was that the LCDR had been complaining for years about the difficulties of handling the through trains from Strood into Chatham and had thereby provided its rival with an impressive case. Also influential was the support of the armed forces, especially the evidence given

102

The South Eastern Railway bridge across the Medway in course of construction. The sawmill
buildings in the foreground were demolished to allow for the Chatham Central branch.

(Rochester Library)

in Committee by the Commander-in-Chief, the Duke of Cambridge. Once
the Act was passed the SER had to negotiate with the Conservators of the
River Medway, the Admiralty and Rochester Corporation. The SER's solicitor
complained in 1888 that 'it took a long time.... to satisfy the Conservators,
and not merely to satisfy their views as regards to what we were to do, but
also their pockets.'

Another part of the SER's 1881 Act also threatened the LCDR in the
Medway area. A 'Northfleet & Snodland loop' was authorised to run from
Northfleet, on the SER's North Kent line, via Cobham and Luddesdown to
Snodland, with a bridge beneath the LCDR main line. It was never built.

The Act for the Chatham branch allowed the SER three years to complete
the works, but a time extension had to be obtained in 1884 due, apparently,
to tardiness in the purchase of land. The waterfront site at Rochester required
special protection, and clause 36 of the 1881 Act stipulated that it 'shall be
constructed so as to admit of free communication....' hence an embankment
could not be used. But having spent between £70,000 and £100,000 on the
line's works, the SER ran into a period of financial difficulty and abandoned
the project. The Strood to Chatham service continued in the meantime; in
early 1888 there were five up and eight down trains with the fastest time to
London Bridge being 1 hour 40 minutes, as opposed to 56 minutes to Victoria
via the LCDR.

The collapse of this scheme was a particular blow to the people of Rochester

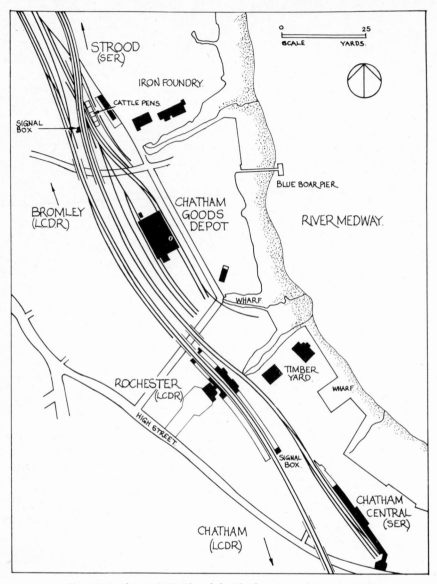

Map 23: Rochester (LCDR) and the Chatham Central Branch, 1895

who, lacking a station they could call their own, felt themselves ill-served by railways. In January 1886 the *Chatham Observer* printed a letter bitterly criticising Rochester Bridge station: 'It is the very climax of inconvenience and awkward construction, and it is in every way as unsuited to the requirements of a city like Rochester as it is antediluvian in design and appearance.'

104

In 1887 the SER applied to Parliament for a renewal of the powers to construct a branch to Chatham. The Bill was bitterly contested, though in typically devious ways. Forbes, of the LCDR, called the scheme an 'unwarrantable act of aggression', but when the Bill reached the Committee stage in April 1888 the LCDR's stand was somewhat peculiar. They chose to oppose this thrust into their heartland on the grounds that it would involve the demolition of their new goods station, which had been built beside the river at Rochester at a cost of £40,000. Mr Pope, representing the LCDR, said 'You are welcome to your powers if you will only carry out your works so as not to destroy our station which, in the meantime, has been erected.... then, instead of opposing you, we would rather assist you.' A statement which must have struck the SER as uncharacteristically charitable!

The counsel for the SER, Littler, was not to be fooled — he saw the construction of the goods station as typical LCDR scheming. 'The Chatham Company completed all this before 1886; they knew we were coming and yet they put this goods shed in with the express purpose of making us pay for it, and we can do it within our limits of deviation if they will let us do it.' He argued that the SER already owned all the land needed except for a small strip through the LCDR's goods yard.

With the new branch only being opposed on the grounds of a goods shed, the Committee passed the Bill; the SER's line subsequently squeezed between the LCDR goods shed and its main-line embankment, crossing the LCDR sidings by means of a viaduct. Forbes was furious about the project's success: 'We could not think that some men would incur such an enormous outlay for such a small result', he complained on 18th April 1888. In 1891 he told the LCDR shareholders '... why in breach of honour they should go to Rochester and spend £500,000 of money upon that outrageous enterprise I am at a loss to conceive.'

The SER's branch actually cost them £171,329 to construct once they had recommenced the works. The Medway bridge, designed by Sir William Cubitt, absorbed £71,000 of this. But to this must be added the sum spent on the project between 1881 and 1885 and the not inconsiderable amount invested in land; Forbes' suggestion of £500,000 for 1m 8.8 chains of line does not then seem so ridiculous.

Trains began running to the branch's intermediate station of Rochester Common (later Rochester Central) on 20th July 1891 and on 23rd February 1892 a special press train ran from London to the Chatham terminus in 53 minutes. The double track branch opened to its terminus at Chatham Central (which was not in Chatham and was very far from being central to anything) on 1st March 1892. The principal feature of the branch was, of course, the lattice-girder viaduct across the River Medway with a span of 170ft; the line was double track although the terminus had only a single platform. Once the branch was completed the SER continued to talk about extensions, even airing the possibility of extending along the waterfront right round to Chatham Dockyard. A short extension was authorised to the nearby victualling yard but never built.

Two views of New Brompton & Gillingham station in 1895-1905, illustrating its position
slightly east of the present Gillingham station site.

(Gillingham Library and E. Baldock collection)

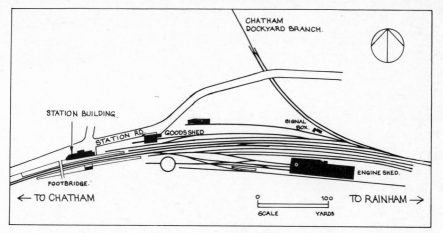

Map 24: New Brompton & Gillingham Station, 1898

The SER's Chatham Central branch induced a sense of panic in the LCDR which at last took steps to improve its facilities in the Medway towns. In December 1890 the Company decided to build a new station on the main line at Rochester and tenders were put out for this in January 1891. The station was opened on the same day as the SER's Chatham Central, 1st March 1892, though it was not altogether well received. A letter to the *Chatham Observer* complained that '... the Company have "improved" their service by making all their *fast* trains stop at a station within a few minutes walk of Chatham station, where they also stop, and only the slow ones at Rochester Bridge.' The new Rochester station was halfway between Chatham and Rochester Bridge stations, so it was felt that the reduction in the latter's services would disadvantage Strood.

In October 1893 the Board received a deputation from Chatham Council, who requested provision of a station at 'Luton Road'. This could only have been at the spot known locally as 'Luton arches', where the railway crosses the Luton valley on a high embankment and viaduct. It was clearly not a good position for a station.

Because of the number of tunnels, viaducts and embankments, the LCDR's facilities in the Chatham area had become rather congested by the 1890s and it was difficult to increase capacity without major engineering. Therefore in 1896-97 the LCDR promoted the 'Chatham Loop Railway' which would have left the main line at Sole Street, curved round to the south of the Medway towns, and rejoined the main line at Newington. This would have been a costly project and, although a Bill was deposited, the LCDR did not proceed with it.

Despite all the railway activity in the Rochester area, it was in fact the eastern side of the Medway towns that was developing as a major traffic centre. Gillingham was the fastest growing of the Medway towns throughout the latter half of the nineteenth century, increasing from 9,321 people in 1851 to 42,643

107

The level crossing east of Gillingham station in 1914.   (E. Course collection)

in 1901 — by which time it was larger than Chatham. Despite this the only
changes which took place were relatively minor such as the renaming of New
Brompton station as 'New Brompton & Gillingham' in 1886 which was,
according to LCDR Minutes for March 1887, part of the town's Jubilee
celebrations. The end of the century also saw an expansion of siding facilities
to the east of the station. Two and a quarter acres were bought for sidings in
1899 and another 20¾ acres in 1900 for a goods yard. But the railway's local
traffic did not keep pace with the growth of population in the area, since the
Medway towns was the one area outside London where electric tramways
competed seriously for traffic against the LCDR.

When the East Kent Railway had opened its main line, Chatham Dockyard
had been left isolated and was therefore at the centre of a number of early
branch-line proposals. In fact a Dockyard branch was suggested as early as 1857
and subsequently reappeared in rumours published by the *Maidstone Journal*
in November 1860. The scheme was again considered in 1866. In the event
it was the threat of intervention by the SER, which was promoting the idea
of a direct link between Woolwich Arsenal — on its own North Kent line —
and Chatham Dockyard that forced the LCDR to commit itself. By February
1873 a Bill had been deposited for a branch from New Brompton into the
'Government Yard', which was estimated to cost £57,000 though there
was to be a Government contribution. A formal agreement with the Admiralty was signed on 30th July 1874, with the Government guaranteeing a
return of 4% on the line. Construction had started by February 1875 and
the line opened on 16th February 1877.[6] Total cost was £54,417-0-7d, which

108

the Government paid off at a rate of £2,176-13-6d per year, though the whole amount seems to have been finally settled by a single cheque paid in 1891.

The Dockyard was well-equipped with its own internal transport network. This included an 'underground canal' and a narrow-gauge railway which was started in the 1860s. In July 1884 the LCDR Minutes recorded:

'Read a letter from the Inspector General of Fortifications dated the 30th May, giving notice of the proposal to make a narrow-gauge Railway to connect the Submarine Mining Establishment at Gillingham with the School of Military Engineering at Chatham and asking the permission of the Company to cross under the Chatham Dockyard line.'

The formation of a working union between the SER and the LCDR had major implications for the railways of the Chatham area. The changes which have occurred since then are described in Chapters Sixteen and Seventeen.

CHAPTER EIGHT

The LCDR in North Kent and Sheppey

i) New Brompton to Faversham

When the East Kent Company first promoted its route it envisaged two append-ages being added to the main line between New Brompton and Faversham; one was a branch across the Swale to Sheerness, and the other was a short branch to Faversham Creek. The latter was clearly an important provision if Faversham was to maintain its position as a port of some influence, and accordingly the East Kent solicited financial contributions to meet its cost from local landowners and businessmen. They wanted £6,000 in February 1858, when Lord Sondes alone gave £1,000. By April 1859 arrangements for land purchase were being made. The date generally given for the opening of the Creek branch is 12th April 1860,[1] though this may be incorrect; LCDR General Committee Minutes of 7th September 1860 record the branch as being 'unfinished' whilst Board Minutes of 16th November 1860 state that it was still 'not handed over.' However it was stated to be in use on 6th December 1860,[2] so it would seem that it opened in early December. As early as 1853 it was realised that the great importance of the Creek branch would be for coal traffic,[3] which was still being brought to Faversham by collier from the North-east; the LCDR hoped to distribute this coal by rail from Faversham Creek and in November 1860 even considered setting up their own coke ovens there. A tramway extension to the Creek branch, serving a brewery and with siding and wagon turntables paid for by local people, was added in 1862. But Faversham remained a minor port, with difficult access and shallow water, so that the Creek branch made little difference to its fortunes.

On the main line itself facilities were initially basic. As we have seen, Newington did not have a station until 1st August 1862 and there were no goods facilities at Teynham or Rainham to start with. Originally it was planned to make Faversham the base for the Company's engine workshops, but these were eventually constructed at Longhedge though Faversham did become the most important engine shed outside of London.

The area seems to have been accident prone to start with. On 4th January 1861 the 9.55am from Victoria was derailed near Sittingbourne; according to the *Railway Times,* which seemed to derive perverse pleasure from the incident, there was 'one man mangled in a truly frightful manner', who later died of his injuries. The following day the 7.55pm from Victoria was derailed at Teynham with three men on the footplate being killed. On 25th January 1862 the 6.40am Victoria to Dover, with only four passengers on board, was derailed at Rainham. In his report on the accident, Colonel Yolland wrote that 'It is apparent that

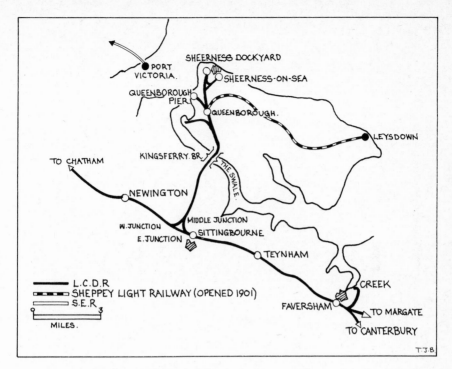

Map 25: North Kent & Sheppey, 1898

nearly every servant of the company that had a responsible duty to perform neglected it.'[4] This was followed by the Ospringe derailment on 9th May 1862, when the 8pm Victoria to Dover was derailed between Sittingbourne and Teynham with one fatality.

Some improvements were made during the 1860s. Faversham became increasingly important with the promotion and construction of the coast line to Whitstable and Margate; thus in April 1862 various improvements were made, including the provision of a buffet, and then in August 1863 the bay platform for the Herne Bay trains were extended. Sittingbourne was also becoming important as the junction for Sheerness, and in 1863 £1,700 was allocated for roofing the station over. Another addition was made at Faversham in 1864 when £1,220 was provided for engine sheds.

Another accident occurred at Sittingbourne on 31st August 1878. Whilst some shunting was taking place a mistake was made with the points and a passenger train ran into a goods train at 40mph. The result was 79 claims for damages, amounting to over £25,000.

During the 1890s the main concern seems to have been about Faversham station, which was proving wholly inadequate for its role as the major junction on the LCDR outside of London. In February 1893 the *Railway Times* referred

111

Faversham looking west in the early 1890s with the original buildings still intact.
(R. Thomas collection)

The rebuilt Faversham with two island platforms serving four through roads and more substantial buildings.
(R. Kidner collection)

to the need for rebuilding and the subject was considered by the Board in November 1894. On 11th May 1895 the Board actually visited Faversham to discuss the improvements, but nothing had been done by the time a deputation from Faversham Council visited the LCDR Board in March 1897. Work finally got started in October 1897 at a cost of £31,000; new signal boxes were provided and the station turned into two island platforms with four faces serving four through roads. A similar plan for the expansion of Sittingbourne, aired in 1900 under the SE&CR, made no progress.

ii) The Sheerness Branch

A branch to Sheerness, particularly with the Royal Dockyard in mind, had been suggested as early as 1844 when the alignment of one was surveyed for the North Kent Railway. The proposal also played an integral part in the East Kent Railway plans in the mid-1850s, although when an Act was obtained on 7th July 1856 it was in the name of the Sittingbourne & Sheerness Railway. This nominally independent concern had a capital of £80,000 and powers for £26,000 in loans. It was to construct a branch of $7^1/_8$ miles from Sittingbourne, across the tidal River Swale, to a terminus close to the entrance of Sheerness Dockyard; there was also to be a short branch to a pier of 240ft on the Swale just south of Queenborough which would allow for the commercial traffic, particularly coal, that could not pass through the Royal Dockyard.

It was clearly obvious that the Sittingbourne & Sheerness would act as a satellite of the East Kent and in December 1858 the two companies agreed that the EKR would work the line and then lease it after five years. Arrangements for the working were, as usual, dependent on the line being completed to a satisfactory standard. The S&SR remained nominally independent until merged into the LCDR by Act of 1876.

Despite the heavy bridge works, good progress was made with construction and the LCDR's Directors inspected the branch in September 1859. Progress had been sufficiently rapid for the junction points to be installed at Sittingbourne in August and by April 1860 the LCDR Board was making arrangements for the engines on the line; it was decided that the tank engines were necessary as there was no turntable at Sittingbourne, and so two were ordered from Hawthorns for £925 each. In the meantime the contractor Crampton loaned an engine called 'Cubitt' to get things started. The line to Sheerness opened on 19th July 1860 with an intermediate station at Queenborough.

An immediate cause of disagreement within the working arrangement was the goods pier just to the south of Queenborough. In April 1860 the LCDR had decided that this pier should extend to 300ft rather than 240ft as originally planned and this delayed its completion until after the rest of the line had been opened. It was still incomplete in August 1861 and in September the S&SR firmly blamed the LCDR for its late completion. The exact date of the opening of the pier and the short goods branch to it are not known, but it was clearly in use by August 1863 when a short loop was planned to allow direct access onto this branch from Queenborough station; normal access was

The east end of Faversham station then and now, with roughly eighty years dividing the pictures; the third rail has been added and the signals changed, but the trackwork has hardly altered and the oasthouses have survived.
(R. Thomas and Author)

from the Sittingbourne direction. This goods pier, which was quite a separate entity from the more famous passenger pier opened further to the north in 1876, was 300ft long and could accommodate seven vessels, three of which would always be afloat in 10-12ft of water. It was never a conspicuous success as the coal trade failed to develop but a siding for the oyster traffic was provided in 1863.[5]

Arrangements between the Sheerness Company and the LCDR were not always satisfactory. In March 1861 the former announced that it would take the LCDR to court for not working its line according to their agreement, but the LCDR claimed that non-completion of the line — including the Queenborough goods pier branch — invalidated the agreement. However by April things had warmed, with the LCDR proposing to lease the Sheerness line for 999 years although an Act to allow such arrangements had already been passed in 1859.

The Sheerness branch joined the LCDR at Sittingbourne, where it ran into the station so that a reversal was necessary for trains working through to Chatham. Facilities were at first basic, but in March 1861 the LCDR agreed to provide some sidings at Milton Meads, near Sittingbourne, for Sheerness traffic. In October 1861 the LCDR decided to provide a platform and signal box at King's Ferry, where the branch crossed the Swale and where the Railway owned the toll rights. Since no passenger station opened there until 1922, it is to be presumed that the 'platform' referred to was a small affair for the use of railway staff needing to get to a very remote spot.

In November 1861 the two Companies discussed their financial relationship once more. The LCDR was dissatisfied with the plan to work the Sheerness line at 55% of receipts for five years and after that to lease it on a scale sliding from £5,000 to £11,000 per annum; instead they wanted the cost to be £4,000 per annum until 1866, £6,000 thereafter. The talks failed since the LCDR was trying to change an agreement that had already been made. During early 1862 the differences were settled, but the LCDR then complained, in April, that £7,890 was needed to put the Sheerness line into a decent state. The state of the track was one cause of concern — but this seemed to be the case wherever LCDR trains ran at this time.

Some further improvements at the Sittingbourne end were suggested in 1862. One was for an extra line into Sittingbourne station so that branch train movements would not conflict with main-line trains and then in November 1862 the Board decided to complete 'Upper Junction' (now Western) and to construct the 'independent line' from 'Lower Junction' (now Eastern) into Sittingbourne. The completion of the Upper Junction, and the loop from there to Middle Junction on the Sheerness branch itself, would allow through running to and from Chatham without reversal in Sittingbourne; no definite date of completion for this spur is available, but Minutes show estimates being prepared in September 1863 so it may have been finished late in 1864. The third line from Lower (Eastern) Junction into Sittingbourne was not completed, even though plans for it were revived in 1876.

The importance of the Queenborough and Sheerness line was increased by the decision to use it for continental traffic, no doubt influenced by its location

A view of Teynham station, a typical late-Victorian wayside scene with the staff posing on the platform. Railway jobs were well sought-after in rural areas where stations rarely employed less than six people. (A. Riley collection)

An accident on the Faversham Creek branch in 1920. Both locomotives still carry the austere SE&CR livery of the First World War. (A. Riley collection)

The first Kingsferry railway bridge across the Swale; the movable central span, which allowed navigation along the River, is clearly visible.

outside the boundaries of the Continental Agreement. The Zeeland Steamship Company was formed on 10th June 1875 to improve the mails service between the Netherlands and Great Britain. On 26th July 1875 a nightly service commenced between Sheerness and Flushing (now Vlissingen) but on 14th November the service was suspended due to a combination of high costs, the loss of a ship and the shallowness of the water available at Sheerness. In preparation for this service the LCDR had started to remodel its facilities at Queenborough in June 1875, including dredging part of the Swale and the construction of a new branch and pier for passenger services to the north of Queenborough station. This enabled the Flushing service to restart via Queenborough on 15th May 1876. The service was beginning to build up a steady custom when Queenborough Pier was destroyed by fire on the night of 18-19th May 1882, so that passenger traffic had to be transferred to Dover; however the LCDR managed to get a temporary landing stage operational within three weeks. When the pier was rebuilt, in 1885, it was extended into deeper water and was 650ft long, at a cost of £100,000. On 1st June 1887 the importance of Queenborough Pier was further increased by the start of a day and night service, using three new paddle steamers and including a German mails service. Another disastrous fire occurred at Queenborough Pier on 17th July 1900, but since the SE&CR had been formed by then it was possible to transfer services to the ex-SER rival facility at Port Victoria; Queenborough Pier was patched up and reopened for the day service on 26th January 1901. An accident that occurred at Queenborough Pier on 13th May 1896 could have been serious; a driver, running onto the pier, misjudged the speed of his train and collided with the buffers. Fortunately the impact was not too great, since there was a real danger of the train disappearing into the murky waters of the Swale.

The LCDR's terminus in Sheerness was conveniently located for the Dockyard, but was remote from the town itself. For the LCDR this was a tolerable state of affairs when the only competition came from the SER's river-boat connection from Strood to Sheerness, but in 1882 the SER opened its new branch to Port Victoria, a spot just across the Medway from Sheerness. Using

117

A very early view of the unusual exterior of Queenborough railway station.

The Scherzer lift-bridge across the River Swale at Kingsferry, with the concrete pillars of the modern road/rail bridge that replaced it. The bridge is shown open for shipping.

(R. Thomas)

M2 class No. 640 (LCDR No. 181) at Queenborough Pier with a boat express in about 1905.
(E. Baldock collection)

a steamer to make the short water connection, the SER launched a fierce assault on the LCDR's Sheerness traffic, having the advantage of a considerably shorter route. An intensive train and boat service commenced on 11th September 1882, with the SER's cheap fast fares at 3/- single and 5/- return whereas the LCDR was charging 3/3d single and 5/- return. In 1890 the SER introduced two new steamers, the *Edward William* and the *Myleta* to the service. Port Victoria was also used by the SER for its own service to Flushing.

Faced with competition, the LCDR had to improve its Sheerness facilities and on 18th July 1882 acquired powers for a short branch into Sheerness town, avoiding the Dockyard station. This opened on 1st June 1883. The original station, at the Dockyard, retained its name of 'Sheerness' until 1st June 1883 when it became 'Sheerness Dockyard'; the new station was always known as Sheerness-on-Sea.

A further dispute arose over the auctioning of the Sheerness pier tolls in 1884. Since it operated a ferry service, these were of interest to the SER but, despite making the highest bid, the SER application was not successful. Apparently this was because the tolls went to the highest cash bidder and the SER offered a cheque, but the South Eastern later denied having offered a cheque at all.

The branch always proved vulnerable to weather; for example storms on 29th November 1897 cut the line between Queenborough and Sheerness, so that no trains ran to the terminus for a fortnight. This produced a revival in

119

Sittingbourne station interior during the early years of British Railways. (A. Riley)

The restricted and cramped layout of Sheerness Dockyard station towards the end of its career. (A. Riley collection)

120

Kirtley No. 506 (formerly LCDR 47) 'Templar' at Sittingbourne in about 1905, probably forming a train to Sheerness. (E. Baldock collection)

the London to Sheerness via Port Victoria traffic, which was languishing by the late 1890s; having been restored, it ran until 1st June 1901.

iii) The Fruit Traffic

As well as being important for hops, North Kent was noted for its fruit. The area between Rainham and Blean Wood, near Faversham, had been a traditional fruit-growing region since the sixteenth century. During the nineteenth century fruit-growing expanded rapidly in Kent, with the acreage of orchards rising from 11,300 in 1872-76 to 25,700 in 1897-1901; small or soft fruit acreage also increased, from 14,920 in 1888-1891 to 22,340 in 1902-6. This was in contrast to the hop trade, which had begun to contract at the same period. Fruit was also grown in areas like the Cray valley, within fifteen miles of the London markets.

Debate over the Metropolitan Extensions Act shows that the LCDR hoped to profit from this traffic, but it seems to have failed to do so. The warnings were evident from the start since in 1860 the SER was carrying only 140 tons of fruit and vegetables to London per day during the high season.

Fruit was unsuitable for rail traffic, not only because it was easily damaged but also because it was carried in fairly small quantities. On the former point Eborall, of the SER, had this to say in 1860:

'The strawberries and currants and sometimes the more valuable cherries — they are carted in spring carts for it is found that the constant transhipment

121

An unusual scene at Sheerness in 1925 with the stationmaster, Mr Parker, harvesting grapes from the station vine. (Southern Railway Magazine)

from cart to railway and from railway to cart damages that description of fruit very materially.'[6]

Within 15-20 miles of London most fruit was delivered by road, the returning vehicles carrying manure back to the farms. From the Faversham area much of the fruit was despatched by water so that the LCDR's share of the traffic was never sufficient to be profitable, generally in the region of about £10,000 per year. Another problem was that the fruit trade was notoriously prone to damage by weather, and so the level of traffic varied considerably from year to year.

A derailment at Whitstable in SE&CR days; notice the basket containing blocks of wood for placing under the wheels of the engine.

(Douglas West collection)

CHAPTER NINE

The 'Coast Line' in

East Kent and Thanet

i) The Ramsgate Line

Most early proposals for railways through Kent were concerned with access
from London to Dover, but in fact the first line to be opened in the County
was a local line from Canterbury to Whitstable on 4th May 1830. This became
part of the South Eastern, which linked up with it by extending from Ashford
to Canterbury on 6th February 1846, going onwards from there to Ramsgate
on 13th April 1846. This left the majority of the Kent coast unserved to any
satisfactory extent, especially Margate which the SER reached only by a branch
from its Ramsgate station — opened 1st December 1846 — and Herne Bay,
which had no station at all. There were many attempts during the Railway
Mania to add extra lines in East Kent and Thanet, such as the Kentish Coast
Railway projected from Stourmouth to Herne Bay with a Ramsgate branch,
and an associated scheme from Sandwich to Sholden (with a Deal branch),
Walmer, Guston and Dover. None of these lines made much progress, but a

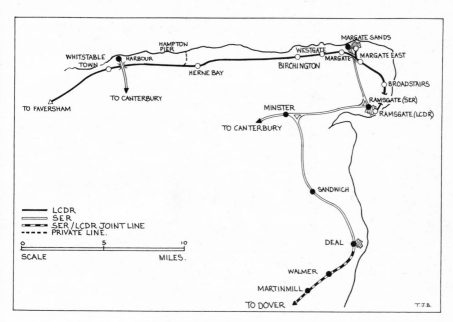

Map 26: East Kent & Thanet, 1898

125

The original Margate station, as illustrated in the 'Illustrated London News' at the time of the line's opening in 1863.

126

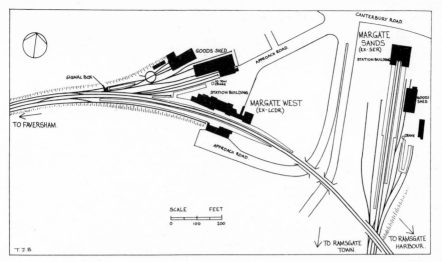

Map 27: Margate Stations, 1906

short branch from South Street, on the Canterbury & Whitstable, to Herne Bay was authorised in 1847 but never built.

The promotion of the East Kent Railway opened up new possibilities, especially as it would now be possible to get to the east Kent resorts without having to take the SER's lengthy diversion via Redhill. It was clear that a line branching off the EKR at Faversham could provide a much better route between London and several resorts than the SER offered. The first step was the promotion by local interests of a line from Faversham to Herne Bay, passing through Whitstable. Herne Bay was a small but fairly thriving resort, which boasted a substantial wooden pier built in 1831. A meeting to promote this branch line was held at the Pier Hotel, Herne Bay, in September 1856 when Mr Holroyd, Secretary of the EKR, outlined a £70,000 plan — acting nominally as a private individual rather than in his EKR capacity. By February 1857 money was being raised and £55,760 had been accumulated — £25,960 from local people and £23,800 from the contractor Crampton, one of Peto's associates.[1]

An Act was obtained, under the name Herne Bay & Whitstable Railway, on 17th August 1857 with a capital of £80,000. The first Board meeting was held on 24th August 1857 with C.J. Hilton of Faversham in the Chair. Although the Company used the name HB&W in its Minute book, it seems to have been universally referred to as the Herne Bay & Faversham because of the two towns it linked up.

Crampton was engaged to do the contracting for two-thirds cash and one third shares, though in August 1858 he informed the Board that Peto had joined him in the contract. Work started late in 1858 and immediately ran into problems with the SER, who complained that the new line would disturb the

127

Ramsgate beach showing the LCDR's station in 1863. Apart from the beach costumes, the scene has changed remarkably little in the course of 120 years.

(R.W. Kidner collection)

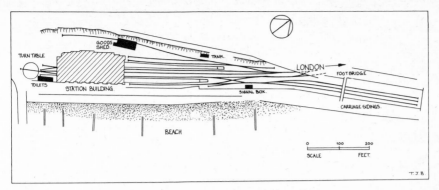

Map 28: Ramsgate Harbour Station, 1906

Canterbury & Whitstable where it passed beneath it. Very sensibly the matter was referred to the Board of Trade who in June 1859 awarded £36-11-5d to the SER.

Meanwhile the *Railway Times,* no doubt encouraged by Samuel Smiles, was looking for scandal amongst the finances. It found, in September 1858, that 700 shares of £20 each had been subscribed for at Herne Bay and 150 at Whitstable, but that 500 remained unsold despite Peto, Betts & Crampton having taken 2,500. Nonetheless ambition was taking root and as early as July 1858 the Company had decided to apply for an extension to Margate.

Undoubtedly an extension to Kent's leading resort made sound commercial sense. Margate had been fashionable since the 1790s and had grown rapidly because steamers made the journey from London relatively easy; as early as 1800 18,000 visitors had arrived this way in one year and by 1860 it was estimated that Margate was visited by 100,000 people a year.[2] Steamers could do the journey in eight hours and were able to compete reasonably well with the SER. The HB&W Board studied the case and in October 1858 estimated that an extension would cost them £105,000 of which they hoped £35,000 would be subscribed by local people; to encourage this they decided to have a Margate person on the Board and Mr Laming was duly elected in December 1858. The Act for this was obtained on 15th August 1859, the Company changing its name to the Margate Railway from the same date. The *Railway Times* alleged that two-thirds of the money was coming from Peto. Also during 1859 a further extension to Ramsgate was considered, but this was not pursued for the time being.

In July 1859 an agreement was reached with the EKR for working the line, although construction was being delayed at the time because most of the navvies had gone off to help with farm work.[3] Initially the Margate Railway hoped to have its line opened to Whitstable by 25th March 1860, but the date was put back several times and a furious exchange with Crampton resulted — Parliamentary powers expired on 17th August. In fact the opening from Faversham to Whitstable just scraped inside the deadline, opening on 1st August

129

View over Ramsgate Harbour station in about 1910. The station was ideally suited for the beach visitor, but its location caused great traffic problems on busy days as can be seen from its congested condition here. (E. Baldock collection)

The beach at Ramsgate today, with the LCDR station buildings still largely intact but converted to other uses. (Author)

1860. The event was celebrated with a special train, departing from Faversham at 3pm, to a temporary station at Clifton Road, Whitstable. A cold meal was served at the 'Bear & Key Inn'.

Having got some trains running along almost seven miles of single track between Faversham and Whitstable, the Margate Railway was in a position to negotiate further with the LCDR. In September 1860 it was decided to rent the whole line out to the LCDR for £18,000 per annum, starting from May 1861; one condition that the LCDR imposed on this was that the line had to be double track to cater for the anticipated Margate excursion traffic. However in October the two Companies revised their decision so that the LCDR would operate the line and receipts would be divided on a 50-50 basis.

The next four miles of the line from Whitstable to Herne Bay were opened formally on 11th July 1861 and to the general public on 13th July. On the former date a special train was run from London, departing at 9.50am, and a meal provided at Herne Bay which cost the Margate Railway £45-10-0d. The people of Herne Bay expected that the opening of the railway would lead to the rapid development of the town; one man who hoped this was George Burge, the railway contractor, who had bought up a large amount of land in the vicinity as a speculative venture.[4] The permanent Whitstable station probably opened at this time, though the one provided at Herne Bay was again a temporary affair. In fact there had been some discussion about the site of the Herne Bay station, with the Board deciding in April 1859 not to have it at Greenhill, which would have been the most convenient point for access to the pier. In February 1862 the Minutes noted that the station was over a mile from the town and that a more convenient one, by which it presumably meant at the Greenhill site, would open 'soon'. In August 1861 it was suggested that a line should be built 'on into Herne Bay',[5] so it would seem there was some indecision on the matter. The decision to open a temporary station, probably close to the road to Whitstable, seems to have been influenced by a number of factors; firstly the line was being extended and doubled, so that a proper station could not be immediately provided anyway, and also the best site — at Greenhill — needed road connections to be laid in. The proper station was at last being built in May 1863 and probably opened in December 1863 when the Board complained about the lack of a decent road from it to the High Street. A dispute then ensued between the LCDR and the Company as to what should happen with the 'old' station, it being suggested that goods facilities were needed whilst the LCDR also wanted an 'accommodation shed' for excursions. The second station was in fact provided by the LCDR. There were no freight services at Herne Bay to start with.

Whilst the Margate Railway had been attending to the opening of the first few miles of its line, it was also casting its eyes onto Ramsgate and on 6th August 1861 obtained an Act for an extension from Margate to Ramsgate Harbour, which included a tunnel of 1,638 yards under the northern part of the town. The decision to promote this line was made late in 1860, although the plan — which had been under discussion for some time — had been shelved only a few months before. It was proposed to gain control of Ramsgate Harbour from its trustees and to open stations at St. Peter's and Broadstairs, a small and genteel resort. The Act allowed the Margate Railway to increase its capital by £96,000 and to raise a further £32,000 in loans. From 26th August 1861 the Company changed its name again, this time to the Kent Coast Railway. The contract for the Ramsgate extension went, of course, to Peto, Betts & Crampton who began to work on the tunnel in Spring 1862. Part of the reason for the line was the prospect of developing Ramsgate as a port for the Ostend traffic, though the Margate Town Clerk wrote to the Board in December 1861 to ask that his own town might also be considered for this purpose.

Part of the agreement with the LCDR had been that the Faversham to Herne Bay line should be doubled and the extensions from there to Ramsgate built as double track. However the Kent Coast was slow to implement this, deferring the decision in March 1861, although when work on the Margate extension started at Herne Bay in August 1861 it was decided to build all bridges for double track. In March 1862 the KCR decided to provide the extra track after all, with Peto being instructed to complete this doubling and the entire line to Ramsgate by 1st September 1863. The subject continued to cause friction with the LCDR, who did not want to maintain a cheaply built line; in September 1862 they complained that the track at Seasalter bridge was dangerous and in March 1863 again commented on the standard of materials being delivered for use in the doubling. Whilst the doubling was completed by adding an up line between Faversham and Herne Bay, the old track was strengthened to form a down line of decent quality.

On 29th July 1862 the Kent Coast gained another Act which allowed it to construct tramways at Ramsgate. It had been decided not to lease the harbour, but agreement over access had been reached in May 1861. Not everyone favoured development of Ramsgate as a port, however, and the *Railway Times* reported in November 1863 that some Ramsgate residents were worried that the resort's social tone would suffer because of the proposed continental cattle trade.

The improvement of the LCDR's access to the Thanet resorts had the usual effect on the SER — it woke up and started to improve its own facilities. The SER identified their Margate traffic as being most under threat, largely because it was 102 miles from London Bridge to Margate by the SER and 74 miles from Victoria to Margate by LCDR. Therefore in 1863 the SER spent £15,000 on a number of minor improvements, including construction of the St. Lawrence spur (opened July 1863) to allow through running to Margate without reversal in Ramsgate; the Margate branch was also doubled.

The formal opening of the extension from Herne Bay to Ramsgate took place on 3rd September 1863, but public traffic did not commence until 5th October; the delay was caused by the Inspecting Officer's doubts about some bridge girders. The double track on the original section of line was brought into use at the same time. There was some debate about intermediate stations, with Broadstairs complaining before the opening that their's was in an inconvenient location; it was at the back of the town, away from the waterfront, and thereby gave an advantage to the rival resort of Ramsgate. Poor St. Peter's fared worse, since they were marked down for a station in 1861 but never got one. The other intermediate stations were at Birchington and Margate. Kent Coast Railway Minutes of 30th August 1864 recorded the opening of Margate East.

The LCDR must have been very relieved when the extension to Ramsgate finally opened since in the first half of 1863 the working profit on the Kent Coast line was a meagre £138! Encouragement of Ramsgate Harbour traffic could therefore only help the line and despite some local opposition the LCDR applied in 1864 for powers to operate Ramsgate-Boulogne steamers, though it never built the tramway to the Harbour authorised in 1862. These powers were conferred on the LCDR by Act of 23rd June 1864, but Ramsgate was not a success as a ferry terminal and all services transferred to Queenborough in 1876. There were regular Ramsgate-Dover excursion steamers.

Some efforts were made to encourage freight in an area that lacked any appreciable industry. On 6th August 1864 goods stations were opened at Reculver and at Graveney, near Whitstable, neither of these facilities being very extensive. Little is known about the ¾ mile branch to Hampton Pier, near Herne Bay, that was constructed in 1864; it was built for the Herne Bay, Hampton & Reculver Oyster Fishery Company. The pier was sold off in 1881, by which time the Oyster Company had presumably gone out of business, and the branch closed. It is possible that the Reculver goods station was also an attempt to develop the oyster traffic, which was very important at Whitstable. Despite these efforts the Kent Coast line remained a passenger railway; receipts on it for a week in September 1865 were £3,080 for passengers and only £180 for freight.

There were some unwelcome attentions from the South Eastern, who encouraged a 'Herne Bay & Canterbury' Bill in 1863 and in 1863-64 sought to improve their position in Ramsgate by promoting an extension to King Street.

Relations between the KCR and the LCDR were not always easy. From the opening of the Ramsgate extension until 1st March 1864, the LCDR worked the line at cost after which it became responsible for maintenance and worked the line according to the 1862 agreement. This situation was upset by the bankruptcy of the LCDR in 1866, which led to the KCR worrying about whether it would receive its share of receipts from through bookings. It was decided that 50% of through traffic receipts would be handed directly to the KCR and not paid through the LCDR's account. The KCR was also dragged into Chancery and during the late 1860s the two Companies discussed revisions of the 1862 agreement. The problem for the LCDR was that the KCR was proving something of a liability — its traffic contributed only £14,334 to the LCDR's gross receipts for the first half of 1866 which were £216,179. The trouble was that the KCR traffic was seasonal, and in the poorer half of 1870 its traffic was so meagre that working expenses absorbed 91.66% of its revenue. However on 13th July 1871 formal agreement was reached for a takeover of the KCR by the LCDR and the last meeting of the Kent Coast Railway took place on 26th June 1872, it shortly after being finally absorbed.

Some problems were encountered with the Sabbatarian movement in the 1860s. In May 1867 the Ramsgate Sunday excursions stopped running due to complaints by local people and by the Lord's Day Observance Society. However

133

by May 1869 the Board of the LCDR was considering the reintroduction of these trains, but the following March decided it would be better to run regular 'cheap' trains rather than excursions. In August 1871 there were more protests from the Ramsgate branch of the Lord's Day Observance Society.

The unpopularity of the excursion train was not unusual. Many resorts like Ramsgate began their development as distinctly 'upper-class' and had an abhorrence of the excursion train and its lower-class passengers; by the 1870s, however, the English upper classes were starting to take their holidays abroad, notably at Nice. Gradually the character of the domestic resorts changed and they became popular with the lower classes, although some wealthy people continued to reside there. It must be said, however, that Margate had always had a fairly 'popular' character. The railway made these resorts cheap and accessible to still greater numbers so that, as J. Pimlott commented in his classic history *The Englishman's Holiday*, '... in the long run snobbishness and conservatism pulled in vain against the forces which made for change.' The expansion of these towns continued quickly after the railways arrived, but it is noticeable that a period of stagnation had set in during the 1850s before the arrival of the Kent Coast Railway; circumstances were similar at Brighton, England's leading resort, which was revitalised by the opening of its rail connection to London.

Population of Kent Resorts Served by the LCDR

	1851	1861	1871	1901
Birchington	885	813	1,137	2,128
Margate	10,099	10,019	13,903	26,734
Ramsgate	11,838	11,865	14,640	16,503
St. Peter's (incl. Broadstairs)	2,975	2,855	3,847	7,193
Herne Bay	3,094	3,147	3,988	8,442

The Bank Holidays Act of 1871 also brought a major increase in traffic to the resorts, though from the Railway's point of view the best traffic was that of the wealthy, long-distance commuter who provided a steady balance to the seasonal fluctuations of the holiday traffic, very little of which was first class.

The LCDR's Kent Coast line continued to suffer 'attacks' from the SER, with a fiercely competitive service being run to Ramsgate and Margate to get the best of the 'residential' traffic. Herne Bay was another prime target and in September 1873 the idea of a branch off the Canterbury & Whitstable was revived, with an estimated cost of only £45,000. This failed, as did the 1884 project for a 'Canterbury & Kent Coast' line which was to branch off from the SER at Grove Ferry to serve Reculver and Herne Bay. To maintain its secure position in northern Thanet the LCDR had to constantly reinvest in its facilities; a new station was opened at Westgate-on-Sea in April 1871 and in 1886 the LCDR embarked on a programme of improvements at Margate, Ramsgate and Herne Bay. With several resorts close together, the railway in this area acquired something of the character of an 'interurban' with stations rarely more than a mile apart and a regular service in operation; this may explain why the LCDR had planned in 1864-65 to open an extra station, a terminus, in Margate but facing towards Ramsgate. There seems to be some debate as to whether this station ever handled traffic[6] but Kent Coast Railway Minutes of 30th August 1864 clearly state that a new station had been opened in East Margate; this was clearly not the same station as 'Margate East' itself, which opened on the main line in 1870, following which the original station became Margate West. Logic would suggest that Margate East replaced East Margate, which would have been inconvenient to operate and which had certainly become a tourist facility known as 'the Hall by the Sea' by 1872.[7]

The SER and LCDR did have their moments of co-operation, and as a result of one of these promoted the Westgate and South Eastern Junction line in 1882 to enable their lines in the Margate area to be linked up.[8]

These numerous minor alterations and improvements did not satisfy everyone. In May 1896 a meeting was held at Ramsgate to complain about the services, but only 22 people turned up. Herne Bay was the centre of attention for a time, especially as by 1895 building development was at last reaching out to enclose the rather isolated station. Excursions were being run to Herne Bay on Sundays, Wednesdays and Thursdays during summer 1896, and its growth was such that further station improvements were made by the SE&CR in 1900. Herne Bay continued to attract the attention of rivals even after the formation of the SE&CR, with various attempts being made to reach it from the south, notably the 'Canterbury, Herne Bay & Whitstable Light Railway' in 1901 and the 'Canterbury & Herne Bay' in 1902. A siding for the Gas Company was opened there in 1915.

The eastern side of Whitstable was being extensively developed by 1893 in the region of Tankerton. The Secretary of the Tankerton Estate Company communicated with the LCDR Board in May 1893, asking to have the Whitstable station moved to a more convenient site; this was refused, so in August he offered a subsidy of £300 per year for five years if the Board would open a new station — but this was also rejected. Not to be daunted, the Tankerton Estate Company put in another request, in October 1897, for a station at Tankerton & Swalecliffe — also without success! A convenient station was, of course, vital to housing development. Whitstable station was eventually moved slightly further east in 1913 and a station was provided at Chestfield & Swalecliffe by the Southern Railway in 1930.

Some further minor extensions took place at the end of the LCDR era. In 1899 five acres were bought at Margate to cater for expanded traffic and at Westgate goods facilities were provided in 1900 because of great building activity in the area.

ii) Deal and Dover
When the South Eastern opened its line to Ramsgate it included in the project a branch from Minster to Deal, which opened on 1st July 1847. This left an

open section of countryside without railways, covering the triangular area between Canterbury, Dover and Deal. When the East Kent Railway began to build its line from Canterbury to Dover there arose a number of proposals to fill this space, one of the first of which was for a branch from the EKR at Adisham to Deal and Walmer.

Generally speaking the EKR was in favour of such proposals and definitely wanted to see a connection into Deal, but not from Adisham. In November 1861 the *Railway Times* reported that the LCDR was backing a proposed line from Ramsgate to Deal and Walmer, which would have made a useful extension to the Kent Coast although duplicating the SER for a few miles south of Minster. During 1861-62 there seems to have been a small scale 'Railway Mania' in the area, with several other projects entering the fray. By December 1861 plans for a Sibertswold (Shepherdswell)-Deal-Sandwich line, for a Deal & Dover, and for a Sandwich & Deal had been prepared. Of these the Deal & Dover most interested the LCDR and it presented a Bill, gaining Parliamentary authority in 1862 with Peto engaged to do the work. In April 1862 the LCDR paid £1,250 to the promoters of the Ramsgate, Sandwich & Deal to withdraw their line, which was seen as the major competitor;[9] old-fashioned bribery was plainly in operation.

However, once it had gained 'defensive' powers to block any SER expansion in the Dover and Deal area, the LCDR lost interest. Local pressure favoured the Sibertswold to Deal line, since it would give more direct access to London, but the Dover, Deal & Sandwich project persisted in its threat to LCDR 'territory'. The LCDR failed to make any effort to start the work on its Deal line, which was bound to be an expensive affair because of the difficulties in bringing the line down into Dover. The LCDR allowed its powers to lapse in 1865 but continued to take an interest in the area, using petitions to keep out potential troublemakers like the Dover, Deal & Sandwich (1864). Plans for a branch from Adisham, which obviously would have had to rely on the LCDR, persisted throughout 1864 and 1865, mostly with Deal as a terminus, though Sandwich was also mentioned. This seemed to offer the cheapest solution to the problem.

The 1866 crisis put a stop to all railway promotion during the late 1860s. This must have worried Deal and Walmer, which were the slowest growing Kent resorts in the decade 1861-1871. In February 1872 the LCDR petitioned against the Walmer, Deal & Adisham, but in 1873 reached agreement for a similar route, though this failed in Parliament. However during this period the relationship between the SER and the LCDR temporarily thawed and a result was the joint promotion of a Bill late in 1873 to connect the SER's terminus at Deal with the LCDR main line at Buckland, near Dover. This was authorised in 1874 following a stiff battle against the Ramsgate, Deal & Dover and the Deal, Dover & Walmer. The project was to cost each Company approximately £250,000.

There was some delay over starting construction and a further Act was obtained in 1878 to allow for this. The first sod was finally cut by Earl Granville, Lord Warden of the Cinque Ports, on 30th June 1878. As part of the project a new curve was provided at Dover to allow SER trains direct access into the LCDR stations and from there onto the Deal line at Buckland Junction. The

Walmer Station during Southern Railway days.   (A. Riley)

Joint line proved to be one of the most difficult to construct in southern England; a horseshoe bend and a gradient of 1 in 70 were necessary to climb out of the Dour valley and then came a tunnel of 1,412 yards at Guston before descent to Deal at 1 in 64. There were intermediate stations at Martin Mill and Walmer.

The ceremonial opening of the new line took place on 14th June 1881 with the public opening the next day, the first train being hauled by an engine of both Companies. The plan of the new line left some doubts in the collective mind of the LCDR, since access could only be gained by reversal at Dover. During construction, as early as December 1880, the LCDR was considering a loop from River to Buckland; this was opened from Deal Junction to Kearnsey Loop Junction on 1st July 1882, though at first the Board of Trade would only sanction the use of tank engines. Kearnsey thus became quite an important junction station but in 1895 its greatest distinction seems to have been that it boasted the shortest signalman on the LCDR, Mr Gambell, who was a mere four feet high.

iii) Other Projects
At times the mere existence of a natural routeway seemed sufficient to attract the attentions of the SER and the LCDR, even if it led to nowhere. This was the case with the valley of the Nail Bourne, running south from Canterbury and sometimes named after Elham, its principal settlement. This valley also offered a route through the Downs towards Folkestone, and therefore the SER needed to 'plug the gap' to keep the LCDR out of its stronghold. The

137

first proposal for an Elham Valley Railway surfaced in 1865-66 and envisaged a line running through the valley and terminating on the coast at Hythe. This project was an adjunct of the LCDR. An Act was obtained in August 1866, an unfortunate timing from which the Company never recovered, especially after its Secretary absconded with some of its funds in 1867.

In 1878 the LCDR became interested in the possibility of a line from River, via the Alkham Valley, to Folkestone — thereby creating panic in the South Eastern camp. Thus in 1879 the SER supported another Elham Valley proposal for a line from Canterbury to Cheriton, on its main line near Folkestone. This eventually received its Act on 28th July 1881, though the LCDR returned with another Alkham Valley proposal in 1883-84. This second Alkham plan was clearly for a main line which would compete for Folkestone traffic on equal terms with the SER, since it was to be double-tracked with a triangular junction at Kearnsey. The *Railway Times* for once supported the LCDR, describing the plan as:

> '...bringing to bear a little of the wholesome pressure of competition as an inducement to the South Eastern to remedy some of those shortcomings which have earned for it an unenviable notoriety and made its name a byeword for bad management.'[10]

The LCDR eventually withdrew its Bill and later tried to enter Folkestone from the west, but only after the SER had been forced to build the Elham Valley line to a higher standard than was necessary for a very minor branch. It opened in sections between 1887 and 1889 but never attracted much traffic, losing its passenger services as early as 1947. The line was nominally independent between 1881, when it was first authorised, and 1884 when it was absorbed into the SER.

138

CHAPTER TEN

Serving the Suburbs

i) Brixton to Loughborough Junction & Peckham

As was explained in Chapter Four, the LCDR's Metropolitan Extensions split into City and West End sections at Herne Hill. The LCDR proposed to link the two main sections together by a short line from Brixton to Loughborough Park, enabling it to operate a service between Victoria and its City stations. This was a very similar idea to a contemporary one of the LBSCR, which planned a South London line from Victoria, via Brixton and Peckham, to London Bridge. The situation was further complicated by the proposals of the Crystal Palace & South London Junction Railway, sometimes an ally of the LCDR, which proposed to connect Crystal Palace with the LCDR via Nunhead and Peckham. By 1863 the LCDR had further added plans for a line from Loughborough Park to Blackheath and Greenwich.

This complicated state of affairs produced a situation where both the LCDR and the LBSCR were proposing to construct lines virtually parallel between the Longhedge area and Peckham. The first part to be opened was the LCDR's 'link line' from Brixton to what is now Loughborough Junction, allowing a Victoria to Elephant & Castle service to operate from 1st May 1863. There was at first no station at Loughborough, but in November 1863 the LCDR decided to provide some platforms on the Brixton spur there and these opened in October 1864. The position of this station on the spur meant that it could not be used by trains between the City and Herne Hill, but only by trains diverging to Brixton and Victoria. A main line station at Loughborough Junction did not open until 1st July 1872, and for a time the LCDR confusingly referred to the platforms on the spur as 'Brixton Junction'. The main-line station was actually known as Loughborough Road until it was renamed on 1st December 1872.

The problem of the parallel routes was solved by the LCDR and LBSCR agreeing to construct part of each other's line. Thus the LCDR was to provide two tracks for the use of the LBSCR between Factory Junction and Barrington Road Junction, east of Brixton, whilst the reverse was true between Barrington Road and Peckham Rye. Just east of Peckham Rye, at Cow Lane Junction, the LCDR's Greenwich line was to continue independently, with the Crystal Palace & South London Junction's branch diverging at Nunhead. In the event the LCDR delayed construction of its Greenwich line so that the Nunhead to Peckham section was constructed as part of the CPSLJR. Services via Barrington Road to Crystal Palace commenced on 1st August 1865, though the intermediate stations for its trains at Denmark Hill and Peckham Rye did not open until December 1865. LBSCR facilities at these two stations did not commence

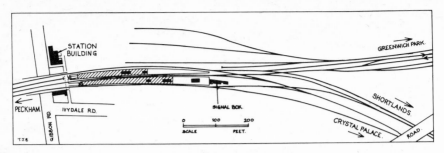

Map 29: Nunhead Station, 1902

operations until 13th August 1866, when its London Bridge to East Brixton (Loughborough Park) service commenced. The section built by the LCDR for LBSCR use was handed over to them on 1st May 1867, extending the line from Barrington Road to Wandsworth Road.

There was no station at Nunhead until 1st September 1871.

ii) The Crystal Palace & South London Junction Railway

The Crystal Palace itself had been served since 1854 by the West End of London & Crystal Palace Railway, most of which became part of the LBSCR. This provided a direct service from Crystal Palace to the West End and offered a reasonable way of getting to the City by way of its link to the LBSCR's London Bridge line at Sydenham. However, with commuter traffic the precise location of the City terminus was of primary importance, and London Bridge no longer seemed so attractive when the LCDR began to promote its City line. The purpose of the CPSLJR was to provide access from the Crystal Palace area onto the LCDR, gathering a slice of the south London commuter traffic.

The project first received attention in August 1861, and in February 1862 the *Railway Times* reported that the Crystal Palace & South London Junction wanted powers for a line from the Crystal Palace to Peckham, and also running powers over the LCDR's lines between Peckham and Brixton which were then under construction or being planned. An Act was obtained on 17th July 1862, for a line of 6¼ miles from Peckham to Crystal Palace; capital was £675,000 and the Chairman was Sir Charles Rich, who was also on the LCDR Board. Agreement was quickly reached for operation by the LCDR, with the CPSLJR to get 60% of the working profits up to a maximum of £34,000. The contract was awarded to Peto & Betts, who started work on the 'Paxton' and 'Crescent Wood' tunnels during the winter of 1862-63.[1]

Meanwhile the LCDR was progressing with plans for its own line between Peckham and Greenwich; the two lines were to run together between Nunhead and Peckham, so under the powers of the LCDR's Act of 28th July 1863 this was to be constructed by the LCDR, the line west of Peckham already being built by the LBSCR for LCDR use. Under an agreement of 1863 the LCDR was

140

also to provide junctions for South Eastern trains to gain access onto the CPSLJR. Early in 1864 the plans were again slightly revised, the LCDR and the CPSLJR deciding to provide two lines each, making four tracks, between Nunhead and Peckham;[2] this plan was authorised in the CPSLJR Act of 23rd June 1864, which also provided for the leasing of the Company to the LCDR. A possible reason for the anticipated need of four tracks was that the Crystal Palace Company planned to open its line to use by other Railway Companies; a Board Minute of 21st June 1865 referred to 'additional line and works consequent upon the provision necessary for the accommodation of the Traffic of the Great Northern and South Eastern Railways.' The LCDR had been negotiating with the SER for better access to Greenwich and offered the prospect of running SER trains to Crystal Palace as a bargaining counter, which was gladly accepted. However in 1865 the LCDR decided to abandon its Greenwich line and so for the time being the CPSLJR was left on its own between Peckham and Nunhead; this decision by the LCDR also made the prospect of running trains from the east onto the Crystal Palace line considerably more remote.

Services to Crystal Palace High Level station began to operate on 1st August 1865, though much of the line was in an incomplete state. The LCDR had not constructed an east to north spur at Loughborough Junction, nor had it built a line authorised in 1864 to run from Camberwell to a junction with its proposed Greenwich branch in the Parish of Deptford since the Greenwich idea had been mothballed. This left the CPSLJR with only indirect access to the City. The Crystal Palace station itself was only half-complete and intermediate stations were not ready at all. The Minutes record that Lordship Lane station opened on 1st September 1865 and Honor Oak, Peckham Rye and Denmark Hill in December 1865. There was at first no station at Nunhead, this being on the section that was nominally part of the LCDR's supposed Greenwich branch, and one did not open until 1st September 1871 by which time the LCDR had at last begun to put some of its proposals into practice.

In November 1865 it was suggested that the CPSLJR could be extended from Crystal Palace to meet the SER at Addiscombe, the first of several similar proposals. At least the line got off to a good start with its traffic since so many people visited Crystal Palace on Boxing Day 1865 that serious overcrowding resulted. However such apparent prosperity was short lived.

Unlike many of the nominally independent companies that the LCDR eventually absorbed, the CPSLJR does seem to have had clear-minded ideas of its own right from the start. Most obvious of these was a determination not to be entirely dependent on the LCDR, especially as there was some strain between the two from the start. An important part of the LCDR's Greenwich branch proposals had been the east to north link at Loughborough Junction or from Camberwell, to allow through running between Peckham and the City; without this, CPSLJR trains could run only to Victoria and not to Ludgate, therefore denying the main purpose of the line. By February 1866 the CPSLJR was seriously worried that this access had not been provided and with the loss of the LCDR's Greenwich Diversion Bill in March 1866 prospects receded still further. Improvements at Canterbury Road Junction, opened on 1st August

Crystal Palace High Level station in about 1905. The broad platforms indicate the expected level of excursion traffic that materialised only infrequently.　　(R. Thomas collection)

1866, did little to alleviate the Crystal Palace Company's anger. By September 1866 the LCDR was in Receivership and could not apply for the new powers needed for the spur, so a bargain was struck with the CPSLJR in which the latter agreed to construct the spur itself and also to surrender its share in the 'Brixton Junction' station (the Brixton curve platforms at Loughborough).[3] This would have involved the CPSLJR presenting a Bill to revive some of the LCDR's powers of 1864 for a connection between Peckham and Walworth, with a link to the SER included, at a cost of £100,000. But in November 1866 the CPSLJR decided not to proceed with the project, clearly influenced by the financial climate.

There were a number of other disputes with the LCDR, especially over the facilities at Crystal Palace High Level. In August 1866 there was a row about the signalling, since only two tracks had full signalling at the terminus and the Board of Trade would not sanction the use of the others. The LCDR had been using the extra tracks and said that if accidents resulted from the lack of signalling then it would be the CPSLJR's fault. The latter's response was to ban the LCDR from using anything except the two authorised lines. Early in 1867 there was another dispute over who should pay for new goods facilities at the terminus.

Meanwhile the CPSLJR was very sensibly seeking to gain advantage from the competitive relationships between the main southern Companies. By February 1866 it had reached agreement with the SER, the Great Northern Railway and

142

the Metropolitan Railway, plainly seeing itself as the southern arm of a cross-London service. However, because the connecting lines authorised in 1864 had not been built the CPSLJR was still isolated from these Companies. The LCDR had promised to provide access for the SER onto the Crystal Palace line in exchange for running powers from off its Greenwich branch onto the SER as far as Woolwich, so yet again the CPSLJR was being held back by the confused state of LCDR affairs. An extra spur would have been provided for SER trains to run from the east onto the Crystal Palace branch.

In September 1867 the CPSLJR turned down a request for a station at Sydenham; one was not opened at Upper Sydenham until 1st August 1884.

In October 1867, as a result of discussions with the LBSCR and the SER, the Board of the CPSLJR decided to go ahead with a junction line to connect it with the SER and the East London line. This plan soon developed into a proposal to deposit a Bill for three purposes:

1. For the 'Brixton link' at Loughborough, to be constructed independently of the LCDR, and for CPSLJR running powers to Farringdon.
2. For arrangements with the LBSCR for a Victoria to Crystal Palace High Level service.
3. For arrangements with the LBSCR, SER, Great Northern Railway, Midland Railway, East London Railway and Metropolitan Railway.

The plan was evidently designed to force the hand of the LCDR, which had been complaining bitterly of the cost of working the CPSLJR and yet had done nothing to improve its traffic prospects. The Crystal Palace Company now intended to buy its own rolling-stock and run through trains to Farringdon on the Metropolitan Railway over its own curve at Loughborough Junction, estimated to cost £51,000. By its arrangements with the LBSCR and the SER it would also be able to operate services to Victoria, Charing Cross, London Bridge and Cannon Street without any reliance on the LCDR.

The entire position of the Crystal Palace line was now at stake and the LCDR was now forced to fight for control of a line that had once seemed a natural ally. The dispute reached legal proceedings, becoming especially serious after December 1867 when the CPSLJR demanded to be allowed to repossess its line and the LCDR refused to vacate it. The LCDR stated that they were working the line 'by request of the CPSLJR, although it was losing them money',[4] a CPSLJR debenture holder started proceedings to regain possession but the case ended in September 1870 when the LCDR was awarded outright use of the line. One of the chief legal problems was that the working agreement between the two Companies had never been legally completed.

Whilst the proceedings were continuing, the LCDR and the CPSLJR were playing their own version of 'Call My Bluff', with threats to cease working or threats to eject circulating rapidly in late 1867. Early in 1868 the LCDR clearly decided on a softer approach, since a CPSLJR Board Minute for 13th February recorded that 'An intimation having been received from the Chatham & Dover Board that they will be willing to confer. . .' The result of this was that in

143

March 1868 the CPSLJR agreed to abandon its proposed link to the SER, but wanted the LCDR to pay half of the deposit for the 'Brixton curve' in exchange; but the LCDR refused to make any financial contribution, being very short of cash, and so the Bill for the curve was abandoned.

Thus by late 1868 the CPSLJR was still very poorly connected, although its Directors had plenty of ideas for improving the situation. Vast building work at Upper Norwood promised to create considerable commuter traffic, making the line more attractive to the LCDR's rivals. Possibilities included a better junction onto the LBSCR's South London line at Peckham Rye which would also allow access to London Bridge. Another proposal was for a line from Elephant & Castle, via Bricklayer's Arms, to Peckham and offering direct access to both Farringdon and the LBSCR. Finally there was also the possibility of creating junctions with the SER which would allow through running from the East London line to the Crystal Palace.

From 1st December 1868, whilst all the talking continued, the LCDR started to work the Crystal Palace line according to a cost basis, abandoning the original agreement. One sweetener, however, was that in November 1868 the LCDR finally agreed to bear the cost of getting a Brixton curve Bill through Parliament. An important step forward was the Act of Arbitration of 26th August 1869, which allowed all disputes between the LCDR and three minor companies — the CPSLJR, the Sevenoaks and the Kent Coast — to go before Lord Cairns and the Marquis of Salisbury; the Brixton curve was authorised the same day. The arbitrators' decision was that the LCDR should work the Crystal Palace line at cost price. Both Companies seemed unhappy about this, the LCDR pointing out that it was an expensive line to operate with working costs absorbing 73.75% of receipts — the figure for the LCDR as a whole being between 60% and 65% at the time.

At least it seemed that there was, at last, some prospect of this ignoble saga being brought to a close. In April 1871 agreement was reached for building and working the 'loop line' and its construction commenced in November; the cost was now estimated at £75,000. It opened on 1st July 1872, necessitating the rebuilding of Loughborough Junction ('Brixton Junction') station. The new station was inspected by the Board of Trade on 7th November 1872 and again on 30th November following complaints about the length of the platforms.[5] In fact these 'spur' platforms were always rather inconvenient and were closed by the Southern Railway in 1925. The construction of the curve gave the CPSLJR some worries, since the original Preference share issue raised only £12,150; interest had to be increased to 6% before more investors could be found. One reason for the LCDR's change of heart about this curve after ten years of indecision was that its original Greenwich branch actually opened — albeit in truncated form — on 18th November 1871 and without the curve it would have been virtually useless. The curve from Loughborough Junction joined the Brixton to Peckham line at Cambria Road Junction; at this point the first 'lock and block' signalling system in the world was installed in 1875, in which the operation of the signals was interlocked with that of the telegraph instruments.

In December 1872 an independent group proposed a line from Dulwich, on the LCDR's main line, to Crystal Palace High Level. Both the LCDR and the CPSLJR petitioned against the Bill and it was lost. The CPSLJR was unconvinced about the parentage of this plan, which it saw as a veiled threat from the LCDR. Accordingly it renewed talks with the South Eastern, the aim being the construction of a junction line to allow through running between Charing Cross and Crystal Palace H.L. which the LBSCR would also have access to; links to New Cross, New Cross Gate and the South London line would have been relatively simple additions. Therefore the CPSLJR initiated a new improvement Bill in November 1873 which included a junction at Peckham to give access to the South London line, a deviation of the 1864 scheme for a junction at New Cross, the widening of the LCDR's Greenwich branch between Peckham and Nunhead, and a branch from Brockley Lane on the LBSCR to the CPSLJR. It was also decided to abandon the 1864 powers for a line going more directly onto the LCDR at Camberwell. These proposals would have given the SER and the LBSCR direct access onto the Crystal Palace branch, with the LCDR left in a decidedly weak position.

The Parliamentary contest of 1874 promised to be a frantic one, especially as the Dulwich to Crystal Palace project had re-emerged promoted, as the CPSLJR Minutes sourly commented, 'nominally by independent parties.' This was not the LCDR's only plan, since it was also applying for powers to construct a loop at Beckenham to allow direct access from the Herne Hill direction into Crystal Palace Low Level (the original WELCPR station). The SER made much of the LCDR's attempts to take over the CPSLJR, arguing that this was in breach of the 1862 Bromley Traffic Agreement — surely as dubious a claim as its later one that Queenborough was affected by a traffic agreement covering the coastline between Ramsgate and Hastings.

The CPSLJR petitioned against both the Dulwich Railway and the Beckenham (or Kent House) loop, with the overall results of the contest emerging in August 1874. The South Eastern, which had argued that its junction proposals were the same as those which had been agreed in 1863 and passed in 1864, withdrew its support whilst the Bill was before the Commons and thus any hopes for the CPSLJR's new line faded. The junction line to the LBSCR at Peckham was also rejected, since the Committee objected to the LBSCR having running powers to the High Level station as well as controlling the Low Level. All that the CPSLJR gained was powers to abandon the unbuilt lines authorised in 1864. The Dulwich Railway Bill was also rejected but the LCDR's curve at Beckenham passed and £11,000 was spent on its construction, though it was probably never used. Thus the CPSLJR was soundly defeated and abandoned by Parliament to endure the cold embrace of the LCDR, into whose arms it had irretrievably collapsed.

Resigned to their fate, the CPSLJR Directors decided in October 1874 to seek fusion with the LCDR, although they had already rejected the latter's tender advances earlier that year. An agreement was reached on 7th December 1874 and the CPSLJR effectively passed into the hands of the Chatham Company in February 1875, its last Board meeting being held on the 26th. Forbes made many comments about the poor state of the Crystal Palace line,

The exterior of Greenwich Park station in about 1935; it had been disused since 1916.

(R. Thomas)

moaning in February 1875 that it cost '75% of its earnings to work, and had fallen into financial difficulties chiefly for having been made with paper instead of sovereigns.'[6] One wonders how Forbes, in control of the LCDR, could make such comments about another Company without blushing profusely.

Various later attempts were made to exploit the potential of the Crystal Palace line. In 1883 the LCDR became very interested in extending the line to Croydon, with the aim of connecting with the Oxted & Groombridge Railway. At a cost of £1,500,000 this was quite an ambitious project which the *Railway Times* interpreted, perhaps correctly, as an attempt to provide traffic for the LCDR's increasing number of London stations. Another attempt to get to Croydon, from Tulse Hill, was rejected by the House of Lords in 1884. The same year there was an attempt to gain access to the Crystal Palace line from the East London Railway, but again this was unsuccessful although the SER revived the idea as the 'New Cross & Crystal Palace Railway' in 1885.

On 1st November 1898 the Crystal Palace station was renamed Crystal Palace (H.L.) & Upper Norwood in recognition of the building work which had taken place there. In general though the line's traffic never developed as much as had been anticipated, because the influence of Dulwich College severely restricted building development in parts of the area it passed through.

iii) The Greenwich Branch
As has been explained, the LCDR had no initial intentions to build any lines east of its City extension between Herne Hill and Blackfriars. However late in 1862 it decided to promote a line from Peckham Rye, on the LBSCR's recently authorised South London line, to Greenwich. This was to make use of the South London line to get to Peckham, so it was agreed that the LBSCR would construct a duplicate line for the use of the LCDR between Barrington Road

146

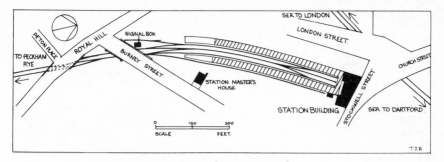

Map 30: Greenwich Park Station, 1906

Junction and Cow Lane Junction, Peckham, although for a time the LBSCR had had its own ideas for a line to Greenwich. The Act for the Greenwich branch was passed on 28th July 1863, allowing an extra £1,220,000 capital. An agreement was reached with the SER which offered to extend its own Greenwich line to Woolwich and grant running powers to the LCDR, in exchange for the LCDR building a 1¼ mile connection so that SER trains could run to Crystal Palace. The LCDR part of this bargain, the connection to Crystal Palace, was authorised as part of the CPSLJR Act of 23rd June 1864 whilst the SER acquired the necessary authority on 5th July 1865 and 16th July 1866.

As has been related, the LCDR soon became markedly unenthusiastic about its Greenwich branch and the Crystal Palace line opened first, making use of the LCDR west of Peckham. The CPSLJR became impatient at the lack of access for SER trains affected its revenue and by 1868 Watkin, of the SER, was becoming angry as well. He decided to seek cancellation of the LCDR's theoretical running powers between Greenwich and Woolwich since the Chatham Company had not kept to the bargain of providing a route for South Eastern trains into Crystal Palace. According to the press, the LCDR's Greenwich branch was delayed by problems concerning Greenwich Observatory which stopped all work between Blackheath and Greenwich.[7] However on 18th September 1871 the LCDR opened its branch from Nunhead as far as Blackheath Hill with an intermediate station at Lewisham Road. The initial usefulness of this line was minimal as there was no means of direct access to the City until the 'Brixton link' between Cambria Road Junction and Loughborough Junction opened on 1st July 1872.

Spurred on by this belated Chatham Company advance, the SER took steps to complete its line between Greenwich and Woolwich, part of the 1863 proposals; the section from Charlton to Maze Hill opened in 1873 and the line was eventually completed in 1878. However the LCDR never completed the spur line at Nunhead so it remained impossible to run through trains between Woolwich and Crystal Palace.

A terminus at Blackheath Hill left the LCDR in a very poor position so in December 1880 it was decided to extend the branch to Stockwell Street,

147

The station approach at Shortlands in about 1914; by this time a substantial suburban community had already grown up around the railway. (E. Course)

The LCDR's Catford station in about 1905, the main intermediate station on the Shortlands & Nunhead route. (A. Riley collection)

Greenwich. An extension of powers had to be obtained in 1886 and the cost for the ½ mile line was considerable, including £200,000 for land alone. The LCDR hoped to open the extension on 2nd July 1888, but it was delayed due to the incomplete state of the station and the service did not begin until 1st October 1888. The Board of Trade imposed a maximum speed limit of 25mph.

The full length of the Greenwich branch had a life of slightly less than thirty years. It was enormously expensive to construct, and so it is tempting to regard it as the LCDR's equivalent to the SER's Chatham Central folly.

iv) The Catford Loop

As suburban traffic developed the LCDR faced the major problem of increasing its traffic capacity between Beckenham and Herne Hill, in which area Penge Tunnel formed a major obstacle to any quadrupling plans. However the promotion of a line to encourage suburban development on the north side of Beckenham fortuitously coincided with the LCDR's needs in this respect.

First mention of a line branching off at Shortlands was made in 1879 but the project did not really get started until 1884. From the outset it was a classic example of a line promoted by local landowners interested in developing their estates for suburban housing and this led to Forbes' comment in February 1884 that '... a thing that was new in his experience was that some of the landowners had given the land for the railway and also contributed towards it.'[8] The Shortlands & Nunhead Railway was expected to cost £411,000 but the Bill was rejected in May 1884, though the LCDR had the unusual consolation of knowing that the *Railway Times* approved of the project as a cheap way round Penge Tunnel.

The scheme was revived at the end of 1888 with the LCDR Directors' Report stating that it was being promoted by 'important landowners.' These included Sir John Lennard and Mr Cator, owners of the Beckenham and Penge estates, and Major Forster. The LCDR Directors' Report of 1st August 1889 gave the project a glowing reference:

'The new line can be constructed at a very moderate cost and will open up a charming suburban residential district; but its chief advantage to the Public and the Chatham Company will be in affording an alternative route into London, and relieving the existing line through the Penge tunnel already at certain hours so crowded as seriously to interfere with the punctual running of the various Express, Local and Goods Services passing over it, and which now impede each other.'

An agreement had been reached with the Shortlands & Nunhead promoters on 13th March 1889 and the Act was passed on 12th August.

At the first Board meeting of the new Company Lennard was in the Chair and Cator was also present. John Morgan, Secretary of the LCDR, was appointed to do the same job for the Shortlands & Nunhead. Lucas & Aird offered to do the construction work for £119,862, but in February 1890 they revised this to

149

£156,862 to cover the cost of three goods stations (£21,174) which the LCDR had refused to pay for. Land costs were £109,000. Further goods facilities were provided at Beckenham Hill under an agreement with Mr A. Cator in July 1892.

There were few constructional problems. A dispute arose in January 1890 since a house was being built on the course of the line at Brockley Lane and this would force the Company to pay higher compensation; it was quite a common trick amongst landowners to run up cheap houses on vacant land if a railway was expected, thereby claiming higher rates of compensation. The railway also affected the course of the River Ravensbourne near Catford, and therefore a mill that was close by. Just south of Catford the line bridged the SER and an inevitable dispute arose over this in July 1890. The Company also had to plant and maintain trees along the embankment where the line passed through the Cator estate.

Forbes was elected to the Board in February 1890 as part of an agreement with the LCDR. Another prominent man to emerge in the S&NR was Aretas Akers-Douglas who started to buy up shares in February 1894 and was Deputy Chairman by 1895; he later became Home Secretary in a Conservative Government.

The line opened on 1st July 1892 and the LCDR immediately became concerned with encouraging building development through goods facilities. Extra sidings for building traffic were laid in at Ravensbourne in 1893 and Catford in 1900. Most of the initial building was done on the Cator estate.

By 1893 the *Railway Times* was commenting on the weak performance of the line, ignoring the fact that suburban development would take time and also that the line's value as a diversionary route was incalculable. An Act was passed in 1896 to allow an LCDR takeover, which was completed by 1st July 1897. Also in 1897 improvements were made to Nunhead station to reflect its new importance as junction for the Crystal Palace and Greenwich branches as well as the Catford Loop.

The Catford Loop was built cheaply with gradients as steep as 1 in 60. But it was only a mile longer than the main-line route through Dulwich and Penge which immediately casts doubts upon the earlier wisdom of building the main line through Penge Tunnel when there was clearly a natural alternative route available. The success of the Shortlands & Nunhead line can be judged from the fact that it was one of the few of the LCDR's later projects which achieved any degree of longevity, and indeed it is still used for express services when these are diverted away from the Penge route.

CHAPTER ELEVEN

A Defensive Campaign:

Sevenoaks, Maidstone and Ashford

'One of the best bits of armour we could put on' — J. Forbes, speaking about the Ashford extension, 1880.

The route of the South Eastern Railway from London to Dover was, when first opened, via Redhill and Tonbridge, leaving a vast tract of Kent countryside between Beckenham and Tonbridge almost unserved. Central to this area was the small town of Sevenoaks which was remote from any direct rail communication to London, and to the east was Maidstone which was served only poorly. During the Railway Mania many suggestions were made for ways of filling up the area including one that would have branched off the SER at Lewisham and gone via Chislehurst, Sevenoaks. Wrotham and Maidstone to Ashford. A meeting at Maidstone in January 1845 preferred a more direct line that would have had a 2,342 yard tunnel at Shoreham and a 151 yard viaduct at Boxley. None of these Mania schemes reached fruition, nor did any of another rash of projects that broke out in the early 1850s; these included the West Kent Railway from London to Bromley and Maidstone via Sevenoaks, and the East Kent & Maidstone Railway.

A more serious threat to the SER's monopoly over the area developed in 1855 in the shape of a Mid-Kent Railway plan for a line to Folkestone with the possibility of a branch to Hastings This would have provided a more direct line to Tonbridge and was supported by Lord Falmouth of Mereworth as well as the merchants of Maidstone. The SER Board was divided in its attitude to the plan.

Positive steps became more easily possible when the East Kent's Western Extension was authorised. A meeting at Sevenoaks in December 1858 supported the idea of a line joining up with the EKR; it was interesting that Lushington and Hilton, both with strong EKR connections, were at the meeting as was Sir Percival Hart Dyke of Lullingstone Castle, member of a family whose LCDR connections lasted many years. The Sevenoaks Railway Company appears to have been presented to the people of the town as a *fait accompli* since its first Board meeting was held in August 1858 — a year before it obtained its Act on 1st August 1859. Capital for the branch from the EKR at Swanley was £120,000 but this was clearly for the records only as the contractor Crampton paid the Parliamentary deposit and thereby secured the contract,[1] afterwards being allotted 4,000 of the 6,000 shares.

Small local lines can grow into major routes, as the East Kent Railway had shown, and the Sevenoaks Railway clearly had similar intentions. In October 1859 the Board decided in favour of a branch from Otford to East Malling;

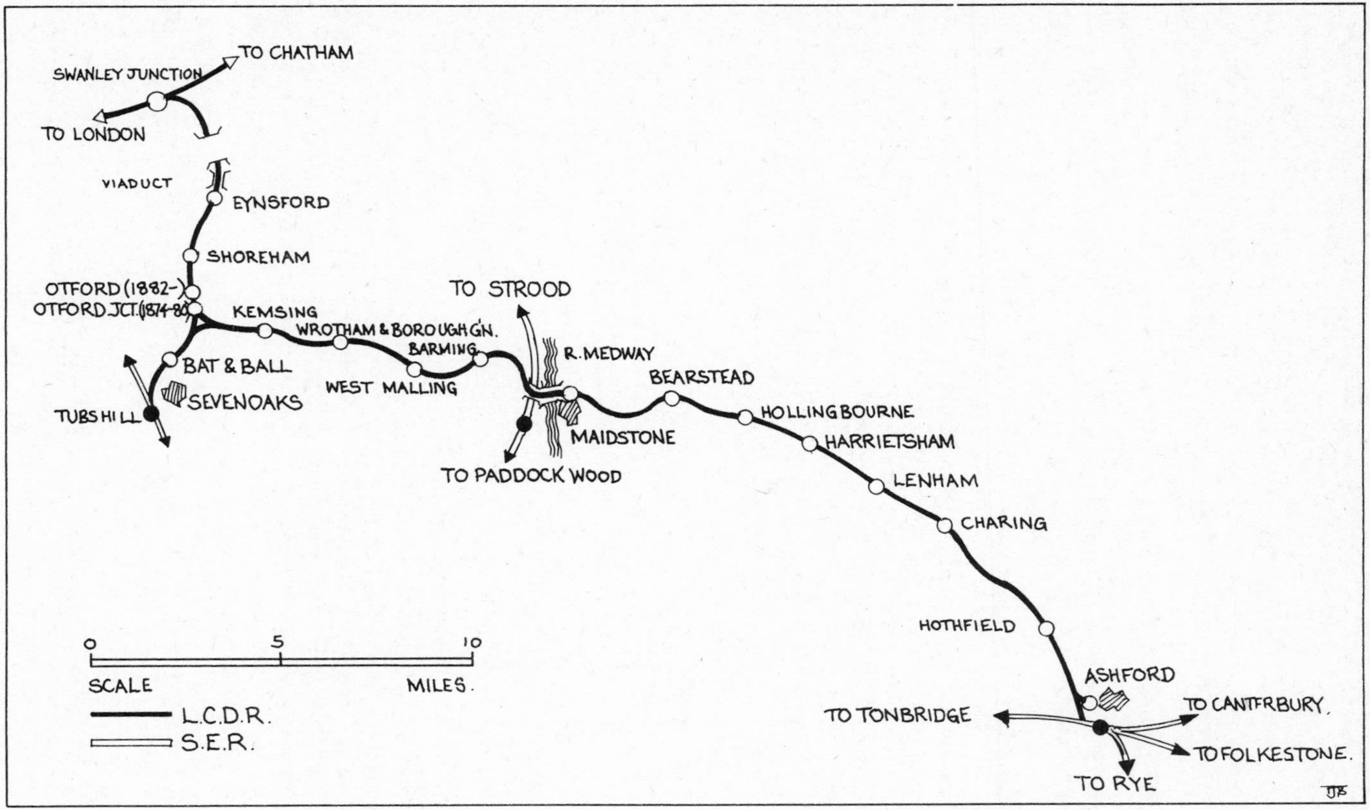

Map 31: Sevenoaks, Maidstone & Ashford, 1898

East and West Malling had a combined population of approximately 4,000 — a healthy prospect for a branch. In 1860 the Sevenoaks Railway presented a Bill for a branch to 'Town Malling' and Maidstone, but this was lost on standing orders having been strongly opposed by the South Eastern.[2]

Therefore the Company concentrated on the completion of its line to Sevenoaks for the time being. Trouble was experienced with a Darenth valley landowner named Mildmay, who made objections as early as February 1859. The Company hoped to pay him for his land by shares since it was short of cash, but not even an offer to stop all express trains whenever his family wanted could induce him to accept this offer. Eventually, in December 1860, he was paid off with £1,000.

The line's works included some very heavy construction activity. There was an 820 yard tunnel between Swanley and Eynsford, near which village the Darenth valley was crossed on a nine-arch viaduct, 75 feet high; work on these features started by the end of 1859 though there was some trouble when it was discovered that bad bricks were being used in the viaduct. South of Eynsford there was a cutting nearly a mile long that was as much as 70 feet deep in places.

By June 1861 discussions were taking place with the LCDR about junction arrangements and in February 1862 plans were prepared for stations at Sevenoaks, Eynsford and Shoreham. Preparatory to opening, an agreement had to be reached with the LCDR. This was signed on 31st December 1859 and, as with many similar agreements, did not become effective until the working Company was satisfied that the line was in a completed state; until then trains were operated at cost.

The line opened on 2nd June 1862 with the customary Directors' Special from Victoria. The terminus at Sevenoaks had not been completed, so temporary facilities were provided until the proper station opened. Shoreham was the only intermediate station that managed to open on time, being followed by 'Eynesford' and Sevenoaks Junction on 1st July 1862, the latter being renamed Swanley Junction from 1st January 1871. The line was opened as a single track though works were built with eventual doubling in mind.

During the later stages of construction the Sevenoaks Railway was again planning expansion. By October 1861 the Sevenoaks and the LCDR were plotting various ways of gaining access to Maidstone and Tonbridge (still generally spelt 'Tunbridge' at this time). LCDR Board Minutes indicate that they were expecting new lines to Tonbridge, Maidstone and Westerham. The problem was that the SER was putting forward a scheme to cut off its lengthy diversion via Redhill with a new main line from Lewisham direct to Sevenoaks and Tonbridge; this would render the Sevenoaks Railway fairly useless so urgent negotiations took place between the threatened Company and both the SER and the LCDR in February 1862. The Sevenoaks Company intended to reintroduce plans for a line from Otford to Malling and Maidstone; it hoped that the SER would use part of this instead of projecting its own line, and then branch off at Ightham to pass via Basted and Hadlow back to Tonbridge and its original main line. The Sevenoaks Railway proposed to install a double-track to cater for the expected traffic, but such a peculiar route was hardly likely to have a serious appeal for the SER.

153

An early view of Wrotham and Borough Green emphasising its original rural setting.
(A. Riley collection)

Eynsford station in about 1910.

(A. Riley collection)

The 1862 Parliamentary contest ended with honours roughly even. The Sevenoaks Company, by Act of 17th July, was authorised to extend to Maidstone and double its line; to mark the expansion its name was changed to Sevenoaks, Maidstone & Tonbridge. On 30th August 1862 the SER's direct main line was also authorised. This would have left a short space in Sevenoaks between the rival stations so it was decided to build a line of just over a mile to connect the two systems. SMTR Minutes of August 1862 indicate this this link was to be the SER's responsibility and that there were in fact to be two links to allow SER trains from both north and south to run onto the SMTR. The northern link was to have been from Riverhead to the SMTR's station.

Of the new projects, the most urgent was the doubling of the original Sevenoaks branch. Some confusion also arose about there being two stations likely to serve Sevenoaks, so that it is interesting that SMTR Minutes started to refer to their own station as 'Bat & Ball' (after a local public house) as early as August 1863 although the official name change did not occur until 1st August 1869 when the SMTR station became 'Sevenoaks (Bat & Ball)'. The SER station was opened on 2nd March 1868 as Sevenoaks & Riverhead. but was known as Sevenoaks (Tubs Hill) from 1890. The link between the two lines, known as the Sevenoaks Junction line, was constructed by Crampton at a cost of £13,462 and opened on 1st August 1869, the delay being due to financial problems for both the contractor and the Company.

The SMTR's first attempt at constructing a line to Maidstone was to be a disastrous story. In January 1863 they leapt out of the frying pan into the fire by rejecting the overtures of Crampton and opted for Peto & Betts; in fact there was a long delay before the contract was finally settled in June 1865 when it was awarded to another combination — Peto, Betts & Crampton! For Betts this must have been almost a garden railway since he lived at Preston Hall near Maidstone, so close to the line that covered ways were constructed to protect the tranquility of the estate.

Following the authorisation of its Maidstone plans in 1862, the SMTR was besieged by various people's new ideas in early 1863. The people of Otford, where the junction between the Sevenoaks and Maidstone lines was to be, wanted a station — they did not get one until 1st August 1882! A plan for a branch to Hadlow also failed to win favour.

Any real progress was made only slowly, work not starting until late 1865 and then the work on the bridge across the Medway being held up by bad weather. Finance was also a problem and it was necessary for the LCDR to guarantee the 5% interest on the SMTR's £210,000 Maidstone Debentures. Not that the Company was proving much of a goldmine for the LCDR — the working profit on the Sevenoaks branch for the first half of 1863 was a mere £26!

The bankruptcy of the Peto empire was a disaster for the SMTR since his financial connections were supporting its Maidstone project. In January 1867, by mutual agreement, the contract between the SMTR and Peto, Betts & Crampton was terminated though Crampton & Sons, trading as a separate firm, were able to continue work on the Sevenoaks Junction line. £20,391 had already been spent on the Maidstone line works but all construction ceased and an

Preston Hall near Maidstone, the home for many years of Edward Ladd Betts.
(Author's collection)

A view of Malling station, probably taken in the immediate post-Great War years.
(E. Baldock collection)

an Extension Act had to be obtained in 1867 to allow more time; the SMTR had difficulty raising the £300 needed for this.[3]

When the LCDR itself collapsed, so too did its satellites. The SMTR duly joined the motley crew and entered into financial disputes with the LCDR on the same pattern as the Kent Coast and Crystal Palace Companies. The LCDR Arrangements Act of 1867 did little to satisfy the SMTR's wishes as, amongst other things, it could not pay for the Sevenoaks Junction line for which it alleged the LCDR owed £1,200. In 1868 there was trouble over the LCDR's refusal to hand over receipts and the SMTR opposed the subsequent Amalgamation Bill.

The rows dragged on into the next decade, centring on the SMTR's claim for the cost of the Junction line and its regular payments for traffic, and the LCDR's view that the line lost money anyway due to competition from the SER. The arbitrators found in favour of the LCDR but another dispute arose over the Chatham Company's refusal to complete the Maidstone line; some SMTR shareholders went as far as to prepare a Bill to allow connections with the SER instead in February 1872.

However, by February 1872 the LCDR had changed its mind on the Maidstone project, and an Act was passed on 25th July 1872. This Act allowed for fusion with the LCDR the following year, though various other current plans such as an Otford to Hadlow branch made no progress. The SER was trying to head off this attempt by the LCDR to get into Maidstone by promoting its own line from Sevenoaks to Wateringbury, much more direct than the routes via Strood or Paddock Wood.

Thomas Bouch, later of Tay Bridge fame, was appointed engineer for the renewed Maidstone effort and Lucas & Aird were appointed contractors. This firm remained prominent in the life of the LCDR throughout the period 1870-1898 though they never wielded the sort of influence that Peto & Betts once had; lessons had been learnt. A dinner was held at Maidstone in January 1874 to celebrate the project; John Aird was present and so was Thomas Crampton to introduce nostalgia to the proceedings! The LCDR agreed to operate the line for £9,000 per annum although it claimed that the Sevenoaks line lost £1,177 for the half year to June 1873.[4]

The last meeting of the SMTR Board was held in August 1873, at which they awarded a contract for £95,739 to Lucas & Aird and the line to Maidstone finally opened on 1st June 1874, twelve years after it had been initially authorised. The formal transfer of the SMTR to the LCDR was not completed until 1879, the Sevenoaks Railway Purchase Act being passed on 3rd April.

The line from Otford to Maidstone (C&D) opened with intermediate stations at Kemsing, Wrotham, Malling and Barming. The station at Wrotham was about 1½ miles from the centre of the village, which then had a population of about 3,200; the result of this was the rapid development of a new settlement named Borough Green around the station. For example, in October 1895 LCDR Minutes recorded that a London architect had bought land at 'Wrotham station' for development; Borough Green is now a larger settlement than Wrotham proving, as at Swanley Junction, the considerable influence of railways on population distribution.

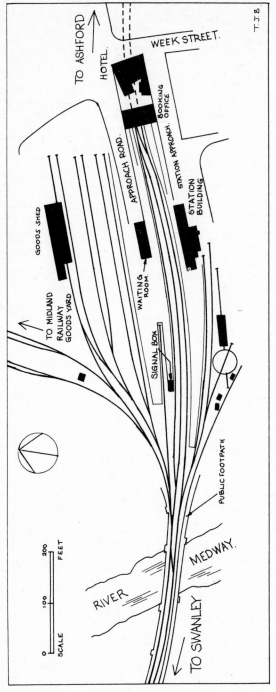

Map 32: Maidstone East Station, 1906

The bridge over the River Medway at Maidstone, photographed during the SE&CR era. This structure was replaced in 1927 when the line was upgraded to allow the running of boat expresses over it.   (A. Riley collection)

The Maidstone branch was built fairly cheaply, as were many of the 'secondary' lines constructed throughout the country in the 1870s and 1880s. Although works were provided for double track, initially only one line with passing places was provided; short stretches of this were at 1 in 85. A feature of the line were the two covered ways at Preston Hall, of 33 and 54 yards in length.

An interesting result of the relationships built up by the Farringdon link was that the Midland Railway opened a coal depot at Maidstone. Initially through working from Sevenoaks to Maidstone was impossible, but from 1st November 1880 a south to east curve was provided at Otford. This allowed the exchange platforms, provided for passengers changing trains but without external access from 1st June 1874, to be closed; a proper Otford station did not open until 1st August 1882.

There were a number of goods facilities along the line including private sidings near Otford and Wrotham, and a public goods siding at Offham.

In April 1876, with the prospect of an extension to Ashford, the LCDR decided to widen the Maidstone line to double track and this was probably carried out by the end of 1877. A significant threat to the prosperity of the line and the SMTR Company, which still nominally existed until 1879, was an improvement in relations between the SER and LCDR. In 1877 amalgamation between the two seemed likely and the SMTR was at first inclined to oppose this since its original purpose had been to siphon off the SER's Maidstone traffic. A bargain was struck however, with the SMTR deciding to promote a connecting line from Dunton Green, on the SER's direct Tonbridge line, to

159

An LCDR passenger train crossing the bridge over the SER at Maidstone; a link between the two lines was authorised but never constructed. (A. Riley collection, source unknown)

Otford and also an extension to Ashford. These two lines would have turned the SMTR into a through route of value even if the SER and LCDR merged. The SMTR agreed not to oppose amalgamation in return for like treatment by the LCDR of its extension plans.[5] Ultimately the problem was solved by the LCDR absorbing the SMTR with a payment of £31,500 in cash and £502,000 in mixed shares.

The SMTR line terminated at Maidstone leaving an obvious gap in Kent's communications between there and Ashford, on the SER's main line. A new line to link up the two towns would be able to follow the foot of the North Downs and pass through several prosperous villages without any major physical obstacles en route. Plans for a Maidstone & Ashford line had been advanced at regular intervals over the years, for example in 1864. On 10th August 1866 an Act was passed for an independent Maidstone & Ashford line, with a Board that included several prominent local men such as the Earl of Romney, from Mote Park, and Charles Martin M.P. of Leeds Castle. This line was planned to connect with the SMTR at Maidstone and the SER at Ashford, though in Maidstone there was also to be a ¾ mile spur giving access to the SER. Clearly the line depended on the success of the SMTR's Maidstone extension, but the atrocious financial climate was too much for both schemes.

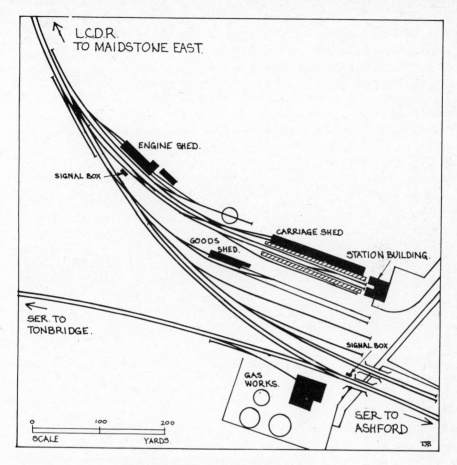

LCDR.
TO MAIDSTONE EAST.

ENGINE SHED.

SIGNAL BOX

GOODS
SHED.

CARRIAGE SHED

STATION BUILDING.

SER. TO
TONBRIDGE.

SIGNAL BOX

GAS
WORKS.

SER. TO
ASHFORD

0   100   200
SCALE   YARDS.

Map 33: Ashford (LCDR) Station, 1895

By 1874 the second route to Maidstone was at last nearing completion and there was renewed interest in a line to Ashford. Both a nominally-independent and an SER-backed scheme were proposed, though the LCDR felt restricted by its traffic agreements and was at first hesitant in its support for the independent project. Other projects for lines from Maidstone to Faversham, in 1875, and Sittingbourne, in 1876, also worried the LCDR. In 1877 the SMTR put forward its own plan for an Ashford line.

The contest built up to reach its peak in 1880. At first the LCDR petitioned against the Maidstone & Ashford Company's Bill, but in May 1880 reached a working agreement with it and changed course. In July 1880 Forbes described the line as 'one of the best bits of armour they could put on.' Rival plans by the SER for branches from Maidstone to Loose and from Ashford to Charing were

161

The ex-LCDR Ashford West station in 1958 after it had been closed to passengers for fifty-nine years, having seen some use as a goods station. (R. Thomas)

rejected in the House of Commons and the Maidstone & Ashford Act passed on 12th August 1880. By this time the LCDR was in virtual control of the MAR so that although the SER gained running powers over it the LCDR's influence was able to block construction of a link-line in Maidstone that would have made this practicable.

An Act of 27th June 1881 provided for the transfer of the Maidstone & Ashford Railway to the LCDR upon completion, the eventual deed of conveyance being signed on 18th February 1885. As early as September 1880 the LCDR lent £24,000 to the MAR and under the powers of the 1881 Act it soon established control of the Board. Forbes became Chairman, Waterlow and Pemberton were on the Board with Aretas Akers Douglas joining in September 1881. A contract with Lucas & Aird was drawn up in January 1882 and just to encourage the process they lent £10,000 for land purchase and bought 45,960 £10 shares;[6] this procedure was handled more discreetly than by Peto & Betts, and the whole Lucas & Aird partnership was designed to avoid unnecessary financial strain. They were paid for the work in monthly instalments of £17,500. Work started in April 1882 and cost £420,000.

The line was opened on 1st July 1884 with many celebrations in Ashford, including a banquet at the Saracen's Head Hotel. Interestingly the MAR also owned the Victoria Hotel and the Railway Guard Inn in Maidstone. The line left Maidstone through a covered way at Turkey Mill and two short tunnels under the town; there were intermediate stations at Bearsted, Hollingbourne, Harrietsham, Lenham, Charing and Hothfield. The LCDR station at Ashford was a terminus, though there was a short spur to allow freight access onto the SER.

This new line was less of a suit of armour and more a rapier's thrust into the South Eastern's flank, because it penetrated deep into their territory and offered prospects of further extension. Lines from Maidstone to Faversham or from Lenham to Faversham were proposed on several occasions during the 1880s in case the SER should launch a counter-attack. Clearly the area was reasonably attractive for railways despite its agricultural nature, since as early as the last half of 1884 the MAR was earning £12,000 per half year for its parent Company. An Act was obtained for a Maidstone to Faversham line in 1881 but despite reconsideration in 1885 this was never built and an Act was passed to abandon the project in 1889. Similarly an independent plan for an Ightham to Hadlow branch in 1885 failed.

But the LCDR was looking beyond Ashford. In November 1887 the LCDR Board became interested in securing running powers from Ashford to Folkestone and this idea was supported by Maidstone Council; passengers were dissatisfied with having to walk between the rival stations in Ashford. Folkestone Council decided to support the idea the following year, but the SER was strongly opposed to any further LCDR incursion onto its metals. Recognising this problem, Maidstone Council amended its demands to pressing only for through carriages in May 1889; Maidstone eventually took the case to the Railway Commissioners and after 1891 LCDR trains began to run through to the SER station. The case was very similar to that of the Toomer Loop in Strood.

Ashford (LCDR) station was made completely redundant by the amalgamation and was its its first victim, closing to passengers from 1st January 1899 with all trains running through to the former SER station. But the Maidstone and Ashford line itself was still to endure some glorious moments, particularly during the Second World War, and has remained a regular route for continental freight trains to this day.

CHAPTER TWELVE

The Gravesend West Branch

The riverside town of Gravesend enjoyed a reputation as a pleasure resort in the early nineteenth century and before the railways Thames steamers brought crowds of visitors down the river for the day, many of whom enjoyed a visit to the famous Rosherville Gardens. However from 1849 the town was well served by the North Kent line of the SER and was of no immediate interest to the LCDR.

The LCDR's Western Extension passed about 4½ miles to the south of Gravesend so that the town did not enjoy the competitive service offered to such places as Canterbury and Ramsgate, although it was possible to take a horse omnibus from Meopham station to Gravesend. In February 1863 a plan was drawn up for a branch from Farningham Road into Gravesend, but it came to nothing. This was the first of several schemes which included the North & South Gravesend (Tunnel Junction) Railway of 1876 and the Gravesend, Northfleet & LCDR of 1880. By 1880 various developments were taking place in the area to stimulate the interest of the LCDR; this included the construction of a major docks system at nearby Tilbury, an influence even though it was on the north bank of the Thames, and a generally increased desire to fight the SER wherever possible. Thus in May 1880 the LCDR Board reached an agreement with the Gravesend Railway Company for working arrangements on their proposed line, and the short branch was authorised on 18th July 1881.

The Gravesend Railway Bill contained some interesting features. One of these was a clause to allow Gravesend Council to take shares in the Railway, though it was decided at a Board meeting in February 1881 to strike this clause out as it was unlikely to be used and might hinder the Bill's progress. There was some debate over where the branch should terminate, the Bill giving Princes Street but the Directors amending this to Bath Street within a week of obtaining the Act so as to save an estimated £47,600 on land and construction costs.[1] The Bill also included a branch from near Springhead Road to a pier at Northfleet, but this was never built — a pier at Gravesend itself making this unnecessary. Capital of £200,000 was allowed for.

The Board started meeting under the Chairmanship of Sir S. Waterlow, M.P. for Gravesend and proprietor of the stationery firm. Board Minutes were written into a minute-book produced by the Waterlow firm, so it is to be hoped that the book was provided free and was not another example of reckless profiteering! It was not an easy start however, for the Company was subjected to several attacks in the form of ridicule from the *Argus* newspaper during November 1881; after careful consideration, the Directors decided it would be wise to abstain from issuing a writ of libel.

164

The former LCDR terminus at Gravesend West, photographed in 1959 after six years of closure; the unique triangular arrangement can be seen.   (R. Thomas)

Another early problem was that Lord Darnley, owner of some land required at the Gravesend terminus, decided to develop it for housing. That he should decide to do so when he already knew it would have to be purchased from him may seem strange, except that Darnley (and the Gravesend Company) knew that land with roads and houses laid out would command a higher price in the compulsory purchase.

By December 1881 Gravesend was in use as a port of call for ships of the Peninsula & Oriental Line and the Orient Line, and the LCDR saw a chance of a share in this traffic. These shipping lines handled long-distance voyages, but it may also have occurred to the LCDR that Gravesend was a useful alternative — outside the bounds of the Continental Agreement — to Queenborough and very suitable for Dutch services. Such thoughts were undoubtedly behind a Gravesend Railway decision, on 8th November 1881, to extend their line to a pier on the Thames and also behind the LCDR's decision to seek to absorb a Company with which they already had close connections and several Board members in common. The Act for the extension, at a mere 154 yards probably one of the shortest ever though it included construction of the pier, was passed on 24th July 1882 and provided for an extra £50,000 in capital. The pier was constructed with three levels to allow for the considerable tidal range on the Thames at Gravesend.

Various competitive schemes troubled the Gravesend Railway Directors during 1881 and 1882. The rival SER Northfleet & Snodland line caused a dispute over land and the Tilbury & Gravesend Tunnel Junction Railway caused

165

Southfleet station on the Gravesend branch; at this stage, summer 1959, the singling of the line was in progress. (R. Thomas)

caused a flutter of panic in March 1882. As relations with the LCDR deepened the Board began to assume a familiar shape, with Major Dickson and Hart-Dyke joining during 1882 to add some experience, along with the inevitable Forbes; Dickson eventually became Chairman.

On 18th October 1882 the line was at last contracted out to G. Barclay-Bruce for £143,500.[2] There was no immediate start to the proceedings however, since the first sod was not cut until 30th June 1883 at West Street, Gravesend. The obscurity of the line was celebrated by the *Railway Times* which described it as running from 'Fakenham to Gravesend',[3] an error of approximately 150 miles!

Yet another Act was passed on 29th June 1883 to allow the transfer of the Company to the LCDR. To pay for it the LCDR raised £245,700 in 4% 1883 Debenture stock during 1884, with one London bank reportedly subscribing for £100,000.

The question of stations then arose, with the Board receiving a letter from the citizens of Northfleet in September 1884, requesting a station at Rosherville. In fact stations were provided at Southfleet, Rosherville and Gravesend from the opening of the line, but no station was built at the junction with the main-line (Fawkham Junction) although a halt was built at Longfield and opened by the SE&CR on 1st July 1913. Rosherville Gardens were of declining importance and brought little benefit to the line. It was double track throughout.

The ceremonial opening took place on 17th April 1886, a special train being run from London which was joined at Fawkham by Waterlow. After arriving at Gravesend, the visitors crossed the Thames aboard the tug *Victoria* to inspect Tilbury Docks, which opened the same day. There then occurred the only untoward event in the line's history when Lord Darnley, disgusted at the treatment he had received over land payments, blocked up the entrance road to the station. He claimed that he should be paid extra money for the roads which he had been building to develop his land and it took until June 1888 for the LCDR to concede to him. In the meantime the line opened to public traffic on 10th May 1886 with a service of fourteen down weekday trains. Boat trains did not start running until 1916.

167

The paddlesteamer 'John Penn', originally owned by Jenkins & Churchward and used briefly on LCDR Continental services circa 1863.

CHAPTER THIRTEEN

Passenger Services of the LCDR

i) Continental Services

For centuries Dover was the traditional port for cross-Channel traffic and the town's prosperity depended upon this trade. The normal route was the short sea crossing to Calais, but in 1846 Dover's importance was enhanced by the introduction of an Ostend service run by the Belgian Government. However the South Eastern Railway decided to develop its own port at Folkestone and to run steamers from there to Boulogne; this was a severe blow to both Dover and Calais, so that the Mayors of both towns were early supporters of the East Kent Railway. In 1856 120,000 passengers used the Folkestone to Boulogne route and only 70,000 the Dover to Calais one.[1]

It seems unlikely that the East Kent Railway initially had any intentions of getting involved with Channel ferries, for such a step would have announced it as a main-line challenger to the SER's monopoly. Instead, the decision to go for this market seems to have arisen as a consequence of the Company's London extensions and pressure from the Dover interests. The subject was first discussed by the LCDR Board in September 1860 and liaison with the Nord Railway of France, the essential partner in a link to Paris, began in October 1860. The Nord Railway thus became involved with both the SER and the LCDR, there being no competitive system of railway promotion in France to foster new allies for the LCDR. The decision to acquire a Channel fleet had clearly been made by December, when a Naval Architect and Marine Engineer was appointed.

In 1861 the Dover Harbour Board was formed. This had seven members, with the LCDR and SER each having one representative. Despite this equality, it became generally assumed in Dover that the LCDR was the more responsive to the town's interests and that the SER would always be the *bête noire* of the piece. The most prized traffic through the port was the foreign mails, and a measure of the influence of this can be seen from the events of March 1861 when the Ostend run was changed from a night to a day service at the insistence of the Royal Mail.

During 1861 the LCDR managed to acquire the Dover-Calais mails contract which had been held by the firm of Jenkins & Churchward since 1854. However the LCDR did not have powers to operate ships until an Act was passed in June 1864, so plans were made for Jenkins & Churchward to operate the service on a temporary basis. Agreement with them was reached on 1st May 1862 and the LCDR raised 4,000 shares of £25 each to help cover the cost of £120,000. Many ships belonging to Jenkins & Churchward were absorbed into the LCDR fleet — indeed they became the LCDR fleet — and are detailed at the end of this section.

LCDR continental services then began on 1st July 1862. Calais harbour was tidal, so the steam tender *Poste* was acquired to assist in the disembarkation of passengers and mail; delays in handling the mails could be heavily penalised according to the rigorous terms of the contract. Traffic grew quickly and in 1864 the LCDR's revenue from the service was £32,352. To avoid unnecessary competition the SER and LCDR agreed from June 1863 to negotiate for the mail contracts jointly; like most of their agreements, this one did not prove binding.

On 13th December 1865 the LCDR's ship *Samphire* collided with an American vessel in the Channel, several people being drowned. Collisions were regular occurrences, but fatalities were generally few.

The cross-Channel traffic was notoriously fickle, and could easily be affected by international tensions or outbreaks of disease on the continent. Thus LCDR continental revenue was severely reduced by the Franco-Prussian War of 1870, which culminated in a siege of Paris. In August 1871 the LCDR lent twenty carriages to the Nord Railway to help it over post-war difficulties. A cholera epidemic in France in 1885 also discouraged traffic at a time when the English colonisation of the French Riviera was gathering pace; that year only 300 of the 700 English villas at Cannes were occupied. In February 1893 the *Railway Times* calculated that a cholera scare had cost the LCDR £10,000 in lost traffic.

In October 1872 the SER acquired a monopoly of the French mails contract, angering the LCDR who claimed that agreements on joint negotiation had been broken. By 1873 the LCDR was trying to develop a new type of traffic in the shape of Sunday excursions to Calais; these incurred the wrath of the Dover Lord's Day Observance Society. A service to the Dutch port of Flushing was introduced in 1875 for the Dutch and German mails; this ran from Sheerness and later Queenborough, so is dealt with below.

By May 1876 the LCDR's Calais services could support two connecting express passenger services, and the Dutch service one. There were Dover departures from Victoria at 7.40am and 8.30pm, with a Queenborough service at 8.45pm.

From the mid-1870s steady investment by the LCDR, the Nord Railway and Dover Harbour Board resulted in the gradual improvement of services. The LCDR was mostly concerned with the ships and, in 1874-75, experimented with some novel designs in an effort to overcome the problem of sea sickness which was then acute on the Channel routes because of the small vessels in use. The general trend was towards larger vessels and experiments were made with twin-hulls and even, in the case of the weird *Bessemer*, a tilting saloon that was intended to maintain stability in the roughest conditions. This ship was not a success, even developing a habit of colliding with Calais pier. Occasional consideration was given to drastic alternatives such as the Channel Tunnel, a project in which the LCDR invested £20,000 in 1875.

The Nord Railway and the French government were responsible for Calais harbour, which was improved in 1882 so that it was no longer restricted by the tides. The LCDR responded by improving its services, so that by June 1885 it was possible to leave Victoria at 10.15am and be in Paris at 7pm. The *Invicta*, one of the LCDR's best ships, was able to do the Dover-Calais run in 69 minutes, although it ran onto a sandbank at Calais in 1888. Powerful new ships *Victoria*

170

and *Empress* were built in 1886-87, and to allow for them the gates of Wellington Dock, Dover, had to be widened ten feet.

The LCDR certainly did very well out of its continental services, proving more than a match for the SER. It took the lion's share of the Paris Exhibition traffic in 1878 and in 1887 the Dover-Calais route carried 235,695 passengers whereas only 116,657 went by the SER's Folkestone-Boulogne route. Another big Paris Exhibition was held in 1889; in preparation for this £1,500,000 was spent on Calais harbour, with the works being opened by the President of the Republic on 3rd June 1889. The Nord Railway built a new station there and agreement was reached with the International Sleeping Car Company for the operation of a *train de luxe* from the same date. This, the 'Club Train', left Victoria at 4.15pm and reached Paris at 11.45pm. The Club Train proved an expensive liability and in 1890 the LCDR calculated that it was costing £14,000 per year to run because of the special ferry crossings that had to be made. The International Sleeping Car Co. was replaced by Wagons Lits in 1892, but the LCDR still wanted to drop out and hoped the service could be transferred to the SER's Folkestone-Boulogne route. Many critics pointed out that this 'exclusive' service was only five minutes faster than the LCDR's normal 11am continental service. The Club Train ceased running on 1st October 1893.

Accidents continued to happen on the Channel services. *Victoria* did £400 damage to Calais pier in 1892 and in January 1895 *Empress* collided with the West Pier at Calais, lost its starboard paddle-box, and then spent five days on a sandbank. Such accidents usually resulted in claims for damages from whoever owned the obstacle that had been hit, and on one occasion the Calais authorities 'arrested' the guilty LCDR ship until payment of compensation had been made.

Travel to Paris was improved in 1892 by the abolition of the French government's tax of 10%. This made it possible to run popular 3rd class trains and the LCDR instituted an 8.30am departure from Victoria, getting to Paris about 7pm. From 1st April 1892 a 3rd class night fare of £2 was introduced. In 1893 the Ostend service was accelerated so that only 2¾ hours were spent at sea, this service being entirely a Belgian responsibility. The same year the LCDR acquired the Calais night mails contract, worth £25,000 per year; the result was that its Night Mail train was accelerated by 35 minutes.

By 1895 talk of amalgamation between the LCDR and the SER had given rise to rumours that the Folkestone services might cease. The LCDR route seemed to be in a strong position, with transits of 54 minutes made possible by a new generation of vessels. The Ostend service had been expanded to thrice daily and in 1897 the Calais Night Mail service was re-equipped.

Figures show a steady increase in passengers on both French and Belgian services:[2]

Dover-Calais					*Dover-Ostend*			
1850	54,036	1880	197,247		1878	26,270	1900	114,516
1860	76,318	1900	316,156		1886	31,745	1910	222,375
1870	108,008	1910	369,069		1890	75,158		

An interesting idea of traffic and operations at the end of the LCDR period can be gained from the following excerpts from the Company's marine records:

Daily Sailings

Ship	Route	Departure	Arrival	Time taken	Carrying
26th January 1897					
Calais	Calais to Dover	2.03am	3.20am	1hr 17m	62 passengers
Chatham	Dover to Calais	3.20am	5.32am	2hr 12m	90 tons
Roubaix	Calais to Dover	8.24am	11.37am	2hr 13m	90 tons
Victoria	Dover to Calais	11.21am	12.41pm	1hr 20m	225 passengers
Calais	Dover to Calais	1.17pm	2.36pm	1hr 19m	206 passengers
Victoria	Calais to Dover	1.41pm	3.04pm	1hr 23m	102 passengers
Dover	Calais to Dover	4.00pm	5.23pm	1hr 23m	102 passengers
Dover	Dover to Calais	11.18pm	0.32am	1hr 14m	66 passengers
23rd August 1897					
Empress	Calais to Dover	2.08pm	3.20am	1hr 12m	103 passengers
Paris	Calais to Dover	2.13am	4.30am	2hr 17m	40 tons
Roubaix	Dover to Calais	6.10am	8.30am	2hr 20m	Ballast
Empress	Dover to Calais	1.38pm	2.49pm	1hr 11m	193 passengers
Victoria	Calais to Dover	1.43pm	2.57pm	1hr 14m	236 passengers
Dover	Calais to Dover	3.56pm	5.10pm	1hr 14m	149 passengers
Victoria	Dover to Calais	11.06pm	0.16am	1hr 10m	82 passengers
Dover	Dover to Calais	11.24pm	0.35am	1hr 11m	120 passengers

Although the LCDR did not operate any ships on the Dutch and German mails services, it was closely interested in them. During 1875 the Dutch government had pressed for a faster mails connection with the United Kingdom and a direct result of this was the formation on 10th June 1875 of the Zeeland Steamship Company. On 26th July 1875 this Company commenced operating a nightly service between Flushing and Sheerness but on 14th November the service was suspended due to a combination of high costs, the loss of a ship, shallowness of the available water at Sheerness and the incompleteness of the pier at Queenborough. The service was restarted via Queenborough on 15th May 1876, but on 18th May 1882 the pier there burnt down and passenger traffic was diverted to Dover. From 1st June 1887 a new day and night service began, using three new paddle-steamers and including a German mails service. During December 1897 the service was temporarily transferred to Dover as bad weather had damaged the track at Queenborough and in 1900 the pier was again destroyed by fire.

The route therefore experienced a number of disasters, both at land and sea. To these must be added the wreck of the paddle-steamer *Stad Vlissingen*, which ran aground and broke up in 1879.

The LCDR's fleet contained a large number of ships over the years which are detailed below. Those listed as far down as *Pioneer* were absorbed into the

LCDR Marine Department having been previously part of the Jenkins & Churchward fleet. From *Foam* onwards they were owned and used by the LCDR with the exceptions of *Castalia* and *Bessemer*, two experimental vessels that were only crewed and used by the LCDR.

Name	Date	Builder	Weight	Comments
Ondine or *Undine*	1844		171 tons	Paddlesteamer (PS), sold 1859
Scout	1843	Orchard Yard	352	PS, sold circa 1864
Garland	1846	Fletcher	292	PS
Jupiter		Miller & Ravenhill	288	PS
Pathfinder	1854	Ditchburn & Mare		PS
Poet				
La Reine/Queen	1854		196	PS, renamed 1864, renamed *Pioneer* 1874
Empress	1855	Salkeld	196	
Prince Frederick William	1857	Thames Ironworks	219	PS, sold 1878
John Penn	1860	Thames Ironworks	97	PS, sold 1863
Maid of Kent	1861	Samuda/Salkeld	364	PS, sold 1898
Samphire	1862	Ravenhill	358	PS, withdrawn 1899
Etoile du Nord or *Petrel*	1862	Salkeld	504	PS, sold 1880
Vivid				On French mails 1864, sold 1865
Pioneer				In use 1864, sold c. 1868
Foam	1862	Samuda/Salkeld	504	PS, sold 1864, scrapped 1901?
Scud	1862	Samuda/Salkeld	504	PS, sold 1864-6
Poste	1862	Thames Ironworks		Steam tender at Calais
Breeze	1863	Ravenhill	349	PS, w. 1899
Wave	1863	Ravenhill	393	PS, w. 1899
Prince Imperial	1864	John Ash	338	PS, sold 1869
La France	1864	John Ash	365/464	PS, sold 1899 for scrap
Chatham	1873	Dudgeon	278	Steamship (SS), cargo, w. 1905
Castalia	1874	Thames Ironworks	1,533	PS, twin hulls with paddles between but could do only 11 knots, sold to Metropolitan Asylums Board 1883 as a Fever Hospital
Calais or *Roubaix*	1874	Dudgeon	299	SS cargo boat, sold to J.S. Forbes in 1890s, bought back by SE&CR 1900, sold to LBSCR 1901

The unusual twin-hulled paddlesteamer 'Calais-Douvres', in use by the LCDR 1877-1887.

(R.W. Kidner collection)

174

Name	Date	Builder	Weight	Comments
Bessemer	1875	Earle, Hull	1,886 tons	PS with tilting saloon, four paddles, sold for scrap 1879
Calais-Douvres	1877	Hawthorn-Leslie	1,924	Twin-hull PS with paddles between, sold 1887 as too slow
Paris	1878			SS cargo-boat, sold 1901
Invicta	1882	Thames Ironworks	1,197	PS, sold to Nord 1896, for scrap 1899
Victoria	1886	Fairfield, Glasgow	1,052	PS, hit Calais pier 1891, to Nord 1896, scr. 1904
Empress	1887	Fairfield	1,219	PS, hit Calais pier 1895, scr. 1906
Calais-Douvres	1889	Fairfield	1,212	PS, first with electric lights, sold 1900, scr. 1909
Calais	1896	Denny	1,002	PS, torpedoed Feb. 1916
Dover	1896	Denny	1,002	PS, scr. 1911
Lord Warden	1896	Denny	1,002	PS, scr. 1911
Le Nord	1898	St. Nazaire	2,004	PS, rammed and sank German U-boat in Great War; sold 1920, wrecked 1923
Le Pas de Calais	1898	St. Nazaire	2,004	PS, accidentally sank French submarine 1910, sold 1923

The Dover to Ostend service was operated by Belgian ships as follows:

Name	Date	Builder	Weight	Comments
Louise-Marie	1867	Cockerill, Antwerp		PS, scr. 1893
Leopold I	1868	Cockerill		PS, w. 1900, scr. 1919
Marie-Henriette	1869	Cockerill		PS, scr. 1893
Comte de Flandre	1870	Cockerill		PS, scr. 1893
Comtesse de Flandre	1870	Cockerill		PS, sank after collision at Dunkirk April 1899
Prince Baudouin	1872	Cockerill		PS, scr. 1897
Parlement Belge	1873	Cockerill		PS, scr. 1897
Ville de Douvres	1886	Cockerill	855	PS, scr. 1910
La Flandre	1888	Cockerill	862	PS, sunk in Ostend harbour by Germans in Great War
Princesse Henriette	1888	Denny	1,100	PS, sunk 1918
Princesse Josephine	1888	Denny	1,100	PS, scr. 1922
Prince Albert	1889	Cockerill	861	PS, sold 1908
Marie-Henriette	1892	Cockerill	1,451	PS, sank 1914
Leopold II	1893	Denny	1,367	PS capable of 22 knots — fastest PS in world at the time, sold 1920
Rapide	1894	Cockerill	1,195	PS, sold 1923
Princesse Clementine	1896	Cockerill	1,474	PS, last to operate on route, scr. 1928

After 1899 further additions were made to both the Belgian and the SE&CR fleets. However, the introduction of screw-driven steamers revolutionised the cross-Channel operations so much that both fleets were almost totally renewed between 1900 and 1918. The first screw-driven vessel in the SE&CR fleet was the 1,650 ton *Queen* of 1902, which was torpedoed on 26th October 1916. Thus the character of the LCDR's former Marine Department was quickly destroyed by the advance of technology within a few years of the amalgamation.

The LCDR's Marine Department maintained a high reputation and its efficiency can perhaps be judged from the longevity of ships like *Foam*, which successfully maintained the service for forty years. The Company was also prepared to experiment, no more so than with a unique and curious trio of vessels built in the 1870s. *Castalia* and *Calais-Douvres* were twin-hulled paddle-steamers, though both suffered from being slow and did not remain on the Dover to Calais run for long. They were part of an attempt to solve the problem of sea sickness by building larger and more stable ships, a problem to which the infamous *Bessemer* was another attempted solution. This was designed by Sir Henry Bessemer with a first class saloon that 'swung' with the waves, but it worked only very poorly.

The LCDR ships maintained the Dover to Calais route in competition with the SER on the Folkestone to Boulogne. The LCDR's *Scud* was used on an early Dover to Boulogne service, but this failed to win the support of the French authorities.

ii) Domestic Passenger Services

The initial passenger service between Strood and Faversham provided for bus links on to Canterbury; the fastest time from Faversham to London Bridge was 2 hours 5 minutes. On 8th December 1860 the Western Extension was opened with a service of five through trains from Canterbury to Victoria daily, the fastest in 2 hours 10 minutes. An interesting local service was introduced at this time – an irregular working between Sheerness and Chatham. All passenger schedules were forcibly relaxed in January 1861 when a speed of 24 mph was imposed throughout the LCDR because of problems with bad track.[3]

The Great Western Railway provided a service into Victoria from 1st April 1863; this initially ran from Southall, but later trains also ran to and from Kensington.

Many of the LCDR's most complex services were connected with the intensive use of the Farringdon link line. On 1st January 1866 through carriages to King's Cross began to run while the Great Northern Railway also ran carriages to Ludgate Hill. From 1st August 1866 a Herne Hill to New Barnet (GNR) service commenced though there was some disagreement with the GNR as to whether third class facilities should be provided. The service was temporarily shut down from 1st July 1867 until 1st March 1868 due to engineering works on the Metropolitan Railway, but on the latter date a reinvigorated service was introduced including GNR trains from Victoria to New Barnet; on 1st June 1869

176

the LCDR commenced running from Victoria to Finchley Road, connecting with the Midland Railway.

The LCDR also had close connections with the London & South Western Railway, which lacked its own City station. From 3rd April 1866 the LSWR began to run seven trains a day from Kingston or Hounslow to Ludgate Hill and from 1st February 1868 expanded the service to include a variety of starting points such as Kensington, Twickenham, Kingston and Clapham Junction. The service between Ludgate Hill and Clapham Junction was taken over by the LCDR from 1st January 1869 but the LSWR continued to operate to Kingston. The LSWR maintained its own booking clerks at Ludgate Hill until 1890.[4]

A review of the May 1869 timetable gives a general impression of the pattern of services. There were eight express trains through to Dover per day, of which six terminated at Harbour and the other two were boat trains through to Admiralty Pier; generally speaking all principal trains had Victoria and City portions which were attached and detached at Herne Hill. The fastest Herne Hill to Canterbury leg was 1 hour 20 minutes by the morning boat express. There were six trains to Ramsgate. About five trains per hour traversed the Victoria-Ludgate-Farringdon route, with some extras running from Loughborough Junction to King's Cross and about one per hour originating from Kensington.

The success of the City lines depended on the frequency of service, so that the LCDR originally intended a service of eighty trains a day into Moorgate. The service, from Victoria to Moorgate, was eventually introduced with about fifty trains per day. By February 1875 the LCDR was operating through to Alexandra Palace on the Great Northern. Over such short distances comfort was not at a premium and in 1875 the Board observed that use of 2nd class was falling. The LCDR was carrying 2,000,000 workmen's fares per year at this time and the Board was under the impression that members of the middle-classes were using these to reduce their costs of travel. On 1st July 1875 a Victoria/Moorgate/Barnet/Hendon integrated service was implemented.

Resorts such as Margate depended not only upon cheap trains to bring in the crowds of visitors but also upon fast and comfortable services to attract upper-class residents. By 1874 Margate was asking for the cheap summer trains to be extended throughout the winter months, but there was also a threat to the Sunday excursions from the Lord's Day Observance Society. To cater for the richer people who resided in Margate or Ramsgate at weekends, a special service was introduced in March 1877; this involved fast expresses, departing from Victoria at 3.15pm on Fridays and returning from Ramsgate on Monday mornings — the down journey being accomplished in two hours. These trains became known as 'The Westgate on Sea and Granville Special Express Trains.'

More traffic came to the Farringdon link line from 1st June 1878 when the South Eastern began a service from Woolwich to Finsbury Park and Enfield, using the spur at Blackfriars. This service only ran until 1907.

Profits on the inner London services were continually squeezed by competition from omnibuses and, later, underground railways. In 1883 the LCDR discovered that it was unable to compete with omnibuses over distances of under six miles, due to their low fares, and by 1884 they were complaining again — this time

177

because of competition from trams. The result was that serious consideration was given to the wisdom of running suburban trains with three classes of accommodation and it was noted that there was a tendency for passengers to switch to 3rd class over short distances; abolition of 2nd class was considered in 1888 and some excursions ran experimentally that summer with only 1st and 3rd class. Competition also depressed fares, so that a 3rd class weekly season for Penge to Ludgate cost only 2/- in 1884.

Consideration of the timetable for August 1890 shows much progress over that of 1869. There were eleven fast trains each way between Victoria and Dover, with five running to Admiralty Pier; best time was 1 hour 40 minutes. Connections into boat expresses from Liverpool, Glasgow etc., were provided via the West London line and Herne Hill. One of the most popular trains was the 'Calais Boat Express', leaving Victoria at 8.30am and, after a stop at Faversham, reaching Admiralty Pier at 10.15am. Ramsgate had twelve through trains, including three 'cheap fast' and four on Saturdays; long-distance commuters were provided for by the 'Kent Coast Express', departing Victoria at 5.15pm (2 hours 30 minutes to Ramsgate) and returning from Ramsgate at 8am to reach Victoria at 10.20am. There were seven through trains to Ashford with an extra two as far as Maidstone, and a market day (Tuesday) local from Ashford to Maidstone. The 5.30pm fast from Victoria reached Ashford at 7.42pm, detaching a Sevenoaks portion at Swanley. On the suburban lines there were fifty-two daily departures from Greenwich, many of which combined at Nunhead with Crystal Palace trains and then ran through to Kentish Town or King's Cross; there were also services from Crystal Palace and Greenwich to Victoria. Some ventured further afield, like the 3.36pm from Victoria (with a Crystal Palace portion which departed at 3.16pm) which ran through to St. Albans at 5.19pm. LCDR carriages also ran to Hendon and South Tottenham. An unusual facility in this timetable was the agreement with the Medway Steam Packet Company which allowed circular tours from Chatham to Sheerness or Queenborough with a choice of rail or sea transport.

In June 1896 the Ramsgate service was accelerated; it became possible to leave Holborn Viaduct or St. Paul's at 5.10pm and reach Ramsgate at 7.05pm.

On 1st April 1897 a new through service between Liverpool/Manchester and Dover started, running via Birmingham, Willesden and Herne Hill. It was possible to leave Birmingham at 7.30am and be in Paris at 7pm. From 1st May a similar service commenced via Queenborough for Flushing.

CHAPTER FOURTEEN

The Life of a

Victorian Railway Company

i) The Leading Characters

Chairmen of the EKR and LCDR

Lord Sondes 1852-1866	Lord Harris 1866-1867
G. Hodgkinson 1867-1873	J.S. Forbes 1874-1904
Sir E. Pemberton 1904-1908	Sir W. Hart Dyke 1908-1922

From 1898 until 1922 H. Cosmo Bonsor was Chairman of the SE&CR Managing Committee.

Secretaries of the EKR and LCDR

G. Holroyd 1852-1863	W. Johnson 1863-1867
G. Brooke 1867-1876	J. Morgan 1876-1900
E. Livesey 1900-1916	J. Dowdall 1916-1922

Biographical Details of Influential Characters

It is not possible, nor is it desirable, to give full details of all LCDR Board members, so only the most influential Kent Directors have been selected together with a few other figures who feature prominently in the Company's history. A Board member is indicated by the letter (B).

Edward Ladd Betts 1815-1872. Born in Kent, Betts became one of the foremost railway contractors in the country with some of his earliest work being done on the South Eastern Railway in the 1840s. He teamed up with Peto in 1846 and the following years brought him prosperity, a mansion at Preston Hall, and a candidacy for the Conservative Party in Maidstone at the election of 1865. He was also High Sheriff of Kent in 1858. Disgraced by the events of 1866, he died at Aswan in Egypt when trying to restore his health.[1]

Thomas Russell Crampton, 1816-1888, was born at Broadstairs and became a brilliant, if erratic, engineer. His first locomotives were built in 1845 and became popular in Europe. He had strong connections with the LCDR as a contractor. He laid the first international submarine cable for a telegraph connection across the English Channel.

Major A. Dickson, 1834-1899 (B), lived at Waldershare Park near Dover, for which he was Conservative M.P. from 1865 until 1889. He had a record of service in the Crimean War and the Indian Mutiny and was also, for a time, Chairman of the Crystal Palace Company. His position on the LCDR Board from 1875 to 1889 ensured that the interests of Dover were well represented. He was succeeded as both Dover M.P. and Board member by George Wyndham.

179

Aretas Akers-Douglas, 1851-1926 (B), lived at Chilston Park near Lenham and became a Director of the Maidstone & Ashford and the Shortlands & Nunhead before moving onto the LCDR Board. He was Conservative M.P. for East Kent 1880-1885 and for St. Augustine's 1885-1911. He was a successful career politician, rising to become Home Secretary under Balfour from 1902 until 1905.

Sir William Hart Dyke, 1837-1931 (B), lived at Lullingstone Castle near Eynsford. His father, Percival, was a Director of the SM&TR whilst William rose through the directorate to become the last Chairman of the LCDR. As a Conservative politician he was Chief Whip 1874-1880 and Chief Secretary for Ireland 1885-1886, but he lost his seat at Dartford in the Liberal landslide of 1906. An extremely wealthy man, he owned about 9,000 acres.

James Staats Forbes 1823-1904 (B). Trained as an engineer draughtsman, Forbes started his career with the Great Western Railway at Maidenhead in 1840 and quickly rose to become Goods Superintendent at Paddington. He moved from there to the Dutch Rhenish Railway, which he left to become General Manager of the LCDR in 1861, though on the condition that he paid regular advisory visits to his old employers. His salary with the LCDR was to be £1,500 per year plus 1% commission on increases in traffic, with a stipulation that the commission was not to be less than £500. By 1869 he was earning £6,000 per year from the LCDR, though this was cut to £3,500 as he was also being employed by the Metropolitan District Railway. He became Chairman of the LCDR in 1874, where his style was characterised as 'indomitable pluck and a persuasive tongue.'[2] In his private life he was a keen practitioner of musical comedy and an avid collector of paintings from the Norwich School. His business career included activities with the Didcot, Newbury & Southampton Railway, the Regent's Canal & City Docks Railway (one of his few failures), and the Presidency of the National Telephone Company for whom he negotiated a nationwide monopoly in 1892. He also found time to be Chairman of three electric light companies and a Director of an insurance company. In 1884 he was reputedly earning £15,000 per annum but in 1898 slipped from power to become merely 'special adviser' to the SE&CR. His only venture into politics was an unsuccessful campaign as a Liberal in Dover in 1873. His nephew William trained on the LCDR before becoming Manager of the LBSCR. He died of pneumonia in April 1904 with the *Railway Times* providing a caustic epitaph: 'Stagnation was his motto, in an age of progress.' His funeral was held near Hayes and a special train brought many distinguished mourners from London — having departed, ironically, from Charing Cross! In his will he left a gross estate of £135,367 including £5,000 as a legacy to the Railway Servants' Orphanage.

Sir Charles Fox 1810-1874. Fox trained as a surgeon before entering into engineering and contracting, where he won fame and fortune for his work in erecting the Crystal Palace — and also a knighthood. His involvement with early EKR contracts suggested rather unsteady finances, but he survived the crash of 1866 and his name lives on through the modern firm of Freeman, Fox & Co.

Lord George Harris, 1810-1872 (B), was a distinguished Kent landowner who joined the LCDR Board in 1860 and became, briefly, Chairman in 1866. From 1854 to 1859 he was Governor of Madras where he became known for his conduct during the Mutiny. The *Dictionary of National Biography* described him as '...a typical English gentleman, honourable, brave and manly; somewhat reserved in manner and faithful to all his duties.' His eldest daughter married Stephen Lushington and the family's connection with the LCDR was also maintained by C. Lushington. Harris typified the old breed of railway directors with local interests and he was one of those ejected after the 1866 disaster.

C.J. Hilton ?-1866 (B). Hilton took control of Faversham cement works in 1849 and by 1862 employed 130 people there. He was mayor of Faversham in 1846 and 1850, and had a family connection with the brewers Shepherd & Hilton (Shepherd & Neame after 1869). He was an early promoter of the EKR and was also Chairman of the Herne Bay & Faversham. He lived at Bickley towards the end of his life.

Grosvenor Hodgkinson ?-1881 (B). Liberal M.P. for Newark 1859-1870, near which he lived, Hodgkinson rose to prominence in the LCDR through his enquiries into the 1866 crash. He was Chairman for six years.

C.M. Lushington 1819-1864 (B). Son of Stephen Lushington of Norton Court, near Faversham. Of the Lushingtons, both father and son were involved with the EKR from its inception, and the son rose to become Deputy Chairman. He was also Deputy Chairman of the London & North Western Railway and Chairman of the Sittingbourne and Sheerness. Both father and son were at some stage M.P.s for Canterbury, the former in 1830-1837 and the latter 1854-1857.

E.L. Pemberton, 1823-1910 (B), lived at Torry Hill and was M.P. for East Kent 1868-1885, as a Conservative. He was knighted in 1898 and became Chairman of the LCDR in 1904.

Sir Samuel Morton Peto 1809-1899. Born in Berkshire, Peto built his first fortune quite literally with the construction firm of Grissell & Peto, in which he was a partner from 1830 to 1846; their buildings included the Lyceum, the Houses of Parliament and Nelson's Column. After 1846 his principal partner was Betts, but he also worked with Brassey and Crampton, particularly on overseas contracts. He was Liberal M.P. for Norwich, near which was his Somerleyton estate, from 1847-1854; during the Crimean War he offered to build railways for military use and so had to resign his seat, but he was compensated for this with a knighthood. He returned as Liberal M.P. for Finsbury 1859-1861, at a time when he was engaged in the promotion and construction of numerous railways. From 1865-1868 he was M.P. for Bristol but he was forced to apply for the Chiltern Hundreds on account of his bankrupt condition. In March 1868 Gladstone described him as 'A man who has attained a high position in this country by the exercise of rare talents and who has adorned that position by his great virtues.' He pieced together his career and returned to contract for the Cornwall Minerals Railway in the 1870s, but again went bankrupt. He died in 1899 without leaving a will and, despite Gladstone's opinion,

LCDR 'Scotchmen' class no. 89 'Kelvin', built in 1866. This early photo shows some pugnacious characters on the footplate! (R. Thomas collection)

B1 class 0-6-0 goods engine no. 153. Built in 1877, this Kirtley designed loco ran until 1923. (R. Thomas collection)

has been remembered in railway history for his somewhat dubious financial practices. This is partly unjust, for Peto also deserves to be remembered for the high standards he set in the care of his employees, as shown by his support for the Truck Acts and the idea of sick clubs for workmen. His fervent Baptist beliefs also led to strict controls on the presence of alcohol on site.

Peto was a classic example of the Victorian 'new establishment' of engineers and industrialists. Had he been born twenty years earlier he may well have encountered the snobbish resistance to outsiders that had at one time characterised the London engineering circles and which had caused George Stephenson himself to be cold-shouldered for a while. But the status that Peto attained is shown to good effect in Selous' famous painting of the opening of the Crystal Palace in 1851, which now hangs in the Victoria & Albert museum. Peto, resplendent in red uniform, stands in the very front of the picture — a confident and dignified figure. The high social position which this painting confirmed for him made the later revelations of shady deals all the more scandalous. In many ways Peto can be seen as representative of the Victorian Age.

Lord Sondes (B) lived at Lees Court, near Faversham, and at Elmham Hall, becoming the first Chairman of the EKR. For a time he was also a Director of the SM&TR. Apparently undistinguished and inexperienced, Sondes proved an easy dupe for the likes of Fox and Peto, resigning in 1866 amidst recriminations.

Sir S. Waterlow, 1822-1906 (B), lived near Wrotham for some time and was a useful LCDR Director on account of his business experience in the Waterlow printing and paper company. As Liberal M.P. he represented Maidstone 1874-1880 and Gravesend 1880-1885 and was noted for his concern about the housing of the lower classes, with which he was much involved in London. Also a Director of the Gravesend Railway.

Sir E. Watkin 1819-1901. Born at Salford, Watkin's forceful — sometimes 'bullying' — management skills allowed him to become one of the great names in railway history. He started with the Trent Valley Railway in 1845, then had spells with the LNWR and the Manchester, Sheffield & Lincolnshire before becoming involved with the SER in 1864. It was his Manchester supporters who first secured him a place on the SER Board and then the Chairmanship itself in January 1866. He combined the Chair with being General Manager from 1873 to 1880. His extensive interests ranged in railways from Manchester to Paris and he also found time for political ambitions. He failed to get elected as a Liberal at Great Yarmouth in 1859, but became M.P. for Stockport in 1864 until losing that seat in 1868 — much against the trend, since it was a year the Liberals swept to power. He was M.P. again from 1869-1873 in East Cheshire and 1874-1895 for Hythe, Kent, during which time he became one of the 'Liberal-Unionists' who supported Joseph Chamberlain. He retired from the SER in 1894, his dream of through railway communication between Manchester and Paris incomplete although he had almost single-handedly created the Great Central Railway.

George Wyndham, 1863-1913 (B), was M.P. for Dover from 1889 to 1913, succeeding Dickson both as M.P. and as Director of the LCDR. In Tory politics he began a career as Balfour's Private Secretary, rising to be Chief Secretary for

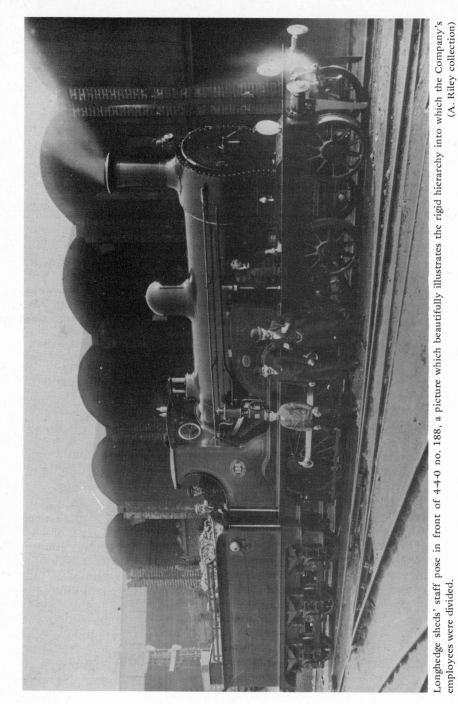

Longhedge sheds' staff pose in front of 4-4-0 no. 188, a picture which beautifully illustrates the rigid hierarchy into which the Company's employees were divided.

(A. Riley collection)

Ireland 1900-1905 with a seat in the Cabinet and responsible for the famous 'Wyndham's Act'. He was also something of a scholar, editing works on Shakespeare and Plutarch.

ii) Locomotive Superintendents

The first man to carry this title on the East Kent Railway was C.R. Sacré, appointed by the EKR Board on 8th May 1858. Born in 1831, he had started work in 1846 at Boston on the Great Northern Railway. His responsibilities on the EKR were limited to the maintenance of the locomotives and he was not given any opportunity to introduce designs of his own. Clearly he had some share in day to day traffic management since he was sacked on 2nd July 1858 following an accident in Fort Pitt Tunnel, Chatham. The same year Sacré was appointed to the Manchester, Sheffield & Lincolnshire Railway. He shot himself in 1889 after being seriously depressed by an accident.

Sacré was succeeded by a Mr Quadling, though no actual date of appointment was recorded. By July 1859 Quadling was in trouble with the Board for questioning the decisions of his superiors, and at this time Edward Betts recommended that Trevithick should be appointed in his place. However Quadling hung on to his office for a few more months until February 1860, when a locomotive on which he was travelling was derailed at Ospringe having worked 'wrong line' from Teynham; he was immediately sacked.

Trevithick was invited to attend for interview but on 29th March 1860 the job was offered to William Martley, who started work on 5th April. Martley had been born in 1824 and had started his career with the Great Western Railway in 1841, subsequently working in Ireland, South Devon and South Wales. Martley proved to be an excellent Locomotive Superintendent and was long remembered for his *Europa* class 2-4-0s which were built to handle the continental express traffic. These famous locomotives ran for over thirty years and four of the class knotched up more than a million miles in service.

Martley was succeeded in 1874 by William Kirtley. Kirtley had begun with the Midland Railway at Derby works in 1854, where he eventually returned as Works Superintendent in 1864. He remained on the LCDR until his retirement in 1898 but through his association with Forbes also secured the post of consulting engineer to the Hull & Barnsley Railway, in which Forbes had a strong interest. Kirtley's main achievement was the construction of a series of 4-4-0 passenger locomotives designated 'M' class, with which he hoped to maintain creditable timings over a line beset with steep gradients and speed restrictions.

All the locomotive types of the LCDR are described in great detail in D.L. Bradley's book on the subject (see Bibliography), so precise descriptions here are superfluous.

iii) Staff

An important Railway Company offered the prospect of a genuine career to

A large proportion of the LCDR staff at Whitstable, with luggage trollies laden with oysters.

(Douglas West collection)

many working class men, even those who began as manual workers. Forbes himself was a classic example of this, starting at Maidenhead station on the Great Western at the age of seventeen and building up his career to create considerable personal wealth. For the working man who was prepared to try to improve himself in the tradition of 'self-help', the opportunities existed; station staff particularly could build up their experience so that it was possible to graduate from being a porter to master of a small country station and so on up the scale. The LCDR often showed a curious ambivalence towards its workers, sometimes treating them benevolently and at other times being parsimonious in the extreme.

In November 1857 the Company started to recruit porters for 16s 0d a week and gatemen at 12s 0d plus a house. These were attractive jobs, since they offered regular employment in a mainly agricultural county that was notoriously seasonal in its prosperity. Agricultural wages in southern England at this time were only about 9s 0d to 10s 0d. But generosity was not to be the order of the day and when, in November 1858, the Board discovered that platelayers on the London & North Western Railway earned only 14s 0d a week, the EKR wages were knocked down 2s 0d to the required level.

Stationmasters were extremely important since they had close contact with the Company's customers. Their duties included managing the station staff and daily checks on the fabric, such as inspecting the water closets. Their standard wage in 1858 was 30s 0d a week, but the Chatham stationmaster earned £150 per year and from 1860 his Canterbury colleague was on £110.

Some concern was shown for the conditions of the Company's staff. For example in December 1858 the Board decided to fit shields onto engines to protect their drivers from the weather and in March 1859 the Board resolved to pay for the services of a chaplain to work with the men. Failure to carry out duties were severely punished however and in April 1861 there was much close inspection after the Board's attention had been drawn to dirty stations and untidy porters. Heavy drinking was a constant problem and was invariably rewarded with instant dismissal, as a General Committee Minute of June 1861 demonstrates: 'Resolved, that Cook, Signal Man at Beckenham had been asleep at his post, and was intoxicated at the time — He was ordered to be dismissed.' Sometimes punishment was even tougher and in 1862 a porter at Meopham got six months hard labour after his negligence caused a derailment. The balance in the struggle between staff and Company was redressed slightly when the Chief Booking Clerk at Victoria absconded with £1,000 in 1863.

Some staff problems were curious. In 1866 the Board considered a 'Petition from Signalman Woodland for a Cork Leg' but sadly their decision was not recorded. In 1871 the Board considered the question of a Staff Superannuation Fund but nothing was done until 1881 when all salaried staff and clerks were ordered to contribute to the Railway Clearing House's Superannuation Fund; manual workers were not provided for.

There seems to have been few industrial disputes on the LCDR, the most serious outbreaks coming after the formation of the SE&CR. One of the few major disagreements was in 1897 when labourers and porters working on the

Kirtley designed 'Europa' class 2-4-0 no. 54 'Asia'.

(R. Thomas collection)

Channel ferries went on strike demanding 3d an hour overtime pay. The LCDR replied by importing temporary labourers from Calais and sixty of the strikers were sacked, but they were later allowed to return to work.

Records of the Traffic Department staff at the end of the LCDR era have survived and show how the promotions system and pay structure worked. A hierarchy was most pronounced in the Locomotive Department, where a top driver could earn 8s 0d a day. These elite drivers included Edward Knivett, based at Dover, who joined the East Kent Railway on 20th May 1858 and retired on 9th September 1898. Even longer in his service was driver William Foster of Longhedge, who started work on 24th June 1860 and did not retire until 31st October 1910. There was clearly a well-defined pecking order amongst the drivers and few earned the top wage; of 24 based at Margate, only two were on 8s 0d whilst at Gravesend the spread was from 4s 6d to 7s 6d. Below the drivers were the fireman, averaging about 4s 0d, followed by Firelighters on 3s 9d, shed labourers on 3s 4d and, lowest of all, engine cleaners on starting pay of 2s 0d per day. The shed foreman, being in more of a managerial position though he might have risen through the ranks, was salaried, the man at Bickley receiving £150 per annum. The Locomotive Department also employed a few skilled men who did not fit into the graded pattern described above; for example Gillingham shed employed a boilersmith on 5s 6d per day, fitters at 6s 4d and a senior locomotive examiner at 28s 6d.

The majority of Carriage staff worked at the London stations, particularly Victoria. Here again there was clear division into levels of seniority with the Senior Foremen at Victoria earning 65s 0d per week. Other staff were paid by the day; carriage-washers ranged from 3s 3d to 4s 4d, on which income was one J. Coad who had been a carriage-washer for twenty-nine years. Carriage fitters earned between 3s 0d per day and 6s 8d. Worst paid of all were the labourers at Dover, on 1s 8d per day.

By agricultural standards the LCDR was a good employer and certainly in many country areas was one of the few alternatives to farm labour. In 1902 average wages for farm labourers stood at 16s 4d per week, lower than all but the most menial of the LCDR's various ranks and tasks.

These staff records also show the relative importance of the various loco depots through the number of drivers assigned to them in 1898:

Longhedge	275	Ludgate Hill	3	Bickley	31
Gravesend	10	Sevenoaks	12	Maidstone	17
Ashford	4	Faversham	39	Gillingham	25
Sheerness	10	Margate	24	Dover Priory	33

The prominence of Bickley was a result of its status as terminus for many of the LCDR's suburban services.

iv) Politics and the LCDR

Politics played an important role in the life of the LCDR, though not necessarily a continuous one. The town of Dover, for example, had a Conservative M.P. sitting on the Board for the majority of the Company's existence, commencing with J. Sadleir in 1855 although he died in 1856 amidst some controversy over his share payments. There was then a lull until Major Dickson, M.P. since 1865, was invited to join the Board in December 1875. Upon his death in 1889, the 'Dover seat' on the Board passed immediately to his successor as M.P. George Wyndham. No other town in Kent could claim such continuous representation and clearly this reflected the importance of Dover to the LCDR, especially if the fact that Dickson was 'invited' onto the Board is taken into consideration. But it was of course a two-way process, since any tame M.P. was a valuable asset for a railway prone to controversy.

Generally speaking the LCDR maintained an independent political line unlike its main rival the SER, where Watkin himself was an M.P. almost continuously from 1859 to 1895. Thus in February 1865 the LCDR Board Minutes recorded that 'Mr Forbes be authorised to impress on the subordinates that all the employees of the Company are at liberty to exercise their franchise as they please.' The LCDR was drawn further into politics by the events of 1873 when some Railway Amalgamation Bills were thrown out by Parliament and the Railway & Canal Traffic Act passed by the Liberal Government. This last was strongly opposed by Watkin although he was himself a Liberal; indeed after 1868 Watkin opposed every Liberal effort to increase Government regulation of the railways.[3] Both Watkin's SER and the LCDR joined the Railway Association, a form of pressure group, as a result of the events of 1873.

Watkin was already an M.P. when he became Chairman of the SER in 1866, a post which he combined with that of General Manager after 1873. Such close involvement with politics was not so customary on the LCDR although Hodgkinson, Chairman from 1867 to 1873, was a Liberal M.P. However in 1873 Forbes, the Managing Director of the LCDR, decided to stand as a Liberal in the traditionally Conservative Dover constituency; this provoked a furious row, since his standing as an M.P. for a town so intimately dependent on the LCDR was seen as unfairly influential. The *Railway Times* was predictably sarcastic, commenting in September 1873:

> 'Although we are quite sensible of Mr Forbes' high estimate of his own gigantic intellect and physical prowess of endurance, we confess that we experienced some slight degree of astonishment when we read his address to the electors of Dover.'

Many others were angry about Forbes' candidature and an irate LCDR shareholder wrote to the *Railway Times* to express disgust:

> 'I think it most inconvenient and detrimental to the interests of the public and the LCDR, that our managing director, who has the absolute control over all the officers and men in the service of the company, should seek to be the member for Dover, where the influence of the company is so great.'[4]

In the event Forbes failed to win election but at least he had the compensation of knowing that a motion put at a General Meeting, censuring his involvement in party politics, was defeated also. However the controversy of 1873 seems to have dissuaded him from any further involvement; after Hodgkinson's retirement in 1874 Forbes combined the Chairmanship with his previous post of Managing Director, so that there was no 'political interest' at the top of the LCDR — unlike in the SER.

In 1885-86 the Liberal Party split on the issue of Home Rule for Ireland and a number of Liberal M.P.s with railway interests followed Joseph Chamberlain into the Liberal-Unionists and a closer relationship with the Conservative Party. These M.P.s included Watkin, and the prevailing trend towards Conservatism was reflected in the M.P.s who dominated LCDR affairs in the last decade of its existence as an independent concern. Wyndham, M.P. for Dover, and Douglas were both extremely able men and were particularly important in that as Kent residents they maintained local interests on the LCDR Board. Akers Douglas was especially notable due to his close involvement with the Maidstone & Ashford and the Shortlands & Nunhead; he was the most active of the two. After the formation of the SE&CR both men remained on the LCDR Board, their managerial responsibilities being much reduced of course. For a few halcyon years, from 1902 to 1905, the LCDR had two Cabinet ministers sitting on its Board: Aretas Akers Douglas as Home Secretary and George Wyndham as Chief Secretary for Ireland. In this respect at least the LCDR must have been virtually unique.

v) The Company's Management

The management structure of the East Kent Railway was rather nebulous, as its Board Minutes indicate. Many decisions seem to have been taken personally by Lord Sondes, a local aristocrat whose knowledge of railways must have been limited. Inexperienced local men like Sondes and the elder Lushington were easy prey for the schemes of contractors like Peto, and it was significant that Sondes was the first man to be ousted in the 1866 recriminations.

Although Finnigan of the SER was appointed Traffic Manager in 1858 there was no experienced General Manager to give advice to the Board until the arrival of Forbes in 1861. Forbes had had a meteoric rise during his twenty years in railway management and was reportedly attracted to the LCDR by a promise of 1% commission on increased receipts; thus even a modest traffic growth, which would automatically derive from suburban development anyway, would yield rich rewards.

Forbes' stature seems to have increased during the 1866 crisis which cleared a lot of his superiors on the Board out of the way. Forbes built up considerable popularity at General Meetings because of his wit, though he had to endure the constant sneers of the *Railway Times*. He nearly became Chairman in 1871 when he won an election by 118 votes to 108, but complaints from the mortgage directors meant that he did not achieve the ultimate office until February 1874. At that time, looking back on his past position with the LCDR, he commented that 'the position of manager of this company from 1863 to 1873 has not been a bed of roses.'[5]

191

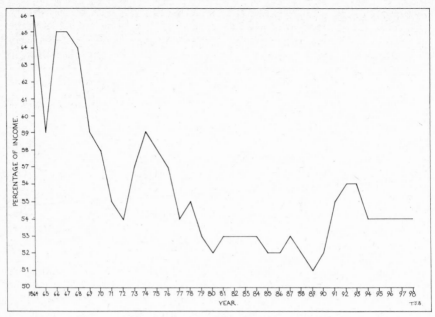

Fig. 1: Working Expenses as percentage of income, 1864-98.

Of course the *Railway Times* was not convinced about his suitability for the job. It felt that he was pleasant to excess, and suspected that his good humour was all a front:

> 'He deals with his constituents [shareholders] as he might be expected to do with weak-minded children or idiots, and diverts their attention from matters in which their interests are involved but which it might be inconvenient for him to have mooted, by platitudes, commonplaces, and truisms plentifully interlaid with self-praise.'[6]

Forbes was effectively put out to grass when the LCDR merged with the SER and died of pneumonia in 1904. In the railway press he was awarded a distinctly uncomplimentary epitaph: 'Stagnation was his motto in an age of progress.' But was this really fair?

A judgement of a railway manager must depend upon the efficiency with which his Railway Company is run. Pure traffic receipts are not enough: natural population growth would be sufficient to show a steady increase in this respect. Thus in the first half of 1874 the LCDR's traffic receipts were £416,112 and in the first half of 1898 they were £762,381; a steady increase at least partially accounted for by the expansion of the LCDR system between those two dates which mark the perimeters of Forbes' period of greatest influence. The key really lies in the efficiency of the Company in turning traffic receipts into profit, and the best judgement of this can be made by studying the percentage

192

of traffic receipts absorbed by working expenses; thus the higher the percentage, the lower the LCDR's efficiency at turning traffic into profit. In 1872 the percentage absorbed in this way was a creditable 54.15%, being a good recovery from the 65.33% achieved in the dark days of 1867. In 1875, Forbes' first full year as General Manager and Chairman, this had slipped back to 57.99%. The best figures Forbes ever achieved were during the 1880s when the figures were consistently between 51.47% (the best ever, in 1889) and 53.28%. However the early 1890s were marked by a depression in traffic and the ratio fell to 56.17% in 1892. The last year of independence, 1898, produced a figure of 54.39% — hardly different to that of 1872.

Thus a picture emerges of a Company that secured a degree of success only to squander much of it. At least part of the blame for this must rest on Forbes, for the majority of new lines that was built under his control were unlikely to be as profitable as those he inherited in 1874: the Maidstone & Ashford is a good example of this. The annual dividends emphasise this, for they rose from £1-8-6d (June 1874) to £4-5-0d in June 1882. They then stagnated at under £4-0-0d again, except for an interlude in 1890-91, until dividends of £4-10-0d were paid steadily in 1896 to 1898. Generally speaking the LCDR proved to be a classic example of a railway company over-expanding to a point where declining efficiency was reached; doubtless competition with the SER was the reason for this.

Perhaps it should be left to the obituarist from the *Railway Times* of 9th April 1904 to assess Forbes' contribution to the art of railway management:

'The Chatham under his administration became a byword and a reproach in the railway world and a standing joke with the general public. Eventually however, he foisted it upon the South Eastern Company in derelict condition, as a result of a bargain which would have been impossible had he been dealing with men of ordinary business capacity. From the Chatham shareholders' standpoint, the amalgamation stood decidedly to his credit, and by bringing it about on such one-sided terms he atoned in slight measure for the deplorable mess into which he had gradually got the Company.'

vi) The Progress of the Company
The working profits diagram shows the excess, or lack of it, of traffic receipts over working expenses for each natural year from 1859 to 1898. These figures only reveal the state of traffic on the line and of course say nothing about the vast sums that were absorbed by interest repayments during the earlier part of the period. Of particular interest is the very poor performance of the LCDR in the early 1890s, when it experienced a reversal in the general trend of increasing profits; the impact of this was made to seem even more dramatic by a result for 1889 which was excellent, partly as a consequence of Paris Exhibition traffic. Thus if a 'Great Depression' really did occur as some historians have suggested for this time, then for the LCDR it only actually bit during the period 1890-93.

Another important factor in the Company's profitability can be discerned by breaking these figures down into their half-yearly components. The second

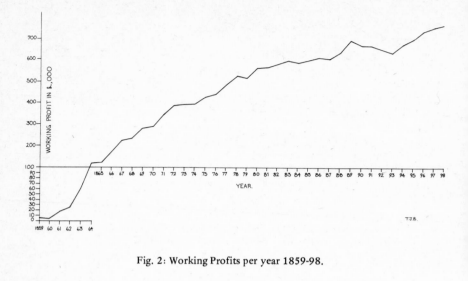

Fig. 2: Working Profits per year 1859-98.

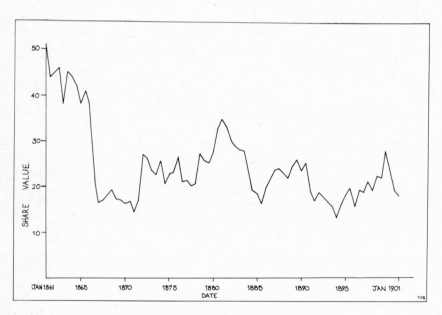

Fig. 3: LCDR Ordinary Share price index 1861-1901.

194

half of the year absorbed the summer traffic and invariably revealed much greater profit than the preceding half year. The most dramatic example of this was in 1861, when the LCDR actually made a working *loss* (at a time when interest charges were massive!) on the first half of £1,201 but a profit of £18,330 on the second half. Generally profits were 25%-35% greater in the second half of the year throughout the Company's history, the figures for 1898 being £321,038 and £442,216 respectively. This trend is well reflected in what can be termed the 'efficiency' of the Company, its ability to keep the amount of receipts absorbed by working costs as low as possible. The *Railway Times* generally reckoned about 54% to be a reasonable target level, but severe first half difficulties often prevented the LCDR from achieving this. Thus in the first half of 1864 80% of receipts were absorbed in working expenses whereas in the second half it was only 52.3%; so throughout the winter the LCDR had to meet severe interest and debenture repayments as well as meeting infrastructure maintenance costs out of very limited profits. A principal contributory factor was that the Company had no regular freight flow to balance the seasonal passenger traffic, and of course skilled train staff could hardly be employed on a seasonal basis; the largest flow of freight was in coal, brought onto the LCDR from other systems — this reached over a million tons a year in 1891.

The LCDR failed to pay any dividend at all until June 1871. The difficulties of the 1890s are again reflected in the dividend figures.

Table Three shows the changing value of LCDR Ordinary shares. The most obvious feature of this is the collapse of the shares between 1863 and 1866; despite the apparent progress of the Company made under Forbes, values in the mid-1890s were hardly an improvement on those of 1866-67. Several of the apparent peaks in share values can be attributed to the stories of amalgamation, fact or fiction, that regularly circulated with respect to the LCDR and SER. Thus the peaks of 1863, 1868, 1876, 1878, 1890 and 1898 all occurred at times when amalgamation was in the air and this lends credence to the *Railway Times* theory that jobbers and stock exchange interests actively encouraged the rumours. The peak of 1881 is explained by a general belief that the LCDR was gaining the upper hand in its struggle with the SER.

vii) Accidents
The principal fatal traffic accidents that occurred on the LCDR were as follows:

9th May 1862 — Ospringe.	*Amethyst* was derailed whilst working a down express. Some vehicles fell off the embankment and three were killed. Bad track was blamed.
13th November 1862 — Teynham.	The driver of *Dawn*, heading the 7.30am Victoria to Dover, was killed in a derailment.
26th September 1864 — Penge.	*Snowdrop*, heading the 7.30am Victoria to Dover, was derailed and the fireman killed.

195

10th January 1866 — Beckenham.	After heavy storms a bridge was washed away and *Tacita*, hauling a heavy goods train, plunged into the void. The fireman was killed.
17th February 1878 — Canterbury.	A points mistake caused the derailment and the death of the man driving engine No. 49.
31st August 1878 — Sittingbourne.	No. 137 on a Ramsgate to London train collided with badly shunted wagons and five were killed, forty injured. The yard foreman was sentenced to three years in prison for manslaughter.
21st May 1881 — Crystal Palace.	Wheels shifting on their axle caused a derailment in which one person was killed and eleven injured.
3rd September 1891 — Ramsgate Harbour	An empty stock working crashed through buffers and a passer-by was killed.
1st August 1895 — Herne Bay.	Passenger and freight trains were in collision. A mixture of scalding water, oil and steam was sprayed into a passenger compartment from one of the damaged locomotives with the result that one person died and two were badly injured.

In terms of loss of life, the most serious incident to occur in the lifetime of the LCDR was the Ivy Bridge disaster near Bromley; this is described in Chapter Three but was not a traffic accident since no train was involved.

CHAPTER FIFTEEN

United at Last: The South Eastern
& Chatham Managing Committee

The 'South Eastern & Chatham Railways' Managing Committee' began operating on 1st January 1899, though it did not receive its Act of Parliament until August. The SE&CR was therefore not really a Railway Company as such but a committee by which two separate railway companies jointly administered their affairs. Both the SER and the LCDR continued to exist, sharing the costs and the receipts of the joint operation on a basis of 59% and 41% respectively. This division applied to all matters, so that when the roof of the SER's Charing Cross station collapsed in December 1905 the LCDR provided 41% of the repair costs. Shareholders still held their shares in SER or LCDR stock, there being no such thing as an SE&CR share. However it was the Managing Committee that supervised the day to day running of the two systems under the Chairmanship of H. Cosmo Bonsor.

One of the immediate problems that the SE&CR had to tackle was the duplicating routes and occasional inconvenient separation of lines that forty years of competition had left behind. Some improvements were obvious and made immediately — none more so than the closure of the LCDR station in Ashford and the diversion of all its passenger services to the SER station with effect from 1st January 1899. Another obvious case for improvement could be found just east of Bickley station, where the LCDR's main line passed beneath that of the SER with no physical connection between the two. The consequent SE&CR plan for the Chislehurst loops was quickly put into effect — starting with the opening of a loop from Bickley towards Orpington in 1902; down trains started to use this from 8th September and up trains from 14th September. Slightly more ambitious were the loops connecting Chislehurst, on the SER, with St. Mary Cray and these did not open until 19th June 1904.

However, after this progress was only slow and in 1908 Bonsor complained that the Act sanctioning the working union had been responsible for slowing down the rate of rationalisation; Kent residents had enjoyed the multitude of lines and stations that competition had brought them and were reluctant to see their services curtailed.

In 1908 Rochester Bridge station was rebuilt in a grand and imposing style; undoubtedly this was a sop to local opinion before the SE&CR introduced its plan to reorganise in the Rochester and Chatham area. Fundamental to this was the closure of the unpopular and inconvenient Chatham Central branch, which was achieved from 1st October 1911. Services on the former SER branch were effectively diverted to run over the LCDR route to Chatham, and to allow for this Rochester station was rebuilt in 1911 with four tracks and two island

197

The celebration of the opening of the Sheppey Light Railway in 1901; notice how the group is exclusively male.

198

The remains of Queenborough Pier station in 1900 after it had been destroyed by fire. The SER rebuilt the pier but it remained in first-rank use only until 1911.

platforms. This apparently radical reorganisation of the Medway towns lines was in fact only the first stage in a process of change that was continued in the 1920s by the Southern Railway.

A number of other SE&CR improvement projects were in hand in 1914 when they were interrupted by the outbreak of the Great War. These are discussed in more detail below, but included rationalisation in the Thanet area and the improvement of continental facilities at Dover by the construction of a new station close to Admiralty Pier.

A number of developments during the SE&CR era affected the Sheppey area. In 1899 the Sheppey Light Railway had been authorised to construct a line from Queenborough to Leysdown at a cost of £52,000 and this opened on 1st August 1901. The purpose of this line was to encourage the development of eastern Sheppey for tourism. The SE&CR leased this line from its inception and in 1905 took it over completely, though circumstances proved this to be a mistake. The original intermediate stations were Sheerness East, Minster on Sea and Eastchurch, to which East Minster on Sea was added in 1902. In 1905 the line became the subject of an experiment with railmotors and two extra stations, or 'halts', were added at Brambledown and Harty Road in March of that year. The railmotors only lasted until 1912, after which conventional tank locomotives fulfilled the line's locomotive needs. Later efforts by the Southern Railway also met with only muted response from the public so that normal services ceased on quite an early date for Kent branch lines — 2nd December 1950.

The Harbour, Dover

General view of Dover Harbour about 1910. The bridge carrying the Prince of Wales Pier branch across the entrance to Wellington Dock can be seen on the right, with the pier itself in the background. (Author's collection)

Also concerning the Sheppey area was the problem of the Kingsferry bridge across the Swale. The Sheerness branch was closed from 2nd February to 11th February 1899 because of difficulties with this, and eventually the SE&CR decided that a replacement was necessary. In 1904 a new bridge of the 'Scherzer rolling lift bridge' type was installed at a cost of £50,000; this was the second of three bridges used by trains on the Sheerness branch.

However the Sheerness branch suffered a reduction in its importance from 1st May 1911 when the Queenborough to Flushing night service was transferred to run from Folkestone instead. This was a deliberate effort to combat competition by the Great Eastern Railway, which was operating an effective service from Parkeston Quay in Essex.

As has been mentioned already, by the late 1800s the LCDR was facing competition on its inner suburban services from underground railways and the electric tram. This was no less of a problem for the SE&CR, who in 1903 obtained preliminary powers to operate trains by electric traction. Little progress was made with the possibility for some time, possibly because of a lack of capital, although from 1909 the SE&CR revealed its intentions by limiting its investment in new suburban stock. It decided to form the South Eastern & Chatham Construction and Power Company to finance the electrification and to generate the necessary power from an electricity plant to be set up at Angerstein's Wharf on the River Thames, but this was another instance of a plan shelved because of the outbreak of war.

Competition from other modes of transport had severely curtailed SE&CR services by the time war broke out and many other services were withdrawn during the course of the war. The earliest victim was the station at Borough Road, which closed on 1st April 1907. The through services via Farringdon and to Snow Hill also suffered a reduction in popularity. Through services to and from the Great Northern Railway ceased in 1907 and those in connection with the Midland Railway went the same way in 1908. In the immediate pre-war years the areas in greatest danger included the local stations on both main routes north and east of Herne Hill and the Greenwich Park branch which, as far as the SE&CR was concerned, was a duplicate line of little real value anyway. The Victoria to Ludgate service was one example of a line where traffic was being abstracted at an alarming rate.

The following table indicates the extent of the decline, though some of the reduction of traffic on the Greenwich branch stations might perhaps have been a natural consequence of the amalgamation in any case:[1]

Station	Traffic Receipts	
	1905	1914
Camberwell New Road	£3,800	£700
Walworth Road	£6,300	£2,100
Lewisham Road	£3,752	£742
Blackheath Hill	£1,921	£372
Greenwich Park	£3,671	£754

Victoria Station, London.

The facade of Victoria station as rebuilt by the SE&CR. This postcard photograph has been modernised by its publishers using the simple technique of drawing in motor vehicles in place of horse buses.

(A. Riley)

In 1918 the SE&CR appointed Alfred Raworth as its electrical engineer and he investigated various possible solutions to the problem, travelling to America in the course of his research. In September 1919 he produced a report which made specific proposals, dividing the areas to be covered into two zones, both of which contained former LCDR lines:

Zone 'A' bounded by Croydon, Addiscombe, Orpington and Dartford, which included the LCDR lines out as far as Bickley;

Zone 'B' bounded by Tattenham Corner, Dorking, Caterham, Tonbridge and Gillingham, would have included the ex-LCDR main line out as far as the last-named station.

On this occasion the electrification would have been partially financed by a Treasury loan of £5,000,000, but there was some delay over proposals for the supply of electricity and in the event the SE&CR's plans were shelved when Government proposals for the reorganisation of the railway system became known.

Whilst major improvements such as this were under discussion, the SE&CR continued with a policy of piecemeal improvement. Examples of this were the rebuilding of Rochester Bridge station in a grand and imposing style in 1908, and the rebuilding of Whitstable station at a new site in accordance with the town's direction of growth.

The likelihood of there being a concealed coalfield under much of Kent had been discussed for many years. The early railway visionary, William James, had brought himself to financial ruin during the early nineteenth century in searching for it without success. In the early twentieth century interest was renewed and in about 1912 various financial interests came together to exploit the coal reserves that had been discovered. One of the first sites to be successfully developed was Snowdown, where a colliery was producing coal by 1913;[2] this was one of the more successful sites, remaining in production for over sixty years. The colliery was very close to the former LCDR main line, on the down side, so it was easily served by a network of sidings. Snowdown Colliery was less convenient for miners since it was in the middle of thinly-populated countryside; to solve this problem, Snowdown & Nonington Halt was opened in 1914. Eventually a mining village was built at Aylesham, where the Southern Railway opened a halt on 1st July 1928.

Stonehall & Lydden Halt, just south of Lydden Tunnel, was also opened in 1914 to serve a colliery — this time the one at Lydden. This, like many of the East Kent coalfield borings, was an economic failure and traffic to the new halt failed to develop; it closed in 1954, the only station on the line between Faversham and Dover Priory ever to do so.

Not all the Kent coalfield lay so conveniently close to the established railway network. To exploit this, the East Kent Light Railway built a surprisingly complex network of lines in the area bounded by Shepherdswell and Sandwich between 1911 and 1931. This Company established a junction with the former LCDR main line at Shepherdswell, to which point it delivered a steady flow of coal from Tilmanstone Colliery for many years.

An SE&CR boat train connecting with the 'Deutschland' on the Prince of Wales Pier branch at Dover; it is shown crossing the swing bridge at the entrance to Wellington Dock.

(E. Course collection)

An SE&CR 'down' express heading eastwards from Shortlands in about 1910, hauled by 4-4-0 no. 731.

(E. Course collection)

The LCDR had always had the public image of a Railway Company held together by string, an image characterised for many years by its nickname of the 'London, Smash 'em and Turn Over.' Nowhere had this image been more apparent than at Victoria, where the Company's main station buildings had been hidden down a sidestreet and a row of wooden huts left to provide the frontage that first greeted nervous 'departure' passengers. By 1907 the role of Victoria was beginning to change as the SE&CR developed it into their first-choice Continental traffic centre and the local traffic declined. Services to the Great Northern Railway vanished from 1st October 1907 and those to the Midland Railway went in June 1908; Great Western and London & North Western services followed shortly after, in 1915 and 1917 respectively. All this was due to changing transport patterns within and through London, but it left Victoria with spare capacity that was not enjoyed at Charing Cross. In transforming Victoria into a prestigious Continental terminal, the SE&CR swept away the wooden huts in 1907 and during 1908 replaced them with a handsome four-storey stone block with a graceful archway over the carriage road.[3] These works were completed by the time the First World War broke out, during which Victoria was extremely busy with regular departures of troop trains to the Channel ports starting in November 1914.

Ludgate Hill was also rebuilt by the SE&CR in 1910-12, again taking note of changes in the public's travelling habits. The main-line platforms were removed, being totally unnecessary with Holborn Viaduct so close, and the suburban platform enlarged. But this rebuilding failed to have the desired effect, the station being killed off by a combination of trams, underground trains and service reductions during World War One. In its rebuilt state it survived in use until 1929; ultimately its position in a spot neither convenient for much of the City nor for any of the West End was probably responsible for its demise.

The outbreak of the Great War in August 1914 brought the heaviest traffic ever to operate on the former LCDR tracks. Unlike in the Second World War, Britain maintained an Army on the Continent throughout the First War, thus forcing extra troop and supply trains onto already crowded tracks.

The vessels of the former LCDR fleet were much involved in the fighting. In 1914 the *Queen* rescued 2,300 people after the *Admiral Ganteaume* had been torpedoed whilst the *Calais* was torpedoed in 1916; *Le Nord* gained revenge by ramming and sinking a U-boat. *Engadine* somehow found its way into the Battle of Jutland and the cargo boat *Hythe* was used in the Dardenelles campaign, where it was lost in October 1915. *Queen*, built for the SE&CR in 1902, was also sunk by a U-boat in 1916.

For the ordinary passenger the Great War resulted in severe curtailment of services which progressively worsened as the War lengthened. The most immediate alterations came at Dover, where the SE&CR was caught in the midst of a huge development programme. In 1904-5 the Company had experimented with running trains to the Prince of Wales Pier, which for a time was used as a port of call by transatlantic liners like the S.S. *Deutschland*. Of far more enduring significance was the SE&CR's decision to redevelop the area on the seaward side of Admiralty Pier and to expand that facility into a new Marine station involving

205

The SS 'Deutschland' calling at Prince of Wales Pier, Dover, circa 1904. (A. Riley collection)

Admiralty Pier circa 1912 whilst extension works were going on in the Harbour.
(E. Baldock collection)

11¾ acres of reclamation. By August 1914 some £300,000 had already been spent, after which the new station was rapidly forced into a state of readiness for handling the Army traffic; it opened in December 1914, but not for public use, and was used for ambulance trains from 2nd January 1915. Public traffic to Dover Marine did not commence until 18th January 1919.

The whole coastal area at Dover became closed to the public, affecting the former SER station at Dover Town which closed from 14th October 1914; it was subsequently used for stabling stock. Sheerness was also quickly affected, all services to Sheerness-on-Sea being diverted to Sheerness Dockyard from 8th November 1914.

On 15th November 1914 Forbes must have turned in his grave, for all Continental services for the public were diverted to Folkestone. In the case of the Belgian services this was rather an academic decision, since the Germans had occupied Ostend on 15th October. All civil traffic via Folkestone was stopped from 29th November 1915.

These emergency alterations were followed up by a programme of service cuts made for reasons of economy. The first of these was the withdrawal of the local service along the old West End of London & Crystal Palace line between Beckenham Junction and Crystal Palace Low Level; this withdrawal, from 1st December 1915, very nearly became permanent closure.

Extra pressure was placed upon the former LCDR main line when a catastrophic landslide closed the former SER line at Folkestone Warren between Dover and Folkestone. This occurred on 19th December 1915 and could not have happened at a worse place; it was possibly an event that bore out the wisdom of the Duke of Wellington, who had argued in the 1840s and 1850s that a second route to Dover was a military necessity. The former SER route remained closed until 11th August 1919, so all Dover traffic had to be funnelled through Priory station and Kearnsey. To relieve the pressure on the ex-LCDR line, a number of new connections were proposed including a west to south spur where the former SER and LCDR lines crossed just outside Canterbury. This was never built, but a north to east spur was opened at the same spot in 1918 to allow for the flow of ammunition traffic from Faversham to the temporary port at Richborough. This spur remained in regular use only until 1920.[4]

On 3rd April 1916 a large number of service cuts were made, mostly in the suburban area. The Victoria to Holborn service was withdrawn completely, involving the closure of stations at Walworth Road and Camberwell New Road; also withdrawn were the through services to the Metropolitan Railway, leaving only a residual service to Holborn Viaduct Low Level on this route — which itself ceased from 1st June 1916. Also from 3rd April 1916, the service on the Greenwich Park branch was reduced to peak hours only with no trains on Sundays.

1st January 1917 was a black day for many of the LCDR minor lines that had duplicated SER routes or failed to develop their traffic. In the interests of war economies, the SE&CR completely withdrew passenger services from the Crystal Palace, Greenwich Park and Sevenoaks branches; Rochester Bridge station also closed from the same date, never to reopen. Another economy was

The 'new image' on the Channel crossing: SE&CR ferry 'Maid of Orleans', one of the new generation of screw-driven vessels, introduced in the early 1900s that quickly eclipsed the old paddlesteamers operated by the LCDR. (Author's collection)

the withdrawal of Sunday services on certain lines, with the Catford Loop and Gravesend West Street branch being immediately affected. Ludgate Hill and St. Paul's also lost all Sunday services.

With the end of the Great War in November 1918, services returned to normal only slowly. Dover Marine opened its doors to the general public for the first time on 18th January 1919, from which date Dover to Ostend ferry services resumed. The various Paris routes operated by the SE&CR returned to normal traffic from 3rd February 1919 as well.

From 1st March 1919 the Crystal Palace High Level branch reopened and the Sevenoaks branch regained its weekday service. However some of the war-time economies proved to be more permanent in their effects: the Beckenham Junction to Crystal Palace line remained closed until 1929 and the major part of the Greenwich Park branch never saw passenger trains again, as was also the case with Rochester Bridge station.

The Great War left many of Britain's railway companies financially exhausted and unable to cope with the huge programme of reconstruction that five years of overuse had burdened them with. Accordingly, in June 1920 the Government published a White Paper on the reorganisation of railways, which suggested the formation of a few large companies by grouping together the old concerns. These proposals were authorised by the Railways Act of 19th August 1921. As part of this Act both the South Eastern Railway and the London, Chatham & Dover Railway — both of which still had a separate legal existence — were to become part of the Southern Railway group from 1st January 1923; the other two principal companies within this group were the London, Brighton & South Coast Railway and the London & South Western Railway.

One of the last acts of any significance by the SE&CR was the withdrawal of passenger services over the spur between Loughborough Junction and Canterbury Road Junction from 1st April 1921. This was one of a number of spurs in the area that had been affected either by the declining use of the railway or by the war economies and which never recovered — the spur between Factory Junction and Latchmere Junction (closed to passengers 5th June 1916) being an example of war economies. The problem did not affect only the ex-LCDR lines, for the Blackfriars spur built by the SER had also lost its passengers from 1st May 1907. The changing pattern of suburban travel was a problem that was passed on to the Southern Railway, which responded in aggressive fashion by a thorough policy of electrification whilst concentrating on the outer suburban commuter rather than the inner city. Thus it was that within a few years the patterns and habits of SE&CR life disappeared.

A wartime alteration was reversed from 2nd January 1922, when Sheerness-on-Sea was reopened and all passenger trains diverted there from Dockyard, which closed.

CHAPTER SIXTEEN

Aftermath

The London, Chatham & Dover Railway effectively ceased to exist from 1st January 1923 and it is not the intention of this book to cover recent events in great detail, but more to look at how subsequent developments have shaped the 'heritage' of the LCDR.

The first Board meeting of the new Southern Railway was held on 4th January 1923. This Board contained three representatives from LCDR interests, compared to five for the SER, five for the LBSCR and eight for the LSWR. One of the LCDR Board members was Sir Francis Dent, who had been General Manager of the SE&CR until 1920; old LCDR connections were maintained by James Staats Forbes' nephew, Sir William, who represented the LBSCR.

An immediate problem inherited by the new Company was yet another disaster that had befallen the Sheerness branch. On 17th December 1922 a Norwegian ship had collided with the Kingsferry Bridge, rendering it completely unserviceable. A temporary ferry service was instituted and trains terminated at halts established at either end of the bridge — Kings Ferry Bridge Halt North and South respectively; this arrangement was rushed into operation by the SE&CR from 27th December, with there also being a ferry connection from Port Victoria. It was left to the Southern Railway to repair the damage, which it did in time for passenger services to recommence on 1st November 1923. That date marked the end for the North Halt, but that on the south side remained and survived to be renamed Swale from 1st July 1929. This halt was resited on 10th April 1960, when British Railways opened the third Kingsferry Bridge and realigned the rail approaches.

Although the SE&CR had made various piecemeal attempts to weld together two virtually separate systems, it had made very little progress in overcoming the more major problems such as in the Thanet area. A plan had existed to make improvements, but had only progressed as far as the construction of two bridges when war intervened in 1914. In October 1923 the Southern Railway Board considered the issue and devised a £400,000 scheme to construct a new link line at Ramsgate and close various appendages of the old SER and LCDR networks. This plan was authorised by the Ministry of Transport on 4th March 1925. The principal feature of this plan was a new line from a point just west of Ramsgate Town station, round the north side of the resort, joining up with the former LCDR line at a point just north of its Ramsgate tunnel. This line and a new station at Ramsgate opened on 2nd July 1926, from which date the Ramsgate Harbour line closed completely (though it was later reused for a private miniature railway) and the former SER line between Ramsgate and

The railways of Ramsgate in the midst of transformation; a Southern Railway train is descending the line into Ramsgate Harbour station whilst construction of the new Dumpton Park curve is well advanced — probably in 1925.   (Southern Railway Magazine)

Margate Sands closed to passengers. There was one new intermediate station, Dumpton Park, which did not open until 19th July 1926.

This was certainly a thorough rationalisation of an area that had once seen considerable competition. It was, however, far from a satisfactory outcome, since the new Ramsgate station was extremely remote from the beach or the harbour. The old LCDR station still survives, though it is now in use as an amusement palace. The former LCDR station at Margate West was completely rebuilt in 1926 and new down-side buildings provided at Broadstairs. Freight trains seeking access to the old SER tracks at Margate did so by a spur which allowed the majority of that line southwards to Ramsgate to be closed completely.

The Southern Railway had also inherited a problem with the SE&CR's run-down inner suburban services. Its efforts to cut back further on these did not always meet with success, since the Metropolitan Railway sued the SR in 1923 for failure to reinstate services over the curve into Moorgate — along which the LCDR had guaranteed to run an intensive operation. The SR bought itself out of this with a £25,000 pay-off to the Metropolitan.

Between Victoria and Brixton the LCDR had had several stations which duplicated similar facilities of the LBSCR on its South London line; most of these had become useless with the service cuts of 1916, and what traffic remained could be handled by the former LBSCR facilities. Thus, late in 1923, the SR ordered the demolition of LCDR buildings at Battersea Park Road, Wandsworth Road and Clapham Road together with the Catford Loop platforms

211

at Brixton. By March 1924 Walworth Road and Camberwell New Road had also been removed, having been disused since 3rd April 1916. The stations between Brixton and Victoria had all closed to passengers from 1st April 1921. The demolition was not a very thorough job as part of the Clapham building is still standing in the mid-1980s.

The Great War had imposed a serious strain on the continental routes of the SE&CR, where a degree of rationalisation and investment was also needed. The SE&CR had started this with its programme of improvements at Victoria in the early 1900s, which culminated with the transfer of all continental trains to that terminus from 8th January 1920, with the exception of the Flushing service which followed suit the next year. However the SR wanted to increase both capacity and the weight of the trains it wanted to run, so a policy of rebuilding of underline bridges commenced. This extended from 1923 to 1927 and included the expenditure of £171,000 on bringing the former LCDR main line into correct order. The most important part of the work was the rearrangement of the Medway bridges at Rochester, with the LCDR tracks being slewed across onto the SER bridge by 1927; the former connection between the SER and LCDR networks had been to the east of the bridges after the SE&CR alterations of 1912 when the connection on the west side had been removed, so under the SR arrangement Rochester Bridge Junction was created on its present site. The old LCDR bridge was not demolished.

The Great War had also shown the value of diversionary routes for continental trains, with the result that £32,000 was spent on improving the Catford Loop to main-line standards and money also spent on constructing a new bridge across the Medway at Maidstone.

But the most important works were at Dover, where the SE&CR had already made considerable steps forward with its Dover Marine project. The SR spent £325,000 at Dover, principally featuring the rebuilding of Dover Priory station. Dover Harbour station was closed from 10th July 1927 and part of the Dover Town station, closed since 1914, demolished to allow double-track access to Dover Marine. Archcliffe Tunnel was removed and a new Motive Power Depot constructed on reclaimed land south of the old Town station, with the Priory MPD being closed as a result. New signalboxes were built at Archcliffe Junction and Hawkesbury Street Junction. Amidst all the changes, the Lord Warden Hotel remained strangely isolated and forgotten.

Plans for the development of Dover did not stop there. In 1932 the SR built a coal staithe on the eastern arm of the harbour, which was reached by the Prince of Wales Pier tramway along Marine Parade. Dover Harbour Board had grand plans to develop Dover as a major coal-exporting port in connection with the Kent coalfield, for which hopes were then high. In 1933 they planned a direct link to the eastern harbour from Kearnsey, a plan which would have involved 1½ miles of tunnel. It never materialised.

Another major SR reconstruction that affected former LCDR lines was in the Lewisham area. In July 1927 the SR received authorisation for the building of loops at Lewisham for a cost of £195,000; these were to allow direct access from Nunhead towards Hither Green, a major freight depot on the old SER main line.

By this route freight from the north, running via Farringdon, could gain access to Hither Green without using the Blackfriars spur and clogging up the tracks around London Bridge. Part of this plan involved rehabilitating some of the old Greenwich Park branch, which was in use for a few coal trains. Approximately one mile of this, to just beyond the former Lewisham Road, was restored but the rest of the branch closed and the bridge across the ex-SER lines removed. The construction of the Lewisham loops was completed by 7th July 1929.

As travel patterns changed, so stations opened and closed. A principal victim of this was the long-ailing Ludgate Hill, which finally deceased on 3rd March 1929. In rural areas a number of stations were opening, such as Aylesham Halt (1st July 1928) and Chestfield & Swalecliffe (6th July 1930). One new station that never opened was Lullingstone on the Sevenoaks line; nearly finished in 1939 it became a victim of the Second World War and planning restrictions which subsequently prevented the growth of housing in the area.

The Southern Railway is best remembered for its energetic pursual of an electrification policy. The first scheme to affect former LCDR lines to any great extent was the Victoria to Orpington via Penge East electrification, opened on 12th July 1925; this covered the former LCDR main line from Victoria out as far as Bickley, from where it used the new SE&CR curves onto the former SER main line into Orpington. The Crystal Palace High Level service was electrified from the same date, involving the closure of the Loughborough Junction platforms on the sharply curved spur to Cambria Road Junction — the new standard length electric trains would not fit cleanly into them. This scheme included the lines into Holborn Viaduct, so that both City and West End lines formerly owned by the LCDR were now electric. The line between Holborn Viaduct and Elephant & Castle was equipped with colour light signals from 21st March 1926, the first part of the LCDR system to be so treated.

Major changes were caused by the Victoria to Beckenham Junction via Crystal Palace Low Level electrification of 3rd March 1929, which replaced the old LBSCR electric overhead system between Victoria and Crystal Palace. This scheme basically covered the old LBSCR Crystal Palace line, but it also included what had formerly been LCDR territory to Beckenham Junction. The Crystal Palace to Beckenham Junction section had been deprived of its passenger services during the Great War, and their revival had to wait until the advent of this electrification scheme. Considerable improvements were necessary at Beckenham Junction, where two extra tracks were provided for the new electric service as far as Penge Junction where the Crystal Palace line diverged from the ex-LCDR main line. Various improvements like this at Beckenham Junction absorbed £105,300. From the same date, 3rd March 1929, electric trains began to run through from Holborn Viaduct to Tulse Hill using the short link from Herne Hill.

These various schemes were essentially inner-suburban in nature, but in the mid-1930s the Southern Railway began to consider expanding its electric network deeper into Kent. The first stage of this was an extension of the third-rail from Bickley to St. Mary Cray on 1st May 1934 but only a limited service was at first involved. However from 6th January 1935 a full electric service

Herne Bay in 1955, awaiting the transformation and reawakening that electrification
brought to the Kent Coast line.   (E. Course)

One of the least successful wayside stations in Kent, Hothfield Halt, photographed in
1955 four years before its closure. For once a station had failed to stimulate commercial
or residential development.   (E. Course)

running through from either Bickley or Chislehurst to Swanley and Sevenoaks Tubs Hill commenced. This was part of a £½ million scheme to electrify both routes to Sevenoaks in the hope that this would stimulate housing development and thus traffic; in fact housing development in areas like the Darent valley failed to get started before the outbreak of World War Two and the LCDR route to Sevenoaks, particularly beyond Swanley, has remained a backwater. One sign of the expected development was the new station constructed at Lullingstone, south of Eynsford, but this never opened.

A minor change that took place in preparation for the Sevenoaks electrification was the removal in 1933 of the old south curve at Otford. This had not seen any regular traffic since 1st July 1912 and since 1923 had only been used for stabling stock.

The final Southern Railway electrification project to affect the old LCDR routes was opened on 2nd July 1939, after which further progress was prevented by the outbreak of war. This final scheme principally involved extensions of electric working from Otford to Maidstone East and from Swanley to Gillingham; linking in with these was the electrification of the Gravesend to Maidstone West or Rochester line. This was a major advance and carried with it a number of wholesale improvements, foremost amongst which was the rebuilding of Swanley Junction to allow electric train sets to be joined and divided there. The old station had been constructed in the 'V' of the junction, so that Chatham and Maidstone line trains called at separate platforms to the east of the junction. In the rebuilding, Swanley station was moved to the west of the point at which the routes diverged, thus allowing Maidstone and Chatham trains to be joined and divided. The status of Gillingham was much increased by electrification since it became the terminus of electric services along both the ex-LCDR main line and the ex-SER North Kent line via Strood. Gillingham station had been completely rebuilt in 1932 with an island platform on the 'up' side and new buildings located on a bridge across the tracks on the pattern the LCDR had employed at Chatham and Bromley South. Thus little extra work needed to be done in 1939.

The former LCDR City stations were much affected by the process of electrification and much realignment of track, as at Holborn Viaduct in June 1932, was needed. St. Paul's was renamed Blackfriars from 1st February 1937. The Southern Railway's main achievement at Victoria was probably to knock a hole in the wall — so that the formerly separate SE&CR and LBSCR stations could function as one. This work was completed in 1925 but until 1938 there was still no running connection between the two halves of the station. In 1930 platform eight, for Continental arrivals, was provided with its own iron and glass canopy and some heated accommodation.

Although the Second World War again brought very heavy traffic to lines in the ex-LCDR area, disruption of services was more limited than in the First World War. The main exceptions to this were the Continental services, which were of course interrupted by the collapse of France in May 1940 and did not resume until 15th April 1946. The other major casualty was the Crystal Palace High Level branch, which closed from 22nd May 1944 until 4th March 1946.

215

A contemporary view of Chatham station from above Fort Pitt tunnel. The island platform layout and the former banana siding can still be traced

(Author)

One short piece of track was revived by the war. This was the spur at Canterbury which connected the former LCDR and SER lines. It was reopened in March 1941 and was last used during this period of its activity on 28th November 1946.[1] Also the old LCDR Medway bridge at Rochester was re-conditioned and adapted for possible road as well as rail traffic in the event of the other two bridges (one road, one rail) being bombed; it was never so used.

The lines and buildings of the former LCDR did suffer some damage from enemy action, particularly in London where a German bomber crashed into Victoria East damaging some of the buildings in September 1940. Holborn Viaduct suffered on the night of 26th October 1940 when the hotel was bombed, and this building's destruction was completed by fire in May 1941. In April 1941 a bomb severely damaged the City line at Southwark Street bridge. The most serious incident occurred on 16th August 1944 when a bridge between Rainham and Newington was destroyed by a flying bomb as a passenger train was approaching; eight people were killed. The ex-LCDR part of Victoria was also hit by a flying bomb in June 1944.

As with the First World War, the Second left Britain's railways exhausted. In 1947 the Labour Government decided on the nationalisation of all Britain's main-line railways and from 1st January 1948 British Railways came into control of the former LCDR territory.

Since 1948 there has been a gradual contraction of the former LCDR network, but this has only really affected its fringes and the main substance of the system has survived. It has not by any means been entirely a period of contraction, since British Railways have virtually completed the electrification of the entire route map.

The importance of Shepherdswell station was reduced by the withdrawal of all passenger services from the East Kent Light Railway from 1st November 1948. This system has been in steady decline since the war, as has the coalfield it served, though it was still considered important enough in 1959 for British Railways to electrify the Shepherdswell sidings on the overhead principle. Since 1951 Tilmanstone Colliery has provided most of the traffic on the rump of the EKLR as far north as Eythorne, though by the early 1980s the line had assumed a virtually derelict condition. The same could be said of Snowdown Colliery, which was also out of use by 1983.

British Railways' economies continued to nibble at the edges of the LCDR empire throughout the 1950s. Next to go, though it was never part of the LCDR of course, was the former Sheppey Light Railway between Queenborough and Leysdown which ceased operation on 4th December 1950.

In early 1953 catastrophic floods hit the east coast of England and cut the Thanet line near to where it crossed the Wantsum Channel. Because of this the old wartime curve at Canterbury was pressed into use for a third time, this time carrying Kent Coast expresses from 23rd February to 20th May 1953 whilst the main line was repaired. Having seen this brief flurry of use it relapsed into decay again and was finally lifted in 1955.

The Gravesend West Street branch closed to passengers on 3rd August 1953.

217

The two railway bridges across the Medway at Rochester in 1968, just before the LCDR bridge (on the left) was reconstructed as a road bridge. (Gillingham Library)

Modern-day Farningham Road: the signal box and the down sidings have gone but the main buildings, now overshadowed by the steel stockyard of the mid-1970s, have hardly changed in 125 years. (Author)

At its northern end it served a number of sidings so it remained in use for freight, though it was singled during 1959. The section between Southfleet and Gravesend closed completely on 25th March 1968, but Southfleet was used as a coal siding by the APCM Company and continued to receive coal trains from the Midlands until about 1976. The points at Fawkham Junction have now been disconnected but the track is still *in situ.*

Margate East station closed on 4th May 1953 and Stonehall & Lydden Halt on 5th April 1954. The next major closure was of the Crystal Palace High Level branch and its intermediate stations on 20th September 1954. The same year the Kingsferry Bridge was again the victim of a collision, following which services to Sheerness were again cut; it was decided however to take the opportunity to commence planning for a new bridge that would serve both road and rail more adequately. The resulting new, and third, bridge was opened in April 1960 and involved the reconstruction of the rail approaches and Swale Halt. Also affecting Sheppey, Queenborough Pier was demolished in 1956 having been out of use since 1933. Hothfield Halt, on the Ashford line, closed on 2nd November 1959.

While these contractions and alterations were taking place, BR was gearing itself for the biggest transformation the old LCDR network had ever witnessed; this was the Kent Coast electrification of 1959. The Southern Railway had brought the third rail as far east as Maidstone and Gillingham, but BR decided to extend this to the coast and include the former South Eastern lines as well. A considerable expansion in the service was envisaged and to cater for this the lines were widened in several places. On 26th April 1959 quadruple track was introduced between Rainham and Newington, virtually the only place between Swanley and Faversham where this was possible, with the track between Bickley and Swanley also being quadrupled on 1st June 1959 — this involved the re-building of St. Mary Cray station. The line between Sittingbourne Middle Junction and Swale Halt was doubled from 24th May 1959. However the loops at Chatham station had to be removed since the cramped layout could not otherwise allow for twelve-car trains; the station was left with a simple siding trailing in on the down side to cater for banana and newspaper traffic. Signalling was also reorganised with there being a number of new power boxes, the most important of which was that at Rochester.

On 15th June 1959 the new services commenced. The principal former LCDR lines to be affected were from Gillingham to Margate and Ramsgate, from Sitting-bourne to Sheerness, and from Faversham to Dover Marine. A new and intensive service was introduced which included some joining and splitting of trains at Faversham. Subsequent modifications included the closure of the steam motive power depot at Gillingham and the removal in 1960 of Canterbury East's overall roof; new platform canopies were brought from the ill-fated station at Lullingstone.

The line between Buckland Junction and Ramsgate was electrified on 2nd January 1961 and included the former Dover & Deal Joint line. Services on this section evolved to include through running via the SER main line, Dover Priory and Deal to Ramsgate; the loop from Kearnsey to Kearnsey Loop Junction was thus of declining importance and closed from 8th August 1972.

The culmination of over 140 years of railway development in Dover. In the foreground can be seen Hawkesbury Street Junction signal box, close to the site of the LCDR's Dover Harbour station. Along the seawall to the right of the picture was situated the SER Dover Town station; the same Company's imposing Lord Warden Hotel still survives, but now relegated to office duties. The later Marine station (now known as Western Docks) is hidden behind it

(Author)

Faversham retains its grace and is still a major junction, shown here with up Kent Coast and Dover trains connecting. (Author)

The last part of the Kent Coast electrification to affect the ex-LCDR network was that of the Maidstone East to Ashford section on 9th October 1961; making use of parts of the former SER system electrified earlier in 1961, this gave the possibility of a third route for boat trains between London and the Channel port. In fact the Maidstone and Ashford line has never really achieved this primary status though it regularly carries continental freight services to and from Dover; even its through electric services via Ashford to Ramsgate had declined to summer only by the 1984 timetable. A new signalbox at Maidstone East was opened on 8th April 1962.

As described elsewhere, there were major changes to the Rochester bridges in 1968 since the old LCDR structure, long-disused, was finally swept away to make room for a second road bridge making use of the same foundations; the last traces of Rochester Bridge station were removed during the same project.

On 23rd March 1969 the last booked train ran from Holborn Viaduct Low Level to Farringdon, though the 'widened lines' did not close officially until 3rd May 1971. Though the trackwork of this hugely expensive line has been removed the right of way has been preserved from violation by building; at the time of writing it seems a very real possibility that this unusual line beneath the heart of London might be revived to carry through trains between the northern and southern suburbs of London just as it did in the days of the LCDR and GNR.

In about 1970 the minor stations on the main line received some improvement.

221

Aylesham had been transformed from a halt to a station in 1968, and in the following years Newington, Teynham, Rainham, Meopham and Longfield were all either rebuilt or much improved.

The former LCDR has survived the problems of the 1970s remarkably well, especially in terms of passenger traffic where services have occasionally been reduced but rarely abolished. Even Chatham station, long one of the grimiest on BR, has benefited from a new bus interchange and a modern ticket office. Freight has also survived, though the wagonload traffic has of course virtually disappeared and, apart from Rochester Goods, it is hard to find a 'goods yard' anywhere. Sheerness Steel help to keep the Sheppey branch alive, despite the almost total demolition of Sheerness station by a train in February 1971, and a steel terminal was added at Farningham Road in about 1975.

The principal single change in the late 1970s and early 1980s has been the refurbishment of the 4-CEP and 4-BEP electric units introduced in 1959. 1984 produced some particularly interesting developments, notably with the reintroduction of Chatham line services through to Holborn Viaduct. There has also been serious discussion about the reopening of the Farringdon link line for passenger traffic.

The character and atmosphere of the LCDR is still surprisingly easy to find. Victoria (East), still strangely tranquil compared to the west side of the same station, is perhaps only comparable to Marylebone amongst the London stations for the strangely forgotten and rather rural garb that it wears for much of the day — broken only by the occasional Continental arrival. Now that the strange foreign carriages of the Night Ferry have vanished it is only foreign accents that reveal Victoria East to be the gateway to the Continent. Of the provincial stations, Faversham is still good evidence of the LCDR style at its best, but the mood of the Company can best be captured by visiting some of the stations that failed — Sole Street or Shepherdswell have hardly changed since the day they were built.

The heritage of forty years of rivalry also remains. At Canterbury it is still possible to use two totally separate stations to travel to London by two entirely independent routes and to arrive at two separate stations at the opposite ends of London's West End. At Ramsgate you can leave in opposite directions and end up in London either way, a situation which is also true at Dover Priory. But just try to get from Chatham to Ashford or Faversham to Sevenoaks... then you'll discover the true heritage of Watkin and Forbes.

Sources, Notes and Index

SOURCES & ACKNOWLEDGEMENTS

The following records of the LCDR and its subsidiaries were examined:

East Kent Railway and LCDR Board Minutes	RAIL	415
EKR and LCDR General Committee Minutes	RAIL	415
East Kent Railway Bill, Evidence 1857	RAIL	415
Metropolitan Extension Bill, Evidence 1860	RAIL	1066
EKR and LCDR General Meetings Minutes & Reports	RAIL	415
Herne Bay & Whitstable/Margate/Kent Coast Railway Board Minutes	RAIL	333
LCDR and Sittingbourne & Sheerness Joint Traffic Committee Minutes	RAIL	625
Sevenoaks, Maidstone & Tonbridge Board Minutes	RAIL	602
Maidstone & Ashford Railway Board Minutes	RAIL	602
Shortlands & Nunhead Railway Board Minutes	RAIL	614
Crystal Palace & South London Junction Railway Board Minutes	RAIL	164
Gravesend Railway Board Minutes	RAIL	221

Plus various timetables, staff and marine records of the Companies concerned.

Other primary sources included:

Maidstone Journal

Railway Times (of which Holroyd of the SER said in 1860, 'I would not publish anything in such a disreputable paper.')

Herapath's Railway Magazine

The Railway News (1904)

Secondary sources:

Of the books listed below, that by Bradley is the best single work on any aspect of the LCDR; so complete is it, that it was felt unnecessary to include detail of locomotives in the present work. The trilogy by Course is also to be recommended.

D.L. Bradley: *Locomotives of the LCDR*, RCTS, 1979.

R.H. Clark: *Southern Region Record*, Oakwood Press, 1966.

E. Course: *The Railways of Southern England*, Batsford, 1973-76.

A.J. Francis: *The Cement Industry*, D&C, 1977.

R. Goodsall: *Whitstable, Seasalter & Swalecliffe*, Canterbury, 1938.

D. Gould: *The SECR in the 1914-18 War*, Oakwood Press, 1981.

J. Hilton: *The South Eastern and Chatham Railway*, Hadlow, 1977.

A.A. Jackson: *London's Termini*, D&C, 1972.

J.B. Jones: *Annals of Dover*, 1916.

R.W. Kidner: *The North Kent Line*, Oakwood Press, 1977.

C.F. Klapper: *Sir Herbert Walker's Southern Railway*, Ian Allan, 1973.

R.M. Lyne: *The Gravesend Branch Railway*, 1975.

J. Marshall: *Dictionary of Railway Engineers*, D&C, 1978.

J.A.R. Pimlott: *The Englishman's Holiday,* Faber, 1947.
R.A. Williams: *The London & South Western Railway,* Volume II, D&C, 1973.

Acknowledgements
I am most grateful to my fellow members of the Railway & Canal Historical Society, particularly to Ron Thomas and Edwin Course. In collecting illustrations I was much aided by Mr A. Riley; all effort has been made to trace the origins of photographs and to acknowledge them where possible. Eric Baldock and the staff of Rochester and Gillingham libraries were also most helpful. I am especially grateful to Mr R.W. Kidner. Help was also given by F. Watson, C. Ewart and S. Blake. Timothy Blake spent many hours on the diagrams.

Braintree, 1984   AG

The following abbreviations are used: where the name of author only is given, details of books are given in the Sources & Acknowledgements section, otherwise:
MJ *Maidstone Journal*
RT *Railway Times*
HRM *Herapath's Railway Magazine*
Mins. EKR and LCDR Board Minutes
GCMins. LCDR General Committee Minutes

Chapter One

1. The SER shared tracks with the London & Brighton Railway to Reigate Junction, now Redhill, and opened to Dover in February 1844. For full explanation of this roundabout route, see Course, Vol. 1, Chapter 1.
2. Deposited plans, Rochester library.
3. House of Lords Evidence EKR Bill 1857; evidence given by Henry Rich, a Director of the SER.
4. Further details of the Gravesend & Rochester Railway are given in Chapter 7.
5. MJ 1848-49.
6. MJ 5th February 1850.
7. MJ 17th September 1850.
8. RT 4th January 1851.
9. RT 11th October 1851 and MJ 14th October 1851.
10. MJ 9th December 1851.
11. Quoted in the MJ, 7th June 1853.
12. House of Lords Evidence EKR Bill 1857, Henry Rich.
13. Quoted in the MJ, 12th April 1853.
14. House of Lords Evidence 1857 EKR Bill, 30th July 1857.
15. RT 3rd December 1853.
16. Harding letter and Fox details from Mins. 25th April 1855. Harding used the spelling 'Folkstone'.
17. RT 8th September 1855.
18. MJ 6th February 1858.

Chapter Two

1. RT 3rd December 1853.
2. Mins. 17th and 25th October 1853.
3. RT 30th June 1855.
4. Cubitt also designed the Canterbury station.
5. LCDR 1860 Bill Evidence, 23rd April 1860.
6. All quotations in this and preceding paragraph from 1860 Evidence.

7. Mins. 27th September 1861.
8. *Illustrated Police News* 15th August 1868; my thanks to Dover Library for this unusual source.
9. Victoria County History and 'Locational Changes in the Kentish Hop Industry', an essay in *Geographical Interpretations of Historical Sources* by Baker, Hamshire & Loughton, D&C, 1970.
10. Ibid. Much has been written about the annual 'Hop-pickers' Specials' which brought seasonal workers from London to the Kent hop-fields, numbering as many as 65,000 persons per year. This traffic mostly affected the SER stations in the Weald.

Chapter Three

1. HRM 20th August 1859.
2. RT 7th March 1857.
3. House of Lords Evidence, EKR 1857 Bill, 27th July 1857.
4. RT 3rd July 1857.
5. Mins. 29th October 1858.
6. 1860 Bill, evidence given by E. Eborall of SER and G. Holroyd of EKR.
7. HRM 20th August 1859.
8. RT 22nd January 1859.
9. General Committee Minutes, LCDR. 3rd September 1876.
10. *Hartley Parish Magazine,* September 1927.
11. Bradley, p. 4; HRM 10th November 1860.
12. Crays Company Mins., 1st November 1859.
13. GCMins., 25th September 1862.
14. A legacy of the Crays Company days was that SER carriages continued to work through to Bickley until 1876.
15. RT 15th October 1887.

Chapter Four

1. Quoted by RT with reference to the LCDR's rapid expansion, 19th Jan. 1861.
2. Bill of 1860 Evidence, RAIL 1066 1815.
3. RT 26th January 1861, but not mentioned in Mins.
4. Mins. 2nd August 1861.
5. Directors' Report to General Meeting, 27th February 1862.
6. Bill of 1860, Evidence for 24th February 1860.
7. Ibid., 19th July 1860.
8. Ibid., 23rd April 1860.
9. RT 8th April 1871.
10. RT 28th February 1863.
11. R. Williams: *The London & South Western Railway,* Volume II, p. 18.
12. GCMins. 11th January 1866.
13. Jackson, p. 200.
14. RT 7th August 1886.

Chapter Five

1. RT 28th August 1869.
2. Debentures are loans raised on the security of the Company's revenues and paying a set rate of interest. They carry priority over all preference and ordinary shares.
3. RT 2nd March 1861.
4. RT 19th June 1858.
5. Lloyd's Bonds were named after John Horatio Lloyd. The Railway Company gave a sealed covenant by which it undertook to pay its contractor at a future date, and the contractor could then use this to raise loans so that he could continue with the works. Interest was much higher than on debentures which were usually at 5-6%, Lloyd's Bonds more frequently being 10% or higher. The ultimate security for these Bonds was the Company's property, leading some commentators to see them as a mortgage on land.
6. RT 12th May 1866.
7. Preference shares give a fixed rate of dividend, having preference over ordinary shares.
8. RT 8th March 1863.
9. RT 14th April 1866.
10. Charles Dickens: *Little Dorrit*, p. 319 (Penguin edition).
11. *The Economist*, quoted in R. Joby: *The Railway Builders*, D&C, p. 115.
12. RT 20th October 1866.
13. RT 22nd December 1866.
14. Letter to the RT, 29th December 1866.
15. RT 21st May 1869.
16. RT 28th August 1869.

Chapter Six

1. The title is taken from the headline of a *Railway Times* article, November 1892.
2. RT 26th November 1859.
3. Letter quoted by Hilton, Volume III.
4. LCDR 1860 Bill, evidence for 20th April 1860, p. 389.
5. Mins. 17th April 1866.
6. Mins. 5th October 1872.
7. This was a reference to Channel Tunnel plans at the time and Government beliefs that it would be necessary to build costly defences to stop the tunnel being used for invasion.
8. RT 1st March 1890.
9. Mins. 7th March 1890.

Chapter Seven

1. MJ 28th January 1845 and 4th February 1845.
2. MJ 22nd January 1850.

3. Mins. 18th June 1858.
4. GCMins. 27th July 1859.
5. LCDR 1860 Bill, evidence given by Eborall, General Manager of the SER. Traffic figures from same source.
6. *Railway & Canal Historical Society Journal,* March 1982, p. 73. An Act of 30th July 1866 also allowed a Dockyard branch but this was not built.

Chapter Eight
1. For example, Clark.
2. GCMins. 6th December 1860.
3. Course, Volume I, p. 75.
4. RT 17th May 1862.
5. The author is indebted to R. Thomas for certain information. See also GCMins. 1863, and SER/LCDR Traffic Committee Minutes 1860-63.
6. LCDR Bill 1860, Evidence.

Chapter Nine
1. RT 7th February 1857.
2. Pimlott, p. 62 and p. 120.
3. Margate Railway Minutes, 17th August 1859.
4. Course, Volume I, p. 101.
5. Margate Railway Minutes, 1st August 1861.
6. Course, Volume I, p. 104.
7. Course refers to a photograph showing the existence of the building in 1872.
8. RT 28th January 1888.
9. Mins. 25th April 1862.
10. RT 12th April 1884.

Chapter Ten
1. CPSLJR Mins. 5th November 1862, 26th August 1863 and 24th February 1864. One of the tunnels was referred to as 'Paxton' tunnel after the engineer who designed the Crystal Palace.
2. CPSLJR Mins. 24th February 1864.
3. CPSLJR Mins. 7th September 1866.
4. Mins. 26th April 1867.
5. Board of Trade dates furnished by R. Thomas.
6. RT 13th February 1875.
7. RT 2nd May 1868.
8. RT 16th February 1884.

Chapter Eleven
1. Sevenoaks Railway Minutes, 21st February 1859.

2. Ibid., 23rd February 1860.
3. SMTR Mins., 28th February 1867.
4. Ibid., 19th August 1873.
5. Mins., 10th January 1877; no SMTR Minutes exist for 1873-79.
6. Maidstone & Ashford Railway Minutes, 13th January 1882.

Chapter Twelve
1. Gravesend Railway Minutes, 25th July 1881.
2. Lyne.
3. RT 14th July 1883.

Chapter Thirteen
1. RT 16th May 1857.
2. Jones. Figures show passengers by all ships on these routes.
3. RT 19th January 1861.
4. Williams, Volume II, p. 19.

Chapter Fourteen
1. R. Joby: *The Railway Builders*, D&C, p. 85.
2. *Railway News*, 9th April 1904.
3. G. Alderman: *The Railway Interest*, RKP.
4. RT 13th September 1873.
5. RT 1st March 1873.
6. RT 15th August 1874.

Chapter Fifteen
1. Klapper, p. 171.
2. Course, Volume III, p. 76.
3. Jackson, p. 302.
4. Course, Volume I.

Chapter Sixteen
1. Course, Volume I, p. 228.

INDEX

Where place names and station names are the same, no separate references are given. Most themes in the life of the LCDR are indexed under 'London, Chatham & Dover Railway' except for its relations with the SER which come under 'South Eastern Railway'. Formerly independent companies that later merged into the LCDR are indexed under the name of the parent company.

Meresborough Books

Proprietors Hamish and Barbara Mackay Miller
7 STATION ROAD, RAINHAM, GILLINGHAM, KENT. ME8 7RS
Telephone Medway (0634) 371591

We are a specialist publisher of books about Kent. Our books are available in most bookshops in the county, including our own at this address. Alternatively you may order direct, adding 10% for post (minimum 20p, orders over £20.00 post free). ISBN prefix 0 905270. Titles in print December 1984:

BYGONE KENT. A monthly journal on all aspects of Kent history founded October 1979. £1.20 per month. Annual Subscription £13.00. All back numbers available.

HARDBACKS

THE LONDON, CHATHAM & DOVER RAILWAY by Adrian Gray. A major study of the development of railways in Kent. ISBN 886. £7.95.

THE NATURAL HISTORY OF ROMNEY MARSH by Dr F.M. Firth, M.A., Ph.D. ISBN 789. £6.95.

O FAMOUS KENT by Eric Swain. The county of Kent in old prints. ISBN 738. £9.95.

KENT'S OWN by Robin J. Brooks. The history of 500 (County of Kent) Squadron of the R.A.A.F. ISBN 541. £5.95.

TWO HALVES OF A LIFE by Doctor Kary Pole. The autobiography of a Viennese doctor who escaped from the Nazis and established a new career in Kent. ISBN 509. £5.95.

SOUTH EAST BRITAIN: ETERNAL BATTLEGROUND by Gregory Blaxland. A military history. ISBN 444. £5.95.

THE WHITE HORSE AND THE KANGAROO by Clive W. Porter. A complete record of the cricket matches between Kent and the Australian touring teams. ISBN 312. £5.50.

KENT AIRFIELDS IN THE BATTLE OF BRITAIN by The Kent Aviation Historical Research Society. A study of nine airfields. Over 100 photographs. ISBN 363. £5.95.

HAWKINGE 1912-1961 by Roy Humphreys. A study of the former RAF Station, 100 photographs. ISBN 355. £5.95.

A NEW DICTIONARY OF KENT DIALECT by Alan Major. The first major work on the subject this century. ISBN 274. £7.50.

KENT CASTLES by John Guy. The first comprehensive guide to all the castles and castle sites in Kent. ISBN 150. £7.50.

US BARGEMEN by A.S. Bennett. A new book of sailing barge life around Kent and Essex from the author of 'June of Rochester' and 'Tide of Time'. ISBN 207. £6.95.

THE GILLS by Tony Conway. A history of Gillingham Football Club. 96 large format pages packed with old photographs. ISBN 266. £5.95. **BARGAIN OFFER £1.95.**

A VIEW OF CHRIST'S COLLEGE, BLACKHEATH by A.E.O. Crombie, B.A. ISBN 223. £6.95.

JUST OFF THE SWALE by Don Sattin. The story of the barge-building village of Conyer. ISBN 045. £5.95.

TEYNHAM MANOR AND HUNDRED (798-1935) by Elizabeth Selby MBE. ISBN 630 £5.95.

THE PLACE NAMES OF KENT by Judith Glover. A comprehensive reference work. ISBN 614. £7.50 (also available in paperback. ISBN 622. £3.95)

LARGE FORMAT PICTORIAL PAPERBACKS

PEMBURY IN THE PAST by Mary Standen. ISBN 916. £2.95.

OLD MARGATE by Michael David Mirams. ISBN 908. £2.95.

OLD RAMSGATE by Michael David Mirams. ISBN 797. £2.95.

EXPLORING OLD ROCHESTER by John Bryant. A guide to buildings of historic interest. ISBN 817. £2.95.

THOMAS SIDNEY COOPER OF CANTER-BURY by Brian Stewart. The life and work of Britain's best cattle painter, with 10 illustrations in colour. ISBN 762 £2.95.

A FIRST PICTUREBOOK OF OLD CHATHAM by Philip MacDougall. ISBN 754. £2.95.

A SECOND PICTUREBOOK OF OLD CHATHAM by Philip MacDougall. ISBN 924. £2.95.

CRANBROOK by Jenni Rodger. A pictorial history. ISBN 746. £2.95.

KENT TOWN CRAFTS by Richard Filmer. A pictorial record of sixteen different crafts. ISBN 584. £2.95.

KENTISH RURAL CRAFTS AND INDUS-TRIES by Richard Filmer. A wide variety of rural crafts. ISBN 428. £2.50.

SMARDEN: A PICTORIAL HISTORY by Jenni Rodger. ISBN 592. £2.95.

A PICTURE BOOK OF OLD SHEPPEY by Michael Thomas. 130 old photographs, mostly from glass negatives. ISBN 657. £2.95.

FIVE MEDWAY VILLAGES by Wyn Bergess and Stephen Sage. A pictorial history of Aylesford, Burham, Wouldham, Eccles and Borstal. ISBN 649. £2.95.

A PICTURE BOOK OF OLD HERNE BAY by Harold Gough. 146 old pictures from the archives of the Herne Bay Record Society. ISBN 665. £2.95.

OLD SANDWICH by Julian Arnold and Andrew Aubertin. 146 old photographs. ISBN 673. £2.95.

AVIATION IN KENT by Robin Brooks. A pictorial history from 19th century ballooning to 1939. ISBN 681. £2.95.

A PICTURE BOOK OF OLD RAINHAM by Barbara Mackay Miller. ISBN 606. £2.95.

THE LIFE AND ART OF ONE MAN by Dudley Pout. A Kentish farmer's son who became successful as a commercial artist and as a children's illustrator. ISBN 525. £2.95.

OLD MAIDSTONE'S PUBLIC HOUSES by Irene Hales. 123 photographs. ISBN 533. £2.95.

OLD MAIDSTONE Vol. 1 by Irene Hales and Kay Baldock. ISBN 096. £2.50.

OLD MAIDSTONE Vol. 2 by Irene Hales. ISBN 38X. £2.50.

OLD ASHFORD by Richard Filmer. A photographic study of life in Ashford over 150 years. ISBN 72X. £2.95.

OLD TONBRIDGE by Don Skinner. ISBN 398. £2.50.

KENT TRANSPORT IN OLD POSTCARDS by Eric Baldock. 146 photographs. ISBN 320. £2.50.

GEORGE BARGEBRICK Esq. by Richard-Hugh Perks. The story of Smeed Dean Ltd in Sittingbourne and its colourful founder, George Smeed. 80 illustrations. ISBN 479. £2.95.

STANDARD SIZE PAPERBACKS

THE GHOSTS OF KENT by Peter Under-wood, President of the Ghost Club. ISBN 86X. £3.95.

CURIOUS KENT by John Vigar. A selection of the more unusual aspects of Kent history. ISBN 878. £1.95.

REAL ALE PUBS IN KENT by CAMRA in Kent. ISBN 894. £1.50.

A CHRONOLOGY OF ROCHESTER by Brenda Purle. ISBN 851. £1.50.

SITTINGBOURNE & KEMSLEY LIGHT RAILWAY STOCKBOOK AND GUIDE. ISBN 843. 95p.

A GUIDE TO HISTORIC KENT by Irene Hales. A guide to the most interesting features of every town and village, with details of each place of historic interest open to the public. ISBN 711. £1.50.

DOVER REMEMBERED by Jessie Elizabeth Vine. Personal memories from the early years of this century. ISBN 819. £3.95.

THE PLACE NAMES OF KENT — see under hardbacks.

PENINSULA ROUND (The Hoo Peninsula) by Des Worsdale. ISBN 568. £1.50.

A HISTORY OF CHATHAM GRAMMAR SCHOOL FOR GIRLS, 1907-1982 by Audrey Perkyns. ISBN 576. £1.95.

CYCLE TOURS OF KENT by John Guy. No. 1: Medway, Gravesend, Sittingbourne and Sheppey. ISBN 517. £1.50.

THE CANTERBURY AND WHITSTABLE RAILWAY 1830-1980: A PICTORIAL SURVEY. ISBN 118. 75p.

ROCHESTER'S HERITAGE TRAIL. (Published for The City of Rochester Society.) A useful guide for the visitor to most places of interest in Rochester. ISBN 169. £1.25.

WINGS OVER KENT. A selection of articles by members of the Kent Aviation Historical Research Society. ISBN 69X. £1.95.

LULLINGSTONE PARK: THE EVOLUTION OF A MEDIAEVAL DEER PARK by Susan Pittman. ISBN 703. £3.95.

LET'S EXPLORE THE RIVER DARENT by Frederick Wood. Walking from Westerham to Dartford. ISBN 770. £1.95.

SAINT ANDREW'S CHURCH, DEAL by Gregory Holyoake. ISBN 835. 95p.

BIRDS OF KENT: A Review of their Status and Distribution. A reprint, with addendum, of the 448 page study by the Kent Ornithological Society. ISBN 800. £6.95.

Further titles are in preparation. Details will be announced in 'Bygone Kent'.